HINGE POINTS IN HISTORY

Amazing leaders who nearly died,
but went on to change the world

by: RK Irvine

Chetnole House Publishing

Rebecca Irvine

Published by Chetnole House Publishing, LLC
Mesa, Arizona

Copyright © 2024 by Rebecca Irvine

All Rights Reserved
Ebook edition

All rights reserved. No part of this book may be reproduced in any form or by any electronic or mechanical means, including information storage and retrieval systems, without prior permission from the author except in case of brief passages embodied in reviews and articles.

This ebook is licensed for your personal enjoyment only and may not be resold or given away to other people. Please purchase only authorized electronic editions, and do not participate in or encourage electronic piracy of copyrighted materials. Your support of the author's rights and hard work is appreciated.

ISBN: 978-1-7323747-8-2

Library of Congress Control Number: 2024916655

Cover design by Molly Phipps with We've Got You Covered Book Design
☐

Dedicated to
Richard L. Finlinson
whose prophetic words served as inspiration for this book
and continue bless my life in innumerable ways.

Table of Contents

Introduction 1

Ch. 1: Harriet Tubman 5

Ch. 2: Mohandas Gandhi 21

Ch. 3: George Washington 39

Ch. 4: Meriwether Lewis 57

Ch. 5: Clara Barton 73

Ch. 6: Benjamin Franklin 91

Ch. 7: Winston Churchill 109

Ch. 8: Brigham Young 125

Ch. 9: Queen Victoria 139

Ch. 10: Martin Luther King, Jr. 157

Ch. 11: Orville Wright 173

Ch. 12: John F. Kennedy 187

Works Cited & Notes 209

Introduction

In the late 1940s, Maya Angelou lived in San Francisco as a single, teenage mom. She worked two jobs to make ends meet. But her life nearly ended while dating a "gentle"-man named Mark. In his earlier years, Mark had aspired to a boxing career. His dream ended when three of his fingers were severed in an automotive plant accident. After that, friends called him Two Fingers.

Maya felt Two Fingers an ideal lover until one day he picked her up from work to take her on a date to Half Moon Bay. The stunning beach, surrounded by rolling hills and redwood trees, had picturesque charm. On arriving, she got out of the car, thinking of the spot as idyllic and romantic. But within moments, Mark accused her of cheating on him and hit her with his prize fighter fists. She soon fell unconscious, awaking briefly to be sworn at and hit in the head with a wooden slat.

Afterward, Mark loaded her unconscious body in the back seat of his car and took her to a restaurant near her home, where he bragged to other men about how he'd got revenge on his cheating girlfriend. Employees of the restaurant who saw Maya in the back seat said she looked dead. The owner of the restaurant, a family friend, immediately called Maya's mother to report the incident.

It took three days for Vivian Baxter, Maya's mother, to locate her daughter. Two Fingers held Maya captive, locked up in his apartment. Too injured to move, Maya offered fervent prayers that help would come.

Miraculously, Vivian found Maya. Two teenage boys had robbed a convenience store, stealing cartons of cigarettes. When the police began to chase them down, the teens randomly threw the stolen merchandise into Mark's car. While searching the area, police found the stolen merchandise. The police soon arrested Mark on robbery charges. By coincidence, he used his one phone call from jail to call Boyd Pucinelli, a bail bondsman and a friend of Vivian's. Mark gave instructions for Pucinelli to go get money from his landlady and provided his home address. Instead of following the instructions, Pucinelli called Vivian. Within a short time, Vivian and three of her meanest-looking pool hall employees arrived at Mark's rented rooms where they knocked down the door to find Maya, bruised, swollen, and unable to walk. Maya's prayers had been answered.

But what if God had not answered Maya Angelou's prayer? What if Mark's beating had led to her death, as a young woman with limited life experience? Maya would never have been able to finish raising her toddler son, Guy. Never have gone on to a brilliant writing career with a deeply poetic style, writing over 20 books and plays. Never worked to help support the civil rights or feminist movements of the 1960s and 70s. Never won a Grammy, Tony, or Pulitzer. Or the Presidential Medal of Freedom. She would never have been remembered in the annals of history.

* * *

Remarkably, Maya Angelou's survival story is not all that unique. Throughout history, the narratives of world leaders are often marked by incidents of immense peril or near-death experiences that serve as pivotal climactic moments: hinge points. Just as hinge points on a door act as the fulcrum for movement and load-bearing, hinge points in history serve to change the course of what might have been, bringing alight new possibilities. Sometimes, as in the life of Maya Angelou, a hinge point enables a capable leader to take on the burden of action and decision-making that will change the world around them. These critical junctures, where life and death hang in the balance, have not only tested the resolve of individuals, but also shaped the destinies of nations and the course of human history.

In the process of writing and editing *Hinge Points in History* the assassination attempt on former President Donald J. Trump occurred in Pennsylvania. In subsequent days, some podcasters discussing the shooting commented on how the near-death experience changed Trump as a person. Would it be possible to go through such a terrifying event and not be changed? Even those who nearly die unexpectedly, who feel fine in the immediate aftermath, likely begin to realize over time that coming close to death changed them: changed their perceptions, their assumptions about life, and the way they react to the world around them. Often such a change becomes a hinge point. It causes individuals to think more long-term—eternally even—and to recognize human frailty more fully. In other words, the experience contributes to building qualities that make for better leaders. Quite possibly, many of the great leaders discussed in *Hinge Points* were outstanding *because* they nearly died.

Call it luck. Call it fate. Call it God. Whatever you want to call it. In some cases, hinge points appear to be caused by divine intervention. Remarkably, hinge points do not necessarily occur because of righteous, upstanding living. Instead, the times when miraculous intercession took place seem to happen because a strong individual had something unique to accomplish or offer. In many cases their actions greatly improved the lives of others or helped to eliminate human suffering. Despite their imperfections, or maybe because of them, these leaders had the opportunity to change the world. As such, I have chosen not to focus on the blemishes or sins of those profiled here. Even flawed individuals can have a purposeful, impactful life.

From battles on the frontlines to assassination attempts and severe illnesses, walking through the shadow of death helped forge character and clarify vision of many amazing leaders. Their appreciation for life enabled them to lead with unprecedented vigor and purpose. By examining the trials and triumphs of these extraordinary figures we gain a deeper understanding of the resilience and tenacity required to navigate the complexities of leadership in tumultuous times. Their stories are a testament to the power of human spirit and the profound impact one individual can have on the world, even after coming face-to-face with their own mortality.

☐

Chapter 1:

Harriet Tubman

On the evening of November 12, 1833, visible all across the United States, a spectacular meteor storm showered in the night sky. In Alabama, *The Democrat* newspaper reported there were "thousands of luminous bodies shooting across the firmament in every direction."[1] Some considered this salute from the heavens to signal the end of the world, while others thought it meant a miracle would soon take place. Maybe both interpretations were correct.

* * *

Harriet Tubman never knew her exact birthday; most enslaved persons didn't. But late in life she supposed her age had to be over 90 because she remembered being around ten years of age on the famous "night the stars fell"[2]—the Leonid meteor shower of 1833. That evening she had snuck away from the plantation to visit her mother and siblings who had been hired out to work on a neighboring farm. After Nat Turner's rebellion[3] took place two years prior, plantation owners had kept a tight watch on their enslaved workers. While Harriet visited with her family, one of her brothers stood outside the door watching for night patrols. As the full moon rose in the sky, and the meteor shower began, Harriet's brother called for her to come and see the stars "all shooting whichaway."[4] Going outside, she saw hundreds of stars falling in the sky and wondered what it meant.

Born Araminta "Minty" Ross, Harriet Tubman's parents were Ben and Harriet "Rit" Green Ross from Dorchester County, Maryland. Rit gave birth to at least ten children, with Minty being one of the last three or four. Although Minty never knew her exact birthdate, records kept by the plantation owner where her mother worked show a midwife paid $2 on March 15, 1822 to care for Rit during childbirth. This date aligns well with Harriet's estimation of being about ten years of age during the Leonid meteor shower.

At the time of Minty's birth, Rit's ownership underwent transition. Technically, the Brodess family enslaved Minty. Edward Brodess, heir to the family fortune, including slaves, had been underage, so during this ten-year time period before reaching his majority, an older stepbrother, Anthony Thompson, had carefully overseen the estate. However, in the same year of Minty's (likely) birth, Edward Brodess came of age, married, and took control of his land, money, and slaves. The Brodess farm spread across 200-acres located 80 miles east of Washington DC, across the Chesapeake Bay. The transition from Thompson to Brodess does not appear to have been a positive one for the Ross family. Records show Brodess did not manage his money well and did not appear to be well-prepared for overseeing a large farm. Additionally, the move meant Rit and her children were separated from their husband and father, Ben, who remained enslaved by Thompson. Two of Minty's older brothers later described Brodess and his wife as cruel and abusive. When she was just a child, Minty's owners hired her out for temporary work, a practice that would provide extra funds to enslavers. On multiple occasions, when working in temporary positions, Minty's life nearly ended.

At about age six or seven, the Cook family took Minty on as a temporary worker. She spent two years wading in swamp waters checking muskrat traps, even through the winter months. At night she would fall asleep on the floor in front of the fireplace, homesick and weeping for her mother's comfort. When Minty contracted measles, the employer disregarded her illness and insisted she keep working. It wasn't until she became gravely ill that Cook sent Minty back to Brodess, where Rit nursed her daughter back to health. It is likely that Minty caught pneumonia as a result of the exposure and illness. Pneumonia is one of the most common complications that occurs as a result of measles, and accounts for more than half of those who die from the disease. That she survived this childhood illness without care from a physician is significant.

Around age nine or ten, Brodess sent Minty to work for "Miss Susan," a young mother who needed help with a baby. Miss Susan frequently lost her temper and whipped Minty on a regular basis. During an argument Miss Susan had with her husband, Minty snuck a sugar cube to eat, thinking the move would go unnoticed. Unfortunately, Miss Susan took note and went for her whip. Minty ran away and hid in a pig pen for four days, until hunger drove her back to work. During the expected beating given by Miss Susan's husband, he "broke [Minty's] ribs and may have lacerated her internal organs and Harriet could no longer work." She returned to the Brodess farm with wounds that "pained her all her life."[5]

The greatest physical damage inflicted on Minty, however, occurred in 1835 at age 13. In the fall of that year Minty's health improved enough again to be hired out to a neighbor—the "worst man in the neighborhood"[6]—whose wife needed help working a flax patch. The labor-intensive job would yield fibers to be used for making textiles, including linen. But Minty preferred the back breaking labor of working in the fields to doing household chores indoors; outside she would be freer to work on her own and not subjected to the women in the "great house."

At some point while working in the flax patch, the cook on the farm approached Minty in the field and invited her to go to the local dry goods store to pick up some needed supplies for the household. Located close to the Bucktown crossroads, west of the Brodess farm, the store stood near the flax patch where Minty worked. The Y-shaped intersection of three roads served as a gathering spot with little more than the store, a Methodist church, and a blacksmith.

At her age, Minty likely neared her eventual full-grown petite height of five feet. In later years, she recalled how she hesitated going with the cook. Minty worried about people seeing her with her hair unkempt, standing on end. Tubman later remarked how after eating a meal she would wipe the grease off her hands onto her hair in an effort to tame her locks and keep them closer to her head. But after a day working on her knees in the flax patch, Minty's hair had got out of control. "My hair had never been combed and it stood out like a bushel basket," she later noted.[7] But, after using a shawl pulled low over her forehead to hide her hair, she agreed to go with the cook anyway and walked barefooted toward the store.

After arriving, a skirmish took place. As Minty stood waiting for the cook, an enslaved man named Jim, owned by local farmer Barnett, left work without permission. The overseer of the estate, McCracken, chased after Jim. "When the overseer found the young slave, he ordered Harriet to help him tie the slave down. Tubman refused, and the slave broke free and ran away."[8] Angered, McCracken reached for a 2-pound weight and threw it, likely at Jim. But instead of hitting its target, the weight slammed into Minty's forehead, nearly killing her. "The weight broke my skull and cut a piece of that shawl clean off and drove it into my head. They carried me to the house all bleeding and fainting. I had no bed, no place to lie down on at all, and they laid me on the seat of the loom, and I stayed there all day and the next."[9]

The resulting injury caused pressure on her brain, which continued for decades, and left a scar that remained visible throughout her life. The blow resulted in headaches and seizures. It also caused her to suffer from fits of narcolepsy, which often made others think of her as half-witted. Thirty years later, in 1865, the *Freedman's Record* reported that her injury "still makes her very lethargic. She cannot remain quiet fifteen minutes without appearing to fall asleep. It is not a refreshing slumber; but a heavy, weary condition which exhausts her."[10] Another report given about sixty years later, in the mid-1890s, noted that her condition continued to cause her to lose consciousness for four to five minutes every half an hour or so throughout the day. Later in life Tubman sought relief from the injury through neurosurgical procedures, but the treatments failed.

Modern medical analysis of Tubman's traumatic brain injury has led to two conclusions. First, the blow to her head likely caused her to suffer from Temporal Lobe Epilepsy (TLE). Classic symptoms of TLE include seizures, headaches, and unexpected sleeping spells, followed by periods of severe exhaustion. Tubman experienced all of these symptoms, as well as an increased sensitivity to spiritual experiences. "Bright lights, colorful auras, disembodied voices, states of tremendous anxiety and fear alternating with exceptional hyperactivity and fearlessness, and dreamlike trances while appearing to be conscious,"[11] as well as hearing heavenly choirs and speaking in tongues, became common for Harriet Tubman after her brain injury. She also mentioned having another common TLE symptom: occurrences when she had out of body experiences, particularly flying like a bird over the landscape. Ever after her injury she had a reputation for being devoutly prayerful and religious.

The second conclusion modern doctors have made about Harriet Tubman's traumatic brain injury is that it likely led to her being an acquired savant. Although a rare condition, acquired savant syndrome occurs when an ordinary individual gains extraordinary new skills and abilities, usually after a serious head injury or stroke. This is clearly seen in Harriet Tubman's post-injury life. Despite having no formal education and having no ability to read or write, she demonstrated time and again an amazing aptitude and recall of geography. She could traverse remote mountains and forests easily in the dark of night. Her ability to use the stars to help to both navigate and tell time were exceptionally accurate. She also developed an effective signaling system using African spiritual songs that informed her Underground Railroad passengers of dangerous conditions ahead; when sung at a faster tempo a song warned of higher risk of discovery. "I was the conductor of the Underground Railroad for eight years, and I can say what most conductors can't say—I never ran my train off the track and I never lost a passenger," she later noted at a women's suffrage convention in 1896.[12]

* * *

After Minty's head injury, unable to work, she returned to the Brodess farm. Edward Brodess, seeing her inability to function, tried unsuccessfully to sell her. With time, however, she managed the long-term effects of her injury. The year after her head trauma, she began working for John T. Stewart of Tobacco Stick (modern day Madison) laboring in a timber gang, which helped her to build strength through cutting wood, driving oxen teams, and plowing fields. She became part of a predominantly male world where she learned about regional communication, trade, and travel networks—information that would eventually enable her to conduct the Underground Railroad.

In 1847 Brodess hired Minty out to Dr. Anthony C. Thompson, the son of her father's former employer. Ambitious and proactive, Minty convinced Dr. Thompson to let her manage her own work schedule if he would guarantee Brodess an annual fee. While employed for Thompson, she worked hard to find job opportunities and saved her money, purchasing her own pair of oxen to help expand her prospects.

Also during this time, in 1844, she met and married John Tubman, a freeman about eight years older than herself. Unfortunately, the couple only had about five years together before circumstances drastically changed. Between 1847 and 1849 Brodess had continually sought to sell Minty as his finances continued to deteriorate.

> "In 1849 Tubman's owner, Edward Brodess, needed to sell slaves in order to cover his debts. Minty heard rumors that she and her brothers were going to be sold. . ... Minty began praying that [he] change his mind 'I prayed all night long for my master till the first of March.' When her prayers did not work she changed it to: 'Oh Lord, if you ain't never going to change tha[t] man's heart, kill him, Lord, and take him out of the way.' A week later, Edward Brodess died."[13]

Although the answer to her prayer, the death of Brodess in March 1849 made Tubman's position even more precarious. Brodess's widow, Eliza, grappled with a mountain of debt and several minor children still living at home. Additionally, legal action regarding Minty's mother's ownership had been taken against Brodess's estate. In financial desperation, Eliza began selling her most liquid assets: the slaves. Multiple advertisements were placed in local newspapers offering several of Minty's family members for sale. Minty soon realized the time had come to take action. She needed to escape, or she would likely be sold and taken in chains to a tobacco plantation in the deep South.

On the night of Monday, September 17, 1849, 27-year-old Minty and her brothers Harry and Ben snuck away from the Poplar Neck Plantation. However, before long Harry and Ben became spooked and changed their minds about trying to escape. They forced Minty to return with them, but her determination to find freedom held steady. Just a few days later she decided to leave on her own. Again, she traveled at night to not be seen by slave catchers. Polaris, also known as the North Star, appeared stationary above the horizon of Blackwater National Wildlife Refuge in Dorchester County. Minty used the never-changing Polaris to help guide her north to Philadelphia and to freedom. "When I found I had crossed that line," she said, "I looked at my hands to see if I was the same person. There was such a glory over everything; the sun came like gold through the trees, and over the fields, and I felt like I was in Heaven."[14]

* * *

For many years Harriet Tubman told people she began using her mother's name, instead of Minty, at the time of her marriage. However, legal documents—and even the advertisement posted by Eliza Brodess offering a reward for the capture of an escaped slave—typically used the name Minty. It is more likely that Tubman began using the name Harriet when she reached freedom in Pennsylvania and needed a familiar pseudonym to use. Little did she know that the name change would be so all-consuming; while Minty Ross faded into darkness, Harriet Tubman stepped forward to take her place in history.

Harriet's desire to help free other enslaved persons began before she arrived in Philadelphia. On her journey north, she had prayed that God would help her bring family members out of Maryland. She felt a spiritual confirmation that this opportunity would be given her; she only needed to wait on God for instruction.

Over the next year, Harriet began making a new life for herself. She took jobs cooking and cleaning, both in hotels and in private residences. In the summer she ventured to Cape May on the New Jersey shoreline to work in a resort. As she labored and saved funds needed to help rescue her family, she also paid close attention to politics as it pertained to slavery. That spring, the US Congress held debate over the Compromise of 1850. Part of the Compromise included the Fugitive Slave Act (also known as the "Bloodhound Bill"), which would require citizens to turn in runaway slaves or be fined and subject to jail time. Newly elected President Zachary Taylor opposed the legislation; but unfortunately, on July 4, after laying the cornerstone to the Washington Monument, President Taylor became deathly ill of a bacterial infection in the small intestine. He died five days later. Vice President Willard Fillmore, whose position on the Compromise differed, soon took office. Much to the dismay of abolitionists and fugitive enslaved persons, Fillmore leant his signature to the legislation. "In response, abolitionists throughout the East and Midwest join forces, forming a more systematized network of assistance for fugitive slaves that will be known as the Underground Railroad."[15]

No one knows exactly how Harriet Tubman became involved with the Underground Railroad. The secretive nature of the organization meant few written records were kept, but it is likely that through the process of helping her own family members to escape, Harriet came into contact with others working with the organization. The first family members Harriet helped escape were niece Kessiah Bowley and her two young children. In November 1850, Eliza Brodess advertised the auction of Kessiah and her children would take place at noon on the Cambridge courthouse steps. Kessiah's husband, freeman John Bowley, and Harriet began corresponding about an escape. The plan had John, an experienced sailor, row his family up the Chesapeake to Baltimore where Harriet would be waiting with accommodations and plans to help the family continue north to Canada. The winter months, especially on the water, meant the family would be traveling in dangerous conditions, particularly with a baby. But the possibility of being sold out-of-state or to an abusive owner made the danger of winter weather the only bearable option.

On the day of the auction, Kessiah stood on the courthouse steps holding her children while the bidding took place. Eliza Brodess's son stood nearby observing. After the sale, the auctioneer and Brodess went on a lunch break. During the interim, John Bowley took his family and disappeared, hiding in the home of a nearby resident. When the auctioneer returned to finalize the sale, he discovered the buyer had been Bowley himself, who could not be located for questioning. Then, the auctioneer tried to start the sale over again, but realized Kessiah and the children were also missing. No one knew or admitted to seeing where she and the children had disappeared to, and a search party had no luck. When nightfall came, the Bowley family snuck down to the waterfront where John launched a small boat or canoe, paddling up the Chesapeake. It took two full nights for him to row his family to safety, but once they reached Baltimore, Harriet met them with open arms and escorted them to Philadelphia. Shortly after they continued to Canada.

Pleased with the success of assisting the Bowleys and fearing the safety of family members still in Maryland, Harriet returned to Baltimore in early 1851—her first time traveling to the South to help rescue enslaved persons. During this trip she helped her brother Moses, and two other men escape to freedom. Emboldened by a second effective venture, Harriet next traveled farther south to Dorchester County in hopes of bringing her husband, John, back to Philadelphia with her. It had been two years since they had been together, and she looked forward to their reunion. As a gift, as well as a disguise, she brought with her a new suit of clothes for John to wear on the journey to Pennsylvania. When she arrived on the Eastern Shore, she sent word to John through a messenger of her presence in the neighborhood. "When Tubman arrived there, though, she discovered that John had taken another wife, a free woman named Caroline. . .. he refused to join [Harriet]; he had moved on and was content to continue with his life in Dorchester County."[16] Spurned, angry, and hurt, Harriet initially wanted revenge. But she soon realized that doing so might lead to her being re-enslaved, so she instead "dropped [him] out of her heart"[17] and gathered a new group of enslaved workers to escort to freedom. She never saw John Tubman again.

* * *

For the remainder of the decade, Harriet continued to work summer and fall months earning money to help rescue her people, including additional family members, from the Eastern shores of Maryland. "In total, she made approximately thirteen trips, spiriting away roughly seventy to eighty slaves, in addition to perhaps 50 or 60 more to whom she gave detailed instructions, nearly all from Dorchester and Caroline Counties in Maryland."[18] The vast majority of her trips were made in an effort to rescue her family. In addition to the Bowley family, she rescued four of her brothers, her parents, and a few other extended family members. Typically, when helping family members or while leading a group north, other enslaved persons asked to join the company. On several occasions she tried to rescue her sister Rachel, who felt reluctant to leave without her children. After multiple failed attempts to get Rachel, Harriet learned her sister had died while still enslaved by Eliza Brodess sometime in 1860. Devastated, Harriet mourned Rachel deeply.

Long after the Civil War, in the mid-1880s, Harriet spent an evening with author James Clarke and shared her rescue methods. Clarke later included these details in his book *Anti-slavery Days*:

> "She said she first obtained enough money, then went to Maryland, where she privately collected a party of slaves and got them ready to start. She first satisfied herself that they had enough courage and firmness to run the risks. She next made arrangements so that they should set out on Saturday night, as there would be no opportunity on Sunday for advertising them, so that they had that day's start on their way north. Then she had places prepared where she knew she could be sure that they could be protected and taken care of if she had the money to pay for that protection. When she was at the North she tried to raise funds until she got a certain amount, and then went south to carry out this plan. She always paid some colored man to follow after the person who put up the

posters advertising the runaways, and pull them down as fast as they were put up, so that about five minutes after each was up it was taken away. She seemed to have indomitable courage herself, and a great deal of prudence."[19]

Additionally, there are reports Tubman carried a pistol, not only as protection from slave catchers but to provide motivation for tired and frightened runaways who wanted to turn back. Dead runaways couldn't tell tales of railroad conductors. On one occasion an exhausted passenger wanted to stop and rest despite having slave catchers on their tail; Harriet aimed the gun at him, saying, "Go on or die." He quickly moved along.[20]

By the year 1854 Harriet's reputation had grown among the abolitionists in the northern states. Some, particularly among slave refugees, called her "Moses" for her reputation of bringing people safely out of slavery to the promised land. A reward of $10,000 had been offered for her capture.

The constant need for money to help run the Underground Railroad meant traveling through northern states to find work, fundraise, and make contacts. Private speaking invitations provided her with the opportunity to earn extra funds and to help promote anti-slavery policies in government. Most of these speaking engagements were with small groups and took place in the parlors of community leaders or in the homes of fellow fugitives. Although she frequented anti-slavery rallies and lectures, she preferred to remain a spectator in large gatherings. Despite keeping a moderately low profile, Harriet also became acquainted with other well-known abolitionists, including Sojourner Truth, Frederick Douglass, and John Brown.

* * *

In rescuing at least 70 enslaved persons and helping them move to safety in Canada, Harriet Tubman had a lasting impact among African Americans. Likely the most significant achievement of her life is felt by her Ross[21] family and relations, which can now claim "scores of living descendants"[22] thanks to Harriet's efforts. But her influence on the Black community and the nation proved to be much broader. If Minty Ross had died from measles and pneumonia in her childhood, or if the two-pound weight that hit her forehead had caused her death at 13, there would have been ripples of change in the history of the United States, most significantly in the Civil War, women's suffrage, and the twentieth century civil rights movement.

By 1860, much of the Underground Railroad had been derailed. Many conductors and safe house contacts had been turned in for helping escapees. Simultaneously, the national conversation on slavery began devolving into violence. In 1859 John Brown led a raid on a federal armory in Harper's Ferry, hoping to encourage enslaved people to rise up and revolt against their owners. The raid failed and the state of Virginia executed Brown in December that year after he prophetically stated, "The crimes of this guilty land will never be purged away but with blood."[23] The following year Abraham Lincoln won the presidency with only a minority of the vote and without taking a firm stance on eliminating slavery. His election caused seven southern states to secede and form the Confederate States of America. Another four states seceded after the Confederate army won the Battle of Fort Sumter.

After a decade as a conductor, Tubman received a new call to serve when the American Civil War began in 1861. As the war progressed and the Union army struggled to find success, leaders sought out those with scouting, spying, and leadership skills. Harriet had spent a decade refining each of these abilities. "In her years of guiding people away from slavery on the Underground Railroad, Harriet Tubman had to arrange clandestine meetings, scout routes without drawing attention to herself and think on her feet. And though she was illiterate, she'd learned to keep track of complex amounts of information."[24] Within a few months of the start of the war, Harriet found herself involved in helping to support the Northern cause, particularly as more enslaved persons in states bordering the North ran away.

In the process of trying to help feed, clothe, and employ refugee slaves, Harriet received an introduction to Massachusetts' Governor John Andrew. Andrew recommended Harriet for a position helping the Union Army gather intelligence. In January

1862, two months before her fortieth birthday, Harriet sailed to Fort Walker in Port Royal, South Carolina. Although in the South, Fort Walker had been captured by the Union in a battle the previous year. After arriving, Harriet got to work helping distribute supplies to Union soldiers. She began a business washing clothes and taught Port Royal's newly freed enslaved persons how to earn a living doing laundry, baking, and sewing.

Tubman initially received rations from the Union Army, but soon gave them up in an effort to gain the trust of other Blacks. To support herself, she baked pies, gingerbread, and made root beer to sell to the soldiers. One of the primary ways Harriet influenced the outcome of the Civil War involved her recruitment of Black soldiers; former slaves trusted her much more than Yankee Northerners. Records show that at least 100 of them joined the Union Army as a direct influence of Harriet Tubman's service. Beyond recruiting new soldiers, Tubman also served as a nurse. "As a nurse, she faced daily arrivals of sick and dying soldiers and civilians, who were ill not from battle wounds (as little combat was occurring in the region during 1862) but from contaminated water and food, poor sanitation and hygiene."[25] Her knowledge of herbs and home remedies helped to heal and ease the discomforts of many who suffered from malaria, measles, typhoid, fevers, and other illnesses.

During her time in South Carolina, Harriet built up a spy ring to help gather intelligence for the Union Army. She and her undercover agents were able to locate and clear mines the Confederate Army had planted in the Combahee River. They also received reports on the location of Confederate supplies and movements of troops. By February 1863, military leaders recognized Tubman's efficiency as a spy, and she received a pass that gave her "free passage at all times, on all government transports."[26]

In June 1863, three Union steamboats carrying 300 Black troops journeyed up the Combahee River into Confederate territory in an effort to rescue enslaved persons, confiscate Confederate commissary supplies and cotton, and destroy local infrastructure. "Tubman oversaw the expedition alongside a colonel she trusted, making her the first and only woman to organize and lead a military operation during the Civil War."[27] The boats safely traversed the river and blew up a pontoon bridge at Combahee Ferry. Soldiers ransacked Confederate supplies from neighboring estates, burning everything they could not carry away. Local enslaved persons on nearby plantations had been forewarned of the mission and came running to the river to be evacuated on the three boats. Over 700 were rescued as a result of Harriet's leadership and planning.

After the conclusion of the Civil War, Harriet Tubman continued to give service at Fortress Monroe in Virginia by nursing Black soldiers. While caring for the wounded, Harriet became frustrated with the disparity of care provided to Black soldiers; the death rates were more than twice as high as that of white soldiers. To complain of the abuses she had witnessed, she traveled to Washington DC to meet with Dr. Joseph K. Barnes, the surgeon general. Because of her action, Barnes initiated reforms at the hospital at Fortress Monroe, both in the recruitment of doctors and in mandated quality of care. Appointed as Nurse Matron[28] at the hospital, Tubman helped oversee the implementation of the changes, which likely saved the lives of many Black patients.

* * *

Immediately at the end of the Civil War Harriet Tubman took up a new cause: suffrage. Even before the war, through her work with the Underground Railroad, Harriet had connected with a network of reformers working to expand voting rights. As a result, she participated in suffrage conventions organized by both Black and white women as early as 1854. Unlike most Black women, Harriet supported the National Women's Suffrage Association (NWSA) established by Susan B. Anthony and Elizabeth Cady Stanton. Their objective to amend the Constitution to include the women's right to vote garnered her support. Harriet toured with the NWSA through New York, Boston, and Washington to help promote women's voting rights. Despite her lack of education, her dynamic way of speaking and telling stories drew crowds. During this time, she developed a close friendship with Susan B. Anthony and expressed her own aspirations for suffrage, noting she had "suffered enough for it."[29] Harriet continued to appear at local and national suffrage conventions until the 1900s when her health declined. Her impact on the movement likely helped to significantly increase support for women's rights, particularly among Black women.

* * *

In 1868 author Sarah Bradford approached 46-year-old Harriet Tubman about writing a memoir of Harriet's life. After agreeing to the project (probably because of the revenue it would bring her) and being extensively interviewed by Bradford, the book *Scenes in the Life of Harriet Tubman* came out a year later. The book generated worldwide acclaim and sold well. Over the next 15 years, particularly when in need of funds, Tubman petitioned Bradford to published new editions of the book. In 1886 Bradford released an expanded biography of Tubman's life, *Harriet Tubman, Moses of Her People*. These two biographical works ultimately helped to deepen public awareness of Harriet as one of the earliest activists and iconic advocates for her people. She became an inspiration for generations of African Americans fighting for equality and civil rights. Although most well-known for her work with the Underground Railroad, Harriet never stopped working as an activist.

After the Civil War "she helped establish schools for the freed Blacks in the South. In 1896, she cofounded the National Association of Colored Women that demanded equality and suffrage for African American women."[30] And about five years before her death she established the Harriet Tubman Home of the Aged to improve the lives of those once condemned to servitude. Here, former enslaved persons would be cared for in their senior years. The number of lives Harriet Tubman improved or saved over the course of her lifetime and beyond is incalculable and deeply deserving of honor.

* * *

On March 10, 1913 Harriet Tubman, ill and penniless, quietly passed away from pneumonia in the Home of the Aged she had established. On hearing of Harriet's passing, Mary Burnett Talbert, an African American civil rights activist and suffragist, wrote, "Harriet Tubman has fallen asleep–the last star in that wonderful galaxy of noble pioneer Negro womanhood has fallen. Phyllis Wheatley, Sojourner Truth, Frances Ellen Watkins Harper, Fannie Jackson Coppin, Harriet Tubman! A fallen star that has shot across the intricate and twinkling dark, vanished, yet left no sense of loss."[31]

Chapter 2: Mohandas Gandhi

The concept of *satyagraha*[1] ("truth forcers") evolved in the mind of Gandhi over a number of years. At its deepest point, the roots can be attributed to his family's Hindu faith and the Bhagavad Gita. The Gita emphasizes qualities such as nonviolence and integrity: "Fearlessness, purity of heart, persistence in the yoga of knowledge, generosity, self-control, nonviolence, gentleness, candor" (Bhagavad Gita 16:1-2). Gandhi's mother's profoundly religious beliefs taught him to treat others kindly and to have tolerance of other faith beliefs. To this tenant, Gandhi added ideas he learned while studying to be a lawyer in London. Some of his studying led him to reading the Bible; of this he most appreciated the Sermon on the Mount in the New Testament. The Beatitudes contained doctrine similar to his familiar Hinduism: "Blessed are the peacemakers: for they shall be called the children of God" (Matthew 5:9). On this foundation of religious doctrine, Gandhi supplemented by reading Thoreau's *On Civil Disobedience* and Tolstoy's works, *The Kingdom of God is Within You* and *Christianity and Patriotism*. The ideas in these writings greatly stimulated Gandhi's thoughts. Eventually, these thoughts motivated his actions.

* * *

During World War I, 46-year-old Mohandas Gandhi established a monastic community, known as an *ashram*, where he could live a religious life devoted to truth. The 36-acre Sabarmati Ashram was located in Gujarat, India between a crematorium and a prison—fitting since Gandhi believed satyagraha like himself were apt to end up at one location or the other. The rustic commune aimed to be self-sufficient as a farm with gardens, fruit trees, and animals. However, because it regularly welcomed poor families willing to live the rigorous lifestyle, finances were stretched. One day Gandhi's daughter announced to him that the group had run out of funds and did not expect any income for the next month. Gandhi responded, saying, "Then we shall go to the untouchables' quarter."[2] Despite his comment, Gandhi half expected Brahma, or the Infinite, would send a benefactor to help; Brahma had done so before on several occasions. And Gandhi's faith held strong. A few days later a visitor came to the ashram to inquire if he could give some help; Gandhi confessed to being very low on resources. The next day the visitor returned and donated 13,000 rupees, enough to cover finances for another year. The community would continue to train new truth forcers and Gandhi's work would carry on.

* * *

Gandhi did not grow up in an ashram. His family had servants and a loving home, but were not wealthy or of a superior caste. Gandhi's father, uncle, and grandfather had served as chief ministers in Porbandar, in northwestern India on the Sea of Oman, and were well-known for their administrative and managerial skills. Gandhi described his father as "incorruptible and [he] had earned a name for strict impartiality in his family as well as outside. His loyalty to the state was well known."[3] Because the chief minister position had been held by a family member for a number of years, Karamchand "Kaba" Gandhi anticipated one of his sons would eventually step into the job. But, after three marriages he only had two daughters. In 1857 Kaba married for the fourth time, and from this union the couple were blessed with four children, including three sons. Mohandas Gandhi, born in October 1869, was the youngest.

In school Mohandas was a "mediocre student"[4] who struggled with his multiplication tables and generally disliked reading textbooks. He did find enjoyment in some of the traditional Indian classical plays about Shravana and King Harishchandra. The plays, which touched on themes of self-sacrifice and devotion to Brahma, were his first introduction to concepts he would later strive to live by in the ashram and as he sought to help others. Despite going to a public school, Mohandas remained introverted and shy in his childhood. He struggled socially and avoided interacting with others, fearing he would be teased or ridiculed for being timid. It wasn't until adulthood that he overcame his reticence.

As it was, Mohandas Gandhi had a fleetingly short childhood. Because weddings were extremely costly in India, Mohandas Gandhi's parents had him married at age 13 in a triple wedding ceremony with one of his older brothers and a cousin. Mohandas's parents arranged a marriage for him to Kasturbai Kapadia, who was 13-years-old as well. Although Gandhi's marriage lasted throughout his life, his relationship with "Ba" had its struggles. His impatience and her stubbornness caused conflict. In South Africa, for example, Gandhi began doing household chores that would normally have been considered below his caste. When he insisted Ba do the chores cheerfully, too, she wept and threatened to leave. Raised in a well-to-do home, she felt the chores should be done by servants. "I will not have this nonsense in my house," he responded tersely.[5] Although he grew to love Ba, he also came to feel the union had come too early: "As I see the youngsters of the same age about me who are under my care, and think of my own marriage, I am inclined to pity myself and to congratulate them on having escaped my lot. I can see no moral argument in support of such a preposterously early marriage."[6]

* * *

From this meek beginning, Gandhi became "the man who has stirred three hundred million people to revolt, who has shaken the foundations of the British Empire, and who has introduced into human politics the strongest religious impetus of the last two thousand years."[7] He is well-known for the nonviolent activism that helped India and Pakistan achieve self-governance from Great Britain in 1947 after 90 years of control. As might be expected, the use of nonviolent strategies to change the balance of power over so large a nation often led to an opposition that escalated into violence. This happened with Mohandas Gandhi on several occasions. But he survived—despite assuming a submissive posture—to help his people in South Africa and India, and in the process inspired many others around the world.

Gandhi's first steps into social action took place in his early 20s while he lived in Durban and Pretoria, South Africa. Pretoria had been settled by Dutch colonists in the mid-nineteenth century. When Gandhi arrived in 1893, more than 150,000 Indian immigrants had also moved to the area causing increased cultural tensions. Having been called to South Africa professionally as a lawyer, the treatment he received there as a result of his race deeply shocked him. In Transvaal he suffered abuse from being verbally assaulted, thrown off trains (despite having a first-class ticket), ejected from hotels, and beaten. Once, a police officer forcefully kicked Gandhi off a public footpath because of his skin color and background. The government, which was controlled by whites, passed a number of racist laws designed to prevent the immigration of those from Asia, and to complicate life for Asians already there. Had he not been under a 12-month contract, Gandhi would have left South Africa earlier. Forced to stay, he patiently bore the indignities as best he could.

In 1894 Gandhi's professional contract neared its end. But at this time, South African leaders planned to pass yet another xenophobic law that would force Indian immigrants to live on specific government-assigned streets and require them to register with the government. Feeling his politics should be indistinguishable from his religious beliefs, Gandhi further believed it his duty to help the Asian immigrants fight against the proposed registration law. That same year he formed the Natal Indian Congress (NIC), a political party with a platform aimed at helping protect the rights of immigrants; Gandhi himself was appointed as the Honorary Secretary. The NIC petitioned South African government officials for changes that would eliminate discriminating policies. Unfortunately, Law 3 of 1885 passed, much to Gandhi's disappointment. He knew bias could not be eliminated by simply changing the legislation; but he also knew discriminating laws would foster prejudice in an already volatile South Africa. He felt the rule of law must be fair and objective, even if those who administered the laws were themselves bigoted.

Knowing the work in South Africa would require a great deal of time and effort, and that he had already been away from his family for three years, in 1896 Gandhi decided to return to India so he could move his wife and two sons (ages eight and four) to Durban. While in India, he informed many about the discriminatory practices immigrants were subjected to, but when word got back to South African leaders, it caused an antagonistic reaction. When the ship carrying Gandhi's family docked in Durban, they were greeted by a hostile crowd. With a stroke of bad luck, a second ship from India carrying 800 more Indians arrived simultaneously. On seeing the second ship, the crowd believed Gandhi purposefully tried to flood South Africa with more immigrants. Angered, they stormed Ghandi on the dock and attacked him, throwing stones, bricks, and eggs. When they pushed him up against a railing, they repeatedly punched and kicked him. At some point, he lost consciousness but remained upright against the rail. Finally, a passerby, the wife of the police superintendent, intervened and stepped between Gandhi and his attackers, using her parasol to protect him from further harm. Her efforts effectively saved his life. He safely escaped the mob violence. Lamentably, that did not mark the end of the danger.

Officials took Gandhi to the home of a friend, where his wife and children had previously escaped to, and where he received medical care. But within a brief time, the angry crowd surrounded the house, shouting for Gandhi to come out so they could burn or hang him. Concerned the crowd would set fire to the house, the police superintendent helped Gandhi escape by sneaking an extra uniform in as a disguise and then removing him to the police station where he was held for his own safety. It took three more days for the crowd to disperse. Eventually, the incident caught the ear of British Prime Minister Joseph Chamberlain in London. In response, Chamberlain sent word to South African authorities to ensure those responsible for trying to lynch Gandhi were fully prosecuted. As would eventually become typical for Gandhi, he refused to take action against the accused. He felt the government and policies were the problem, telling the prosecutor, "I do not hold the assailants to blame. They were given to understand that I had made exaggerated statements in India about the whites in Natal and calumniated [defamed] them. If they had believed these reports, it is no wonder that they were enraged. The leaders . . . are to blame."[8]

Over the next several years, Gandhi continued to work as an attorney with the NIC to improve conditions for Asian immigrants. He founded a newspaper, *Indian Opinion*, which he published in English and three Indian languages. Despite his busy life, he longed for the opportunity to do humanitarian work on a permanent basis. Through self-study he trained himself in first aid, nursing, and midwifery, and volunteered his time at the local hospital. He found volunteer work brought him inner peace. Then, in October 1899, the Second Boer War began between the British Empire and the Boer states of the South African Republic (Transvaal) and the Orange Free State. "Though Gandhi's sympathies were with the Boers who were fighting for their independence, he advised the Indian community to support the British cause, on the ground that since they claimed their rights as British subjects, it was their duty to defend the Empire when it was threatened."[9] To show material support for the war, Gandhi helped organize the Indian Ambulance Corps, which had over one thousand volunteers. Although initially the services of the Indian Ambulance Corps were rejected by government officials in Natal, eventually their efforts were utilized as stretcher bearers.

During the war, the corps worked to rescue the injured during the Battle of Spion Kop. Gandhi and his men repeatedly went onto the battlefield under enemy fire, bringing back the wounded, moaning soldiers to receive care at the base hospital. Reports of the corps' service were well-documented and lauded by British newspapers, with one reporter commenting on seeing Gandhi specifically:

> "'After a night's work which had shattered men with much bigger frames,' Mr. Stent recalled, 'I came across Gandhi in the early morning sitting by the roadside eating a regulation army biscuit. Every man in Buller's force was dull and depressed, and damnation was invoked on everything. But Gandhi was stoical in his bearing, cheerful, and confident in his conversations, and had a kindly eye. He did one good.' He wore a khaki uniform, a jaunty, broad-brimmed cowboy felt hat, a Red Cross armband, and a drooping mustache."[10]

For risking his life to help others during the Boer War, Gandhi received the Kaiser-i-Hind War Medal. Although he had hoped the sacrifice and service of the Indian Ambulance Corps would lead the European community to be more accepting of the immigrants, Gandhi found that not to be the case. Yet, when the Zulu rebellion took place in 1906, the corps once again stepped forward to assist the military.

For the next seven years Gandhi continued to lead the South African immigrants in satyagraha—passive resistance. His third arrest occurred in 1909. "He made such good use of his time in jail with study and prayer that he was able to declare that 'the real road to ultimate happiness lies in going to jail and undergoing sufferings and privations there in the interest of one's own country and religion.'"[11] While still imprisoned, British General Jan Smuts offered to repeal the mandatory registration law if immigrants would willingly register on their own. Gandhi and other leaders of the protest agreed to the compromise, leading to anger among some immigrants who did not trust Smuts. One Indian immigrant friend, Mir Alam, swore to kill the first person who willingly sought registration. Gandhi told Alam, "I would happily die at the hands of a friend but in no case I would leave the path of truth."[12]

Three months later, the time came to register. Gandhi and several other leaders journeyed to the registration office. On the way there, Mir Alam and some of his supporters blocked the road. When Gandhi invited Alam to accompany them to register, Alam hit him on the side of the head with a stick. Gandhi immediately fell unconscious, but the group continued to attack him. Mir Alam likely would have carried out his oath to kill Gandhi if others on the road had not intervened and restrained Alam. During the assault Gandhi lost his front teeth, had several ribs broken, and his lips ruptured. Those who had attacked Gandhi were arrested, and despite Gandhi's efforts to get them freed, they were sentenced to six months in prison. Once again, Gandhi's life had been preserved.

* * *

In the late 1890s Gandhi began to transform himself into the man most people are familiar with as he pondered over *brahmacharya* (literally meaning conduct consistent with Brahma; the first of four ashrama studies). His felt self-restraint would draw him nearer to God: "The concupiscence of the mind cannot be rooted out except by intense self-examination, surrender to God and lastly, grace," he wrote in his autobiography.[13] He stopped dressing like a British barrister and donned the white wrap frequently associated with poor Indian immigrants as a way to restrain his desire for finer clothing. He limited his diet to nuts and fruits, and at home he took on many of the more mundane, distasteful tasks, including his own laundry and emptying chamber pots. The Gandhi home had no running water, making many of the daily chores more challenging, not to mention unsanitary. Similar conditions existed at the ashram Gandhi established after moving back to India in July 1914, about the time his people began addressing him as Mahatma, or "great-souled." These conditions may have been what led Gandhi to have a life-threatening attack of dysentery in 1918 at the age of 49.

The illness began as a mild bout, after which Gandhi fasted, hoping his body would be able to cure itself. He had previously experimented with fasting as both a health remedy and as a form of developing self-restraint. After breaking his fast, however, he immediately had an acute attack of dysentery—an infection in the intestines. Unfortunately, that same day he needed to travel to Nadiad in Kheda, Gujarat. With difficulty he walked to the train station for the journey. After arriving in Nadiad, he had to walk another half mile to the Hindu Anath Ashram as his pain steadily increased. By the time he arrived the attack worsened. "Instead of using the latrine he usually used, which was a long way off, he asked for a commode to be placed in the adjoining room, as he couldn't walk the distance."[14] Although offered medical care, Gandhi refused, feeling he should suffer for what he considered his own foolish behavior. He went on a complete fast again as a form of self-inflicted punishment. Despite fasting, his appetite completely failed, his strength disappeared, and he suffered from a low-grade fever. He feared death would be imminent.

Concerned for the Mahatma's well-being, his friends in the ashram called in a few doctors. The known treatment for dysentery in India in 1918 included a series of injections of emetine hydrochloride; however, Gandhi feared the injections would contain some sort of serum that would be against his dietary restrictions. For religious reasons—he had taken a vow to live brahmacharya—he refused the injections and instead began listening to friends reading aloud to him from the Bhagavad Gita. "He was unable to read and was hardly inclined to talk, as uttering even a few words caused him strain. He seemed to have lost all interest in life."[15] While in this state of near death, one of Gandhi's doctors came up with an inspired idea:

> "I must say that for acute amoebic dysentery there is no treatment so sure as a few injections of emetine hydrochloride. We were almost at our wit's end how to give Mahatmaji emetine. Suddenly it struck me that, if we proposed to him an enema, he would gladly allow us that procedure. So we proposed to him that we would only give him an enema. He at once agreed, and we added to the enema water a full dose of emetine and morphia. This little procedure had such marvelous effect on our patient within the next twenty-four hours that he voluntarily asked for a repetition of the same enema procedure for five successive days, with the result that his dysentery was cured and he was able to travel in a week's time."[16]

Dysentery is infection and inflammation of the intestines, which causes diarrhea that may contain blood or mucus. Most cases of amoebic dysentery, as Gandhi had, occur when people ingest food or water contaminated with feces. Complications of dysentery typically include dehydration, liver abscess, and permanent damage to the kidneys. In India at the time, dysentery caused nearly one in every seven deaths.[17] The fact that Gandhi survived an acute attack of dysentery after refusing treatment for many weeks is remarkable. His doctor's inspired idea enabled Gandhi to carry on a work that would eventually help India gain its independence from Great Britain.

* * *

In 1920, Gandhi's appreciation of British rule over India shifted. During the previous year, the Amristar massacre took place in India. Peaceful Indian protesters had been entrapped then shot by troops under the command of British Brigadier General Reginald Dyer. Shooting continued even when the protestors tried to flee, ultimately causing the death of at least 380 people and injury to over 1,200 more. News of the tragedy reached London and Winston Churchill described the massacre as "an extraordinary event, a monstrous event, and an event which stands in singular and sinister isolation."[18] Although an inquiry took place and British Parliament voted to condemn Dyer's actions, the level of brutality and lack of any real accountability caused many in India, including Gandhi, to think differently about British rule. The Mahatma advocated strongly for independence. Seeing the anger of his people, Gandhi sought to find a way to lead them in a way that would channel their ire toward nonviolent strategies. In December 1920, while attending the Nagpur Congressional session, Gandhi made a bold promise: If India's noncooperation remained nonviolent, the country would be self-governed within a year. Trusting in Gandhi's assurances, the people followed his lead.

Sadly, Gandhi overpromised.

After a year passed, India remained under British rule. But the Mahatma, working with the Indian National Congress's leader Jawaharlal Nehru, continued to try and persuade British leaders that the prolonged repression of his people would deepen the antagonism between their cultures. And, despite going to prison for sedition multiple times, his efforts gradually yielded results. "Throughout the 1920s and 1930s Britain introduced a range of measures that gave more and more independence to India. The number of Indians who were eligible to vote was increased. Indians began to serve on the Council of the Viceroy and also got jobs as ministers in the government."[19] Regardless of these changes, nationalism continued to increase. The people wanted independence and self-governance.

In April 1930, 60-year-old Gandhi used civil disobedience to protest the Salt Act, which prohibited Indians from collecting or selling salt. After informing Viceroy Lord Irwin he would break the Salt Act, Gandhi and 78 other men set out on a 240-mile march to Dandi, a small town on the Arabian Sea. As the march progressed, more and more people joined in. By the time the group reached Dandi, the Mahatma led a crowd of over ten thousand. There on the sandy beach, he picked up a piece of natural salt rock from the mud, breaking the Salt Act. The march inspired millions of Indians, and soon civil disobedience broke out across the country causing havoc. Nearly 60,000 Indians were arrested, including Gandhi. But as news spread around the world, an international outcry arose over the injustice of his incarceration. After eight months in prison, Gandhi received his release. British leaders "acknowledged Gandhi as a force they could not suppress or ignore."[20]

Protests continued in the 1930s and throughout World War II. Gandhi encouraged the people to boycott British clothing by weaving their own fabric. He urged Indian families not to send their children to British schools. Finally, in 1945, British leaders realized Indian independence would be inevitable. Parliament passed the Government of India Act, which started India on a path to self-rule. In 1946, Jawaharlal Nehru received an appointment as the prime minister over an interim cabinet, with Lord Louis Mountbatten as Viceroy. On August 15, 1947, India was granted full independence, although Mountbatten agreed to stay in India as Governor-general during a transitionary time period.

The shift from British rule to independence presented a challenging period for India, primarily due to the diverse cultural groups within the country. One reason the British were reluctant to leave India included fear the country would erupt into a civil war between Hindus (three-fourths of the population) and Muslims (one-fourth of the population). India remained deeply divided along religious lines. Gandhi had been able to successfully align the religious groups after WWI; but, when he was in jail for nearly two years in the early 1920s, the factions broke with each other. Gandhi had not been able to bring the coalition fully together again. As Great Britain prepared to withdraw from India in 1946, violence between the Muslims and Hindus grew. In an effort to make a more peaceful transition, Britain established two new independent states: India, which would be predominantly Hindu, and Pakistan, which would be Muslim. Gandhi felt deep sorrow over the partitioning of his country; he fasted and visited unsettled areas of the land to help establish peace. Sadly, this work led to his death. Mahatma Gandhi was assassinated shortly after India received its independence from Britain. In January 1948, while walking with a crowd of 1,000 of his followers to a prayer meeting, Nathuram Godse, a Hindu nationalist, shot Gandhi three times in the chest. Gandhi, age 78, died immediately.

* * *

On the occasion of Gandhi's death, Prime Minister of India Jawaharlal Nehru said, "Friends and comrades, the light has gone out of our lives, and there is darkness everywhere."[21] Nehru was correct. The loss of Gandhi led to darkness. The next 40 years in India were filled with war and political turmoil, particularly between Hindus and Muslims. Without Gandhi, India seemed to have lost its moral compass. In considering the shadow that fell with the death of Gandhi in 1948, it is interesting to weigh what may have happened if his life had ended earlier. Would the darkness have been intensified? Certainly, "it would be a travesty of historical method to say that had there not been Gandhi, someone like him would have appeared on account of historic necessity."[22] But what if Gandhi had been lynched in South Africa in 1896, or had been killed in the Second Boer War? What impact would this have had on history?

As an historical figure, Mahatma Gandhi is unique. He was a politician without an electorate, a leader without authority. His family background played an important role in why he had the ability to realize position in Indian society. But his significant historical impact did not stem from his family. Three unique leadership qualities help make Gandhi a one-of-a-kind trailblazer: his charisma, his invention of a radical resistance characterized by restraint (satyagraha), and his willingness to lead by example.

Gandhi's charisma and character are what helped him to use his leadership role to influence the nation. "It was Gandhi's capacity to pierce the hearts of everyone, including those who were personally engaged in violence and killing, that lay at the heart of his charisma."[23] His magnetism and integrity helped him to move beyond cultural identifiers: despite being from the business or commerce caste (known as *bania*), the Pathans and Sikhs both admired and respected him. Although an educated, wealthy lawyer, he pledged to live a life of poverty. More importantly, while millions of people joined in his movement, Gandhi never tried to be populist. This lack of cultural or personal identifiers extended to those he associated with in a democratic manner; he treated the grocer and the governor in the exact same way. This helped those who made his acquaintance to feel loved and valued. Julia Close, wife of American journalist Upton Close, expressed it eloquently: "In his presence I felt a new capability and power in myself rather than a consciousness of his power. I felt equal, good for anything – an assurance I had never known before, as if some consciousness within me had newly awakened."[24]

In addition to his charismatic treatment of others, Mahatma Gandhi introduced a method of nonviolent civil disobedience, which he called *satyagraha*. The purpose of his resistance strategy was to help his people secure basic human rights. To clarify, the word civil, which has multiple meanings, refers to the relationship between citizens and the state; civil disobedience, therefore, means disobedience to the state or government. Although some misinterpret civil disobedience to mean pacifism or polite noncompliance, this is not the construct Gandhi and many of his followers were trying to communicate or make happen. Gandhi encouraged his people to purposefully disobey unreasonable or suppressive laws, and to willingly accept the punishment that would result from doing so. Throughout the process he would calmly point out the unfairness of the laws to government officials. Eventually, by forcing the truth of the impact of the prejudicial legislation to the forefront, leaders would recognize and change laws that deprived human rights. The satyagraha strategy proved successful in both South Africa and in India. "Gandhi proved that even the strongest nations cannot win in the face of a united people determined to plan and control their destiny through nonviolence."[25]

Having invented the concept of satyagraha, Gandhi felt passionate about demonstrating its effectiveness. He willingly led by example to show his followers what it looked like in practical application. He spent more than seven years of his life in prison because he himself led his people into satyagraha. One example of this occurred in 1913. At the time, South African immigrants were still required to register and to pay a crippling tax. On top of this, a court ruling removed government recognition of Indian marriages (many of which were polygamous). In late fall Gandhi gathered followers and indentured servants (who went on strike) to his Phoenix ashram, where they would begin a march to the Transvaal-Natal border and cross without permission. Thousands followed Gandhi to the border:

> "By 6 November the march had reached Volksrust, on the border with the Transvaal. Whites in the town threatened to 'shoot the Indians like rabbits.' Still they pressed on and the border was crossed without violence. By the end of November the towns in Natal were at a standstill, troops had been rushed from the Eastern Cape and Pretoria and the mines had been turned into temporary prisons. Strikers were bludgeoned, beaten and intimidated; some died. Gandhi and his closest supporters – including several whites – were imprisoned."[26]

As the demonstrations continued Gandhi served as the cook in jail for his fellow-protesters. Eventually, a Reuters news bulletin of the protests reached India and caused a national outcry. India's Viceroy Lord Hardinge broke protocol and spoke out against the treatment of Indians in South Africa. Finally, in December, General Smuts called for an inquiry into the causes of the movement. On January 16 the following year, Gandhi had negotiated a deal, ending the tax and allowing polygamous marriages. Satyagraha had proved effective.

* * *

How would history have changed without Gandhi's influence on the world? As might be expected, the biggest differences would likely be seen in India itself. Although some speculate that without his influence India might still be considered part of the British Empire, others disagree. In fact, there is a possibility that a more violent rebellion against British rule in the 1920s or 30s may have led to independence sooner; however, this would have resulted in more bloodshed—not just in fighting against Britain, but also Hindu-Muslim conflicts over ensuing political power. As it was, Great Britain created both India and Pakistan in an effort to extend independence without causing too much violence between the two factions. The geopolitical landscape of Asia today would be very different if Gandhi had not led the movement to end British rule.

An early death of Gandhi would have also had a heavy impact on the cultural and political environment in India today. Three examples stand out. First, Gandhi advocated for having a secular government that allowed for religious pluralism. Despite receiving tremendous pushback, he greatly desired harmony between the Hindu and Muslim believers. Although he did not see this in his lifetime, today India is closer than ever to achieving this reality.

Secondly, Gandhi worked hard to overcome his personal feelings of racism, both against untouchables and Black Africans. As he worked to overcome his own flaws, he taught that every citizen has the right to dignity and the opportunity to pursue prosperity. These teachings have been broadly accepted in India over the last 60 years.

Lastly, Gandhi encouraged the government to provide better sanitation and environmental sustainability. The preservation of trees in India is one tangible result of Gandhi's love of nature; he planted many varieties on his ashrams. In the first half of the twentieth century, India had been overharvesting trees in an effort to build and modernize; seeing the depletion, Gandhi taught that trees were a resource that should be managed. In the 1960s and 70s Sunderlal Bahuguna, inspired by Gandhi, worked tirelessly to help India preserve and plant more trees. Although his life should not be reduced in meaning or impact to that of a lifestyle guru, in some ways his example and writings have led to the conditions India enjoys today.

Beyond the borders of his homeland, Gandhi has had widespread influence. His use of nonviolent resistance to change public opinion and laws that limit human rights have been significantly utilized. Martin Luther King Jr., for example, frequently noted that his work to improve civil rights conditions in the United States directly resulted from his adaptation of Gandhi's satyagraha. In fact, in February and March 1959, Dr. King and his wife took a five-week tour of India specifically to see sights where Gandhi had lived and worked. On arriving at the airport, King told reporters, "To other countries I may go as a tourist, but to India I come as a pilgrim."[27] In addition to Martin Luther King Jr., Nelson Mandela's motivations stemmed from his knowledge of Mahatma Gandhi. "Mandela referred to Gandhiji[28] as his role model and was inspired by Gandhiji to lead South Africa's journey to independence, and was sometimes referred to as the 'Gandhi of South Africa.'"[29] After being released from prison, Nelson Mandela utilized the Gandhian principles of forgiveness and compassion to help lead a movement to end apartheid in South Africa. It would be difficult to imagine what civil rights might look like around the world without Gandhi's impact on these two influential followers.[30]

Mahatma Gandhi's influence extended to other leaders who have greatly shaped history:

- Gandhi inspired Mother Teresa. The year of Gandhi's assassination is the same year Mother Teresa answered a spiritual call to serve the poorest of the poor living in India. "The philosophy, ideology and message of Mahatma Gandhi were reborn in Mother Teresa."[31] Mother Teresa even dressed similarly to Gandhi, donning a simple white cotton sari.

- In 1989 the Dalai Lama received the Nobel Peace Prize. During his acceptance speech he paid tribute to Gandhi, specifically noting how inspiring Gandhi's work had been to him. "Mahatma Gandhi is the personification of nonviolence and compassion in my opinion. In his life, Gandhiji exemplified both the principles of nonviolence and compassion. I consider him to be my mentor, and I consider myself to be a small follower of his."[32] The Dalai Lama also said that Gandhi's work continues to be relevant today and that many world problems could be solved using Gandhi's approach.

- Cesar Chavez has reported that his political awakening took place after watching a newsreel he saw at a young age. The newsreel showed Gandhi protesting against British rule over India. Chavez, seeing the effectiveness of the methods, modeled many of his own on Gandhi, including boycotts and hunger strikes.

Over the years, *Bapu* ("Father") Gandhi has become known as the Father of India. His global influence has continuously grown since his death in 1948. In fact, his greatest legacy extends far beyond the boundaries of India, profoundly influencing global movements for civil rights and social justice. His philosophy of nonviolent resistance, or satyagraha, became a powerful tool for oppressed communities worldwide. Gandhi's impact is a testament to the enduring power of nonviolence as a means to achieve social change and justice. Essentially, his dedication and work laid the foundation for the civil rights movement and its furtherance of global human dignity.

Chapter 3:
George Washington

George Washington should have died young. Neither genetics nor colonial era healthcare were in his favor. Great-grandfather John Washington, representative in Virginia's House of Burgesses, died at age 44. Grandfather Lawrence Washington only lived to age 39 after a life of politics and service in the militia. George's own father, Augustine "Gus" Washington, served in the British Navy and ran several plantations, but his life ended at 48. Even George's beloved stepbrother Lawrence died at 34 of tuberculosis. Somehow George Washington lived to the relatively old age of 67. But during his life he survived multiple near-death experiences, leaving him to make his mark on history.

One of Washington's earliest bouts with illness occurred in 1751, during the only international trip he ever took during his lifetime. His stepbrother Lawrence asked 19-year-old George to accompany him to Barbados. Suffering from tuberculosis, Lawrence hoped spending the winter in the warmer weather would help him to recover. Since Lawrence's wife had recently given birth and couldn't accompany him on the trip, George agreed to go instead. During the six-week voyage on the *Success*, a small trading ship, Washington learned navigation skills. He also studied the diverse types of fish being caught, including dolphin, sharks, and barracudas.

"The crew unexpectedly sighted the east coast of Barbados at four o'clock on the morning of November 2, at a time when the captain's calculations placed the ship nearly 150 leagues to the east."[1] The border of Cobblers Reef on the east side of the island made for hazardous sailing. Cobblers, or black sea urchin, thrived in the double-barreled reef running parallel to Barbados's southern coast. The reef made it extremely dangerous for ships because of the potential for running aground and the rough waters over and around it, even in calmer weather and ocean currents. As a result, everyone on board the *Success* was "greatly alarm'd with the cry of Land," as George recorded in his diary.[2] Although the moon shone nearly full that night, by 4 a.m. it had already set below the horizon. The crew somehow spotted land in the dark hours of the morning. Otherwise, the ship could have met with disaster on the reef.

After sailing around the southern tip of Barbados, the *Success* dropped anchor in Carlisle Bay, near Bridgetown, Barbados's capitol. The Washington brothers finally set foot on land on November 3 after the difficult and rough voyage. At the time, Barbados's sugar cane plantations made it one of the wealthiest corners of the British empire. George Washington had never visited a city as large as Bridgetown, which made Williamsburg, Virginia look like a small hamlet in comparison. The size of the city and the cultural differences were fascinating to Washington. Accommodations were found with the commander of Fort James, located just outside the city. Commander Crofton introduced George to society, helped him make connections, and gave him the opportunity to learn more about military forts and leadership.

Lawrence Washington soon received an invitation to visit from Gedney Clarke, an uncle of Lawrence's wife and a resident of Bridgetown. Although Mr. Clarke noted his wife had been suffering from smallpox, the Washington brothers decided to visit anyway. In the 1700s "smallpox was a dreaded disease . . . Even among survivors, the suffering was immense."[3] As an extremely viral illness, it causes high fever, severe headaches, vomiting, achiness, and pustules on the skin. At that time, the death rate of those with smallpox was nearly one in five.[4] Thus far George had avoided the horrifying pox. But within two weeks of visiting the Clarke home, he began to experience symptoms. In his journal he recorded simply, "Was strongly attacked with the small Pox."[5]

The disease started with a high fever and a severe headache. Within a few days, ugly red pustules appeared on his scalp and forehead. "For three weeks the feverish young man, confined to bed, was nursed back to health by the 'very constant' presence of Dr. John Lanahan."[6]

Afterward, George remained forever scarred with light pock marks on his face. Some modern-day doctors hypothesize that the illness may have sterilized Washington, since he never fathered a child. But, in the long run, the disease was somewhat of a blessing to him: the attack conferred lifetime immunity to future infection. Later, when smallpox tore through the American army multiple times during the Revolutionary War, Washington avoided getting sick with an illness from which he could have easily died.

* * *

Nearly two years after his return from Barbados, Governor Dinwiddie of Virginia called on George Washington to deliver an important document. Dinwiddie needed an emissary sent to France's General St. Pierre, commander of the French forces stationed at Fort Le Boeuf near Lake Erie. Prior to the French and Indian War (which began in 1754), the French had begun building posts along the Allegheny River to assert ownership of the Ohio River Valley. In essence the French were usurping lands clearly included in the Pennsylvania and Virginia colonies. Dinwiddie hoped to be able to use diplomatic means to help eliminate future clashes over the land. As a 21-year-old major in the Virginia militia, George accepted the assignment. He departed on October 31, 1753, for the 500-mile journey, accompanied by seven escorts, including an interpreter and an explorer. Lieutenant Christopher Gist served as a guide.

Unfortunately, the winter weather blustered and blew, making the journey on horseback difficult. Washington's frontier journal mentions dense forests, snowstorms, flooded valleys, and swollen rivers as they traveled along the Venango Path through Ohio country. While en route to Fort Le Boeuf, Washington met in council with Iroquois Chief Tanacharison (also known as Chief Half-King). "The previous year the chieftain had signed a treaty with the British, making him their nominal ally, and he had sternly warned the French against incursions in the region."[7] Although less than half of Chief Tanacharison's age, Washington's height (6'2"), demeanor, and courtesy secured the leader's respect. In fact, the chief gave Washington the same nickname his great-grandfather, John Washington, had been given: Conotocarious, meaning 'town destroyer' or 'devourer of villages.' Washington felt honored to bear his great-grandfather's name. Tanacharison also agreed to escort Washington's party on the last leg of the journey.

The group finally arrived at Fort Le Boeuf the second week in December. General St. Pierre received the company graciously and invited them to stay for several days; but he refused to discuss the conflict over the Ohio Valley or to remove troops from the area. Eventually, St. Pierre gave Washington a response to deliver to Governor Dinwiddie[8] and the Virginians prepared to set off for home. Their horses had grown weak on the demanding journey to the fort, so the French loaned the group canoes to take as far as Venango, saving the horses from having to carry heavy loads. They finally departed December 16. Chief Tanacharison and his men stayed in the area to hunt.

Throughout the visit to Fort Le Boeuf, Washington grew concerned the French were getting ready to build additional posts in the upcoming spring. He knew the Governor needed to be warned. After returning the canoes at Venango, Washington and Gist decided to leave the others behind and take a faster route back to Williamsburg and share the news. But with their horses still too weak, crossing the Allegheny Mountains in winter on foot would be treacherous. Washington reported that within a few days, "We fell in with a Party of French Indians, which had laid in wait for us, one of them fired at Mr. Gist or me, not 15 Steps [paces away], but fortunately missed."[9] Gist tackled the gunman, likely saving Washington's life. The two were able to escape unharmed by traveling all the next day and night to get away, moving fast enough that their tracks could not be followed. On December 29, Gist and Washington came to the partially frozen Allegheny River. They spent an entire day building a raft to use, hoping it would speed their journey. They were wrong.

> "They finally launched out into the rapidly moving icy waters, but the raft was quickly dashed into an icy jam, threatening to sink the small craft. Attempting to stabilize it, Washington thrust his push pole into the river but the raging water seized the pole, knocked Washington off balance, and

pulled him overboard into the icy current. Grasping one of the raft logs, Washington was able to save himself."[10]

Unable to navigate to shore, the two guided the raft to a small island in the middle of the river instead, where they spent a very wet and cold night. "The Cold was so extream severe, that Mr. Gist got all his Fingers, & some of his Toes Froze, & the Water was shut up so hard, that We found no Difficulty in getting off the Island on the Ice in the Morning, & went to Mr. Frazers."[11]

Washington finally delivered General St. Pierre's response to Governor Dinwiddie on January 16, 1754. The entire trip had taken 11 weeks. Dinwiddie had George give a full report, and when he learned a journal had been kept of the expedition, Dinwiddie ordered it published. The journal, printed in various colonial newspapers, including *The Maryland Gazette*, eventually made its way to the House of Burgesses. As a result, it circulated widely, both in the colonies and in London. Leaders lauded Washington for his bravery and efforts. "Clearly, to have survived these mishaps, Washington must have been a physical prodigy, made of seemingly indestructible stuff."[12]

Sadly, conflict between the British colonies and France continued to grow. "Despite Washington's gallant efforts, official negotiations had failed; possession of the disputed territory would now be determined through war."[13] In the weeks after George's return from his journey to Fort La Boeuf, reports of further French infiltration into the Ohio Valley continued to reach Governor Dinwiddie. By spring the French began to build Fort Duquesne at the confluence of the Allegheny and Monongahela rivers. The location was considered strategically important for controlling the Ohio River Valley. In May, Dinwiddie again sent George on a mission to take control of the territory. Unfortunately, the significantly larger French military overpowered the Americans, and after a nine-hour siege, and many men dead, Washington surrendered. The French and Indian War had officially begun.

By February the following year, additional troops arrived in Virginia from England. Two regiments under the command of Major General Edward Braddock planned to take action against the French and reclaim the Ohio country. In preparation for warfare, Braddock held a council with colonial governors in

Alexandria where he explained his four-pronged plan of attack. General Braddock himself would lead one of the four campaigns, in which the British would attack Fort Duquesne. Having heard of George Washington's previous experiences and familiarity with the frontier, Braddock asked Washington to become one of his aides during the operation. Twenty-three-year-old Washington accepted the position. But fearing others might perceive his acceptance as a sign of his desire for power, Washington decided to decline any pay.

On hearing her son had decided to accept such a dangerous assignment, Mary Washington visited Mount Vernon to try and persuade George to change his mind. He explained that he felt God wanted him to be in the military, and that he would be protected. "The God to whom you commended me, madam, when I set out upon a more perilous errand, defended me from harm, and I trust He will do so now. Do not you?" George asked in response.[14] Mary pledged to continue praying for her son's safety and bid him Godspeed on his mission before heading back to her own home.

The prayers of a loving mother were effectual.

In June 1755, after several months traveling toward Fort Duquesne, Washington became ill with dysentery. George shared in a letter to his brother John that he had been "seized with violent fevers and pains in my head."[15] The attack so incapacitated him that he spent two weeks lying in the hospital wagon as the regiment moved forward. Medicinal bleeding further weakened him. Narrowly avoiding death, George finally recovered enough to try and catch up with Braddock, who traveled with an advance company. Having been slowed down by mountainous terrain, Braddock had taken a division of 800 forces ahead so as not to lose the element of surprise in the planned attack. George, still in a weak condition, caught up with Braddock about 12 miles away from Fort Duquesne.

On July 9 a battle between the French and the British took place at the Monongahela River. Despite warnings from both Benjamin Franklin and Washington, General Braddock had refused to recognize the dangers of a wilderness warfare. As the British troops marched forward in their bright red coats, banners raised high, the French launched an ambush. On signal of an ear-piercing war cry given by a Native American, a shower of musket balls rained down on the British. Soon the redcoats were in a state of confusion. Braddock rode to the front of the column and took charge, but all of his staff (except Washington) had been shot. The surprise attack gave the French a firm upper hand in the two-hour clash. Eventually, General Braddock suffered severe injuries and had to be removed from the battlefield on a litter. He later died from his wounds. It was "a fight more one-sided than had ever occurred in the history of woodland warfare."[16]

Washington, justified in his warnings to Braddock, tried his best to follow orders. He bravely went back and forth across the battlefield amidst the shower of musket balls, trying to rally the troops. "Because of his height, he presented a gigantic target on horseback, but again he displayed unblinking courage and a miraculous immunity in battle."[17] During this chaos he had two horses shot out from under him. Despite his heroism, he could not stem the tide; he guided the few remaining troops in a retreat to the division that had been left behind. In total, of 1,300 men, over 700 British officers and troops had been lost; only 33 French died.

After the battle ended, four bullet holes were found to have pierced Washington's hat and uniform. But despite being physically exhausted from his illness and the exertion of leading the retreat, the young colonel remained unharmed. Fifteen years later the Native American chieftain who fought against the British that day remarked on the protection Washington received:

> "The chief had ordered his Braves to fire at Washington but 'a power mightier far than we shielded you.' Believing he was under the 'special guardianship of the Great Spirit,' they stopped shooting at him. The old chief prophesied that Washington would become the chief of nations and that 'a people yet unborn will hail him as the founder of a mighty empire.' Washington was 'a particular favorite of heaven, and who could never die in battle.'"[18]

The chieftain's prophecy eventually came to pass. Throughout his life and service in the Revolutionary War, Washington never received a wound in battle.

* * *

In June 1775, as the Revolutionary War began, Congress named 43-year-old Washington commander in chief of the Continental Army. Although the obvious choice to lead the troops, at least three other men were considered. Washington seemed to know the job would be his; he wore his uniform to Congress and had recently purchased military strategy books. "[I]t has been a kind of destiny, that has thrown me upon this Service," he wrote in a letter to Martha.[19] But he acted with great humility. When John Adams rose to speak on behalf of Washington as a candidate, George left the room so the delegates could speak freely about him. It wasn't until later when others began addressing him as 'General Washington' that he knew he'd been given the position. He accepted formally in writing:

> "Mr. President: Tho' I am truly sensible of the high Honour done me in this Appointment, yet I feel great distress from a consciousness that my abilities and Military experience may not be equal to the extensive and important Trust: However, as the Congress desires if I will enter upon the momentous duty, and exert every power I Possess in their service & for the Support of the glorious Cause: I beg they will accept my most cordial thanks for this distinguished testimony of their Approbation."[20]

General Washington soon became central to the importance of the Patriots. John Adams wrote, "The liberties of America depend upon him, in a great degree."[21]

The same month of his appointment, Washington traveled to New York, arriving the same day Governor William Tryon returned from a yearlong trip to Great Britain. Both Washington and Tryon made formal processions into the city. The back-to-back parades upset Tryon when hecklers jeered at him. Tryon blamed Washington for the harassment. After meeting Tryon, Washington had the impression that the Tory governor should not be trusted. Washington's intuition was correct. Tryon had been spying for the British. Like other New York loyalists, Tryon likely felt that by removing Washington the rebellion would soon come to an end.

Within a few months of serving as commander in chief, a traitorous plot came to Washington's attention. Before long, others followed.[22] General Washington soon realized the need for and the importance of counterintelligence and espionage. He formed a secret committee with the goal to uncover strategic communications between Loyalists. Attorney John Jay (who later would be America's first named Supreme Court Justice) led the covert group.

In the summer of 1776 Washington marched the Continental Army back to New York in anticipation of a fleet of British ships arriving to occupy the city. By this time Governor Tryon had abandoned his home under cover of night and began living on a British merchant ship. Tryon had been told by spies that the Continental Congress specifically sought his arrest. Since there wasn't a naval arm of the American military, Tryon felt safe living in exile on-board the British ship. He also continued to exert his influence and gather information to help Britain. Tryon had regular visits from known loyalists, including New York's mayor David Mathews.

That June two members of Washington's Life Guard,[23] body guards Thomas Hickey and Michael Lynch, were arrested for using counterfeit money. While incarcerated in Bridewell prison, Hickey boasted of helping the British to another inmate, Isaac Ketchum. Ketchum used this information to negotiate a more lenient sentence, and returned to the prison as a spy to try and get more details from Hickey. John Jay's secret committee gathered additional evidence about the plot. In short order, Hickey faced court-martial and was found guilty of mutiny and sedition. Following the trial, General Washington made an example of Hickey by hanging him in front of a crowd of 20,000 spectators.

Exact details of Hickey's plot were kept under wraps and only a few references to it exist in contemporary documents. Washington may have kept the details private because he worried it would cause more disruption or fear among the colonists. Several mentions, however, are found in personal letters of the time, including a letter written by Dr. William Eustis to Dr. David Townsend on June 28, 1776. Eustis, who had witnessed the hanging of Hickey, wrote:

"You doubtless have heard of the discovery of the greatest and vilest attempt ever made against our country. I mean the plot, the infernal plot, which has been contrived by our worst enemies. . ... Their design was, upon the first engagement which took place, to have murdered (with trembling I say it) the best man on earth: Gen Washington was to have been the subject of their unheard of sacricide."[24]

Some say Hickey's conspiracy seems greatly exaggerated. Historians know for sure that Hickey reported at least eight other members of the Life Guard were part of some sort of plot, and at the very least they planned to defect to the British. There were also reports the plan included blowing up bridges and destroying American powder magazines when the British fleet arrived in the harbor. During Hickey's trial, accusations arose against Mayor Matthews for funding Hickey's plot. Authorities arrested Matthews and found him guilty of treason and subversion. Mathews later confessed, "He had formed a plan for the taking of Mr. Washington and his guard prisoners, which was not effected by an unforeseen discovery that was made."[25] If this plan had been effectively deployed, and Washington kidnapped and turned over to the British, he could have been executed. The official punishment for treason against the Crown involved capital punishment by hanging, drawing, and quartering.

* * *

After multiple miraculous incidents on Revolutionary War battlefields, General Washington led the Continental Army to victory. Near the end of the war, some of the officers under George Washington's command assembled to discuss a plan to revolt. Despite promises, Congress had failed to provide them with pensions and back pay. Washington met with these officers and delivered a famous speech in which he both sympathized with them and helped them see that mutiny did not represent the best course of action. The speech likely prevented the war from continuing. As it was, the American Revolution officially ended on September 3, 1783, with the signing of the Treaty of Paris. On December 23 Washington surrendered his commission as commander in chief and went home for Christmas.

* * *

It is hard to imagine how the Revolutionary War, or the infancy of the United States, might have been different without George Washington's presence. What alternate path might history have taken in absence of such a great man? Many have considered this question over the past 200 years. President Calvin Coolidge, for example, once gave his opinion:

> "Washington was the directing spirit, without which there would have been no independence, no Union, no Constitution, and no republic. . ... We cannot yet estimate him. We can only indicate our reverence for him and thank the Divine Providence which kept him to serve and inspire his fellow man."[26]

In consideration of Washington's impact on history, it is helpful to first understand what unique offerings he made in his lifetime. The two most important contributions Washington is known for are his service as commander in chief of the Continental Army and as the first president of the United States. The innovation required of Washington in both roles is remarkable to consider. "Everything Washington did was, in a sense, being done for the first time."[27] He frequently trailblazed, set protocols, and established baselines that future leaders could build upon. For example, the Continental Army became the first in history to be patched together from militia provided by separately governed colonies. And never before had a country been led by an elected president with limited terms. Being such a pioneer posed significant challenges and caused him immense stress. "Few," he wrote, "can realize the difficult and delicate part which a man in my situation had to act."[28]

George Washington's strengths as a leader included both his moral character and a willingness to follow. He had learned early the responsibility, integrity, and necessity of carrying out duties as assigned by superiors. Frequently in his journals he would outline the tasks given to him by his commanders. He understood the importance of completing these tasks to the best of his ability, and then reporting back to those in authority. "Obedience to orders was a lesson he had learned early and this principle became fundamental to his nature."²⁹ This lesson instilled in Washington a sense of humility often lacking in other leaders. For example, at the end of the Revolutionary War, Washington appeared before Congress, as the highest governing body in the land, and surrendered to them his sword. He remembered his commission as the commander in chief of the Continental Army had been conferred on him by Congress. Many other military leaders in history would likely have seen an opportunity to usurp Congress's power by force. Washington could have easily placed himself on a throne of power. After all, many Americans had addressed him as "His Excellency" during the War. Instead, he honored the leadership of elected officials. "It was a decision that even led his recently defeated foe, King George III, to comment that Washington was 'the greatest character of his generation.'"³⁰

In addition to his strength of character, Washington's vision as a leader made possible both the defeat of the British and the birth of a nation. "The visionary leader is skillful in designing and creating an organizational culture which will make possible the attainment of the leader's vision and ideas."³¹ When Washington first saw the bedraggled American "army" encamped at Roxbury, near Cambridge, he had to suppress his shock and dismay. As he rode on horseback through the camp, boots shining and sword strapped to his side, he found himself "surrounded by an unruly, vociferous mass of men who didn't take well to orders. . . .and elected their own officers, choosing farmers, artisans, or storekeepers."³² He had expected men with at least *some* military experience. Instead, he recognized that he would be building an army from the ground up.

Washington's skill in bringing together the disparate, ragtag troops, providing training, structure, and leadership, came from having vision. He had studied and prepared to determine what would be required to defeat the British. He understood that the vast majority of military strategies his army could employ would be unsuccessful if the Continental Army lacked unity and discipline. In fact, most military analysts do not describe Washington as a great strategist or tactician. But where he excelled as a leader was in organizational structure and management. Despite a lack of funding, poor direction from the

Continental Congress, disease, and low morale, Washington's vision for the army succeeded. They outmaneuvered the strongest military power in the world and achieved independence.

Similarly, when elected as the first president of the new nation, Washington's vision of what the country could be led his every decision. Washington had foresight enough to see the need for a cabinet. The Constitution mentioned nothing of a board of directors, or cabinet, just that the president had the ability to get opinions from executive department heads. Using this justification, on September 11, 1789, President Washington sent his first cabinet nomination to the Senate. That same day, Alexander Hamilton received unanimous appointment as Secretary of the Treasury. By late November, Washington held his first cabinet meeting with the department heads. In addition to Hamilton, Thomas Jefferson served as Secretary of State, Henry Knox as Secretary of War, and Edmund Randolph as Attorney General. Although not known to be one of the great intellectuals of the era, in the choice of these remarkable men Washington had surrounded himself with gifted minds. In like manner he chose the first Supreme Court justices. Washington had the ability to recognize excellent ideas, to inspire important stakeholders, and to bring about necessary compromises. He worked with the American public, state leaders, Congress, and foreign governments to bring together the much needed political and financial support that made the government function as intended. Under his leadership, the Constitution of the United States of America, a government that existed solely on paper prior to 1788, came alive and operated effectively.

* * *

After considering Washington's near-death experiences sailing to Barbados, contracting smallpox, crossing mountains in frigid temperatures, fighting the French and Indian War, escaping plots against his life, and more, was President Coolidge right? Was Washington's influence beyond estimation? Certainly, an earlier death of Washington would likely have made winning the Revolutionary War more challenging for the Continental Army. Without considering Washington for the position of commander in chief, it is possible one of the other candidates—possibly John Hancock, Horatio Gates, or Charles Lee—would have been chosen. Would Hancock, Gates, or Lee have had the vision and organizational behavior skills to bring the American Army together? Probably not. Hancock had served as the president of the Continental Congress, but he had limited military experience and struggled with health problems. Gates had the ambition, but proved to overestimate his own abilities, as shown during the devastating defeat of the American Army at Camden. Additionally, Charles Lee had serious character and competence issues. The British captured Lee, held him prisoner for nearly two years, and then used him in a conspiracy to remove Washington from command.

Washington's indispensable character became especially important at the end of the war when he yielded military power back to Congress. Would John Hancock, Horatio Gates, or Charles Lee have done the same? Most historians feel Washington displayed unique behavior among his peers in that moment. "Without Washington's character, fortitude, and calming presence, the American Revolution would likely have degenerated into civil unrest and a military dictatorship. The dream of freedom and a republican form of government would've been stillborn."[33]

What about the indispensable role Washington played in helping get the Constitution adopted and ratified? Who else could have assumed that responsibility? Washington had, in fact, waivered on being part of the Constitutional Convention. He felt deeply that the Articles of Confederation governing the country were dismally weak, and agonized the nation might be in danger of failing altogether. But he (correctly) worried that if he committed to attend it would lead to his life being swept "back into the tide of public affairs."[34] And, some leaders with whom he corresponded hypothesized that such a convention would be considered illegal; attending could be a huge risk to his reputation. But by February 1787 he had made the decision to attend. With that decision, he was all in for a full reform: a new constitution. When he arrived in Philadelphia cheering crowds lined the streets as the Liberty Bell clanged a welcome.

Once Washington had been elected as the president of the Constitutional Convention, he limited his oral participation. As was characteristic of his personality, he remained silent during most of the debates. His primary contributions to the Constitutional Convention prevailed in helping others understand the need for a strong national government, and in lending credibility to the convention as a well-intentioned meeting. "His attendance at the Constitutional Convention did much to allay fears and concerns that a monarchy or dictatorship was being erected in Philadelphia."[35]

If somehow America had won the Revolutionary War without Washington's leadership, who would have taken his place as the president overseeing the Constitutional Convention? As president of the Executive Council of Pennsylvania, and one of the primary advocates for the convention, Benjamin Franklin would likely have been a leading candidate. "[T]he nomination came with particular grace from Pennsylvania, as Dr. Franklin alone could have been thought of as a competitor," James Madison recorded.[36] Franklin's celebrity lent greater credibility to the legitimacy of the meeting, while his many years of diplomatic experience would have qualified him to lead the effort. However, his age and poor health (he suffered from gout and kidney stones) might have disqualified Franklin. In fact, Franklin did not show up the first day of the Constitutional Convention due to illness.

* * *

If Washington had died young, during the French and Indian War or early on in the Revolutionary War, he could not have been elected as the first President of the United States. Numerous historians feel no other contemporary American could have taken the oath of office in 1789. No other person in the 13 states had the name recognition or held the confidence of the public. Americans had already seen proof of Washington's leadership skills during the war and they had witnessed his willingness to walk away from a position of immense power. He alone could become the father of the country.

Washington's presence in the lives of Americans is still widely felt today. Envisioning what life would be like without the impact he has had on American culture seems impossible. Beyond the likely fact that the United States of America would simply not exist without George Washington's influence, consider the following points from his presidency alone:

- Members of congress ratified the Constitution in 1788 on the contingency that a Bill of Rights would be added. As president, Washington worked to make that happened, thus ensuring many of the basic rights Americans enjoy today. Without the Bill of Rights, the government would likely have overstepped limitations of its power secured by the freedoms of speech, press, religion, the right to bear arms, etc.

- President Washington supported moving the capital of the nation to its present location and took an active part in its initial design. If he had died before becoming president, Washington DC and the State of Washington would likely not be named after him.

- Without having been president, numerous landmarks and monuments, such as Mount Rushmore, would not include or be named after him. Washington's face would not be on the dollar bill, the quarter, or other commemorative coins and postage stamps.

- As president, Washington began some traditions still associated with the office today, including using the title "Mr. President," taking the oath of office with a hand on the Bible, and keeping to a limit of two four-year terms.

- If Washington had not left office willingly after two terms, it may have served as a precedent to greatly change history. His unwritten two-term limit eventually became the 22nd Amendment to the Constitution in 1951.

- Washington decided to give his first inaugural address in front of Congress, thus establishing the tradition of what has become known as the State of the Union Address.

- After essentially dismantling the military after the end of the Revolutionary War, Washington endeavored to create, maintain, and develop a professional national military force. His military principles remain at the center of US forces today.

- Washington insisted on the formation of a chaplaincy for the Continental Army to encourage his men to build and maintain a relationship with God. Similarly, he established the tradition of discipline in the military. He subscribed to a philosophy of "reward and punish every man according to his merit, without partiality or prejudice."[37]

* * *

On December 14, 1799, 67-year-old George Washington passed away from an infection and excessive bleeding. Washington took unprecedented action in his will to free the enslaved persons working at Mount Vernon on the occasion of Martha Washington's passing.[38] In the economy of the day, he knew this action would probably condemn Mount Vernon to failure and foreclosure. Although many rightly criticize Washington for benefitting from slave labor throughout his life, the statement sent from the grave served as a guiding principle for the next generation of leaders. The noble principles of freedom and liberty should be extended to all. Even in death, George Washington served his nation by setting an example of honor and duty.

Chapter 4: Meriwether Lewis

As the Lewis and Clark Expedition—officially known as the Corps of Discovery—drew close to an end, sailing down the muddy Missouri River toward civilization in St. Louis, Meriwether Lewis and William Clark had no idea much of the country already thought them dead. As they navigated the last 1600 miles, they were surprised to see at least 150 traders, trappers, and mountain men heading upriver in their own boats. Then, on September 17, 1806, the Corps met trader John McClellan who "was Somewhat astonished to See us return and appeared rejoiced to meet us. ...this Gentleman informed us that we had been long Since given out by the people of the U.S. Generaly and *almost forgotten*"[1] (emphasis added). Ironically, despite crossing an unknown land with a harsh climate, dangerous wildlife, steep terrain, and warring Native tribes, the group returned having lost only one of its members—not to any of the inherent dangers of the journey, but to what was likely a burst appendix. Despite this extraordinary survival rate of the Corps members, Meriwether Lewis, as one of the remarkable leaders of the crew, nearly died at least seven times during the journey. His experiences alone seem to indicate a higher power watching over him to ensure the successful completion of the expedition.

* * *

On October 21, 1803, the United States of America nearly doubled in size when Congress, under the direction of Thomas Jefferson, ratified the purchase of the Louisiana Territory from France for $15 million. The French had only owned the region for about two years, having previously purchased it from Spain. But the terrain remained virtually unknown except to localized Native American tribes. No published detailed maps existed.[2] No documentation of animal or plant life had been made. No records of its resources could be found. President Jefferson understood that to be able to defend, utilize, and traverse the Louisiana Purchase, exploration would be required. And he knew exactly who to choose to lead the mission: Meriwether Lewis.

Truth be told, Meriwether Lewis did not receive any formal education until age 13. His father died when Meriwether was five-years-old, possibly one of the reasons he was prone to sadness and bouts of depression throughout his life. Prior to his teenage years, he spent much of his youth in Georgia as an outdoorsman: hunting with his dogs, helping his mother in her medicinal herb garden, and appreciating wildlife near his home. "When only 8 years of age, he habitually went out in the dead of night alone with his dogs, into the forest to hunt the racoon & opossum. …In this exercise no season or circumstance could obstruct his purpose, plunging thro' the winter's snows and frozen streams in pursuit of his object."[3] From his earliest years, Lewis showed deep curiosity about nature and the world around him. Although taught at home how to read and write in his childhood, much of his youth seems to have prepared him well for what would be the peak experience of his life: leading the Corps of Discovery on its two-year expedition across the Louisiana Purchase. By the time he reached adulthood, Lewis "knew the wilderness as well as any American alive during his day, including Daniel Boone and William Clark."[4]

Of course, living two years in nature while trying to cross territory with an unfriendly climate, steep mountains, and wild animals meant Meriwether Lewis's life would be frequently endangered. But his reputation for keeping a cool head had been proven from a young age. A beloved family story relates that a bull rushed at eight- or nine-year-old Meriwether while he crossed a field. "His companions watched breathless as he calmly raised his gun and shot the bull dead."[5] Another time, then age 10, the settlers in the area were too few in number to safely live separately, so they gathered to protect themselves from being attacked by Native Americans. One dark night, after a settler lit a fire for cooking, the group heard a shot ring out and immediately prepared themselves for defense. Only Meriwether had the good sense to put out the fire and cloak the group in the safety of darkness. Later, he served in the Virginia militia during the Whiskey Rebellion of 1794, and then as a captain in the US Army from 1795 through 1800. By the time the Louisiana Purchase finalized, Lewis had been tempered and strengthened to survive in a wide variety of life-threatening, treacherous situations.

* * *

The Corps of Discovery, a group of about 45, departed in May 1804 and traveled from Wood River, Illinois, to the Pacific Ocean. They followed the Missouri River northwest across the Great Plains until they reached the Rocky Mountains (near modern-day Great Falls, Montana). The Rocky Mountain region rises abruptly above its adjacent lands, particularly the plains on the east and northeast where the group first approached. At that point, the mountain region is nearly 373 miles (600 km) wide. The summits of the Rockies rise high above the Northern Plains, which at the time served as home to the American bison herds. After reaching the head of the Missouri River, the Corps had to abandon their boats and barter with Natives for horses to cross the Bitterroot Mountain range in modern-day Montana and Idaho. One of the Corps members, Sergeant Patrick Gass, described the topography as the "most terrible mountains I ever beheld."[6] In crossing the rugged Rockies, the steep cliffs they encountered endangered Meriwether Lewis's life on more than one occasion.

Lewis's first (literal) cliff-hanging incident took place in the very first month of the journey, on May 23, 1804, as he neared his thirtieth birthday. On that Thursday, according to Clark's journal, the Corps passed a Missouri landmark known as Tavern Cave. Clark ordered the boats to stop about a mile upriver from the cave to wait for Lewis, who had scaled the sandstone cliff to get a view of the river and explore the cavern. He scaled the cliff to about 300 feet above the river. As he hung over the water he slipped, plunging about 20 feet before breaking his fall by stabbing his knife into the face of the cliff. The fast-thinking move more than likely saved his life. It is likely the shallow water below would not have been deep enough to break his fall safely.

Just over a year into the journey, Lewis again miraculously lived after slipping on a narrow ledge on a bluff. On June 7, while near the mouth of the Marias River (in modern-day Montana), Lewis and Private Richard Windsor survived a very close shave. Lewis described the event in his journal:

> "In passing along the face of one of these bluffs today I sliped at a narrow pass of about 30 yards in length and but for a quick and fortunate recovery by means of my espontoon [a polearm, or close-combat weapon] I should been precipitated into the river down a craggy pricipice of about ninety feet. I had scarcely reached a place on which I could stand with tolerable safety even with the assistance of my espontoon before I heard a voice behind me cry out god god Capt. what shall I do[?] on turning about I found it was Windsor who had sliped and fallen abut the center of this narrow pass and was lying prostrate on his belley, with his [one] wright hand arm and leg over the precipice while he was holding on with the left arm and foot as well as he could which appeared to be with much difficulty. ... I expected every instant to see him loose his strength and slip off."[7]

Lewis calmly maintained his composure as he guided Windsor to safety. Afterwards, he directed the remaining men to backtrack. The detour required them to wade through the chest-high water below. Once again, Lewis had cheated death.

Lewis's last close call with precipitous terrain occurred on the return trip on Monday, June 30, 1806. On this occasion, he did fall—off a horse and 40 feet down a mountain. He wrote briefly describing the incident: "[I]n descending the creek this morning on the steep side of a high hill my horse sliped and both his hinder feet out of the road and fell, I also fell off backwards and slid near 40 feet down the hill before I could stop myself such was the steepness of the declivity; the horse was near falling on me in the first instance but fortunately recovers and we both escaped unhirt."[8] That he dodged injury is remarkable. Falls are the most common horse accident incidents that cause harm to their riders. This includes brain, neck, and spinal injuries, as well as head trauma. As in Lewis's case, some of the most harrowing injuries involve falls from a moving horse or having the horse fall on the rider. But he survived once again to continue on with the expedition.

* * *

Thomas Jefferson provided detailed instructions to Meriwether Lewis for documenting information about plant and animal life found on the journey. Additionally, the President asked Lewis to carefully observe the natural resources of the region; Jefferson had strong personal interest in the subject.[9] "Other objects worthy of notice will be the soil & face of the country," Jefferson wrote to Lewis "…[T]he mineral productions of every kind; but more particularly metals, limestone, pit coal & salpetre; salines & mineral waters, noting the temperature of the last, & such circumstances as may indicate their character."[10] Lewis took these instructions very seriously, but in doing so he put his own life in grave danger.

On Friday, August 22, 1804, Captain Clark journaled: "Set out early, wind from the south. At three miles we landed at a bluff where the two men sent with the horses were waiting with two deer. This bluff contained alum, copperas, cobalt, pyrites, the alum rock soft, and sandstone. Capt. Lewis in proving the quality of these minerals was near poisoning himself by the fumes and taste of the cobalt, which had the appearance of soft isinglass. The copperas and alum are very poisonous."[11] It appears that Lewis had collected mineral samples from the bluff and, while trying to analyze the crushed samples, accidentally breathed in or consumed enough of the powder to poison himself. Smell and taste tests are still legitimate scientific techniques to determine a rock's composition, but they can be risky. Pyrite and marcasite are abundant in this area of South Dakota, and when these minerals interact with iron sulfides under specific conditions, they can generate small amounts of arsenic. In Lewis's case, it is suspected he ingested enough arsenic to nearly poison himself.

Low exposure to arsenic can produce headaches, vertigo, nausea, and acute diarrhea. Lewis's exact symptoms were not detailed. However, according to Clark, "Capt. Lewis took a dose of salts to work off the effects of the arsenic [used to test the quality of the ores they had found]."[12] There is no indication in the journals of how well this treatment worked, but it is clear luck favored Lewis. In more severe cases of arsenic poisoning the symptoms can include a wide variety of life-threatening issues. The only additional information given is that on August 25, 1804, Clark noted, "Capt. Lewis much fatigued from heat, . . . he being in a debilitated state from the precautions he was obliged to take to prevent the effects of the cobalt and mineral substance which had like to have poisoned him two days ago."[13] Apparently, the poisoning left Lewis feeling poorly for several days—but he survived.

* * *

One of the most terrifying near-death events Captain Lewis survived occurred on a solo scouting trip in June 1805 along the Missouri River in Montana. While exploring Lewis came across a series of five waterfalls, the first of which he called Crooked Falls.[14] "I now thought that if a skillful painter had been asked to make a beautiful cascade that he would most probably have presented the precise image of this one," he later wrote in his journal.[15] As he continued on his course, he shot a buffalo through the lungs. As he waited for the animal to bleed out and die, he discovered a large brown bear approaching from only 20 paces away. Lewis immediately took up his shot gun to take aim, then remembered he had not yet reloaded. The bear was too near and moving too quickly to give him time to do so. He decided to retreat toward a tree some 300 yards away, but the bear quickly gained on him. "I had no sooner turned myself about but he pitched at me, open mouthed and at full speed. I ran about 80 yards and found he gained on me fast. I then ran into the water. The idea struck me to get into the water to such depth that I could stand and he would be obliged to swim, and that I could in that situation defend myself with my espontoon."[16] Once Captain Lewis positioned himself waist deep in the water, he turned to take on the raging bear.

At this point a miracle happened: the bear "suddenly wheeled about as if frightened, declined the combat on such unequal grounds, and retreated with quite as great precipitation as he had just before pursued."[17] Surprised, he waded back to the riverbank and watched the bear run for its life. "I saw him run through the level open plain about three miles till he disappeared in the woods on Medicine River. During the whole of this distance he ran at full speed, sometimes appearing to look behind him as if he expected pursuit."[18] Lewis wondered at the mysterious behavior of the bear and could never account for its change in demeanor. Instead, he decided to never let an unloaded gun put him at such a disadvantage again, and began the 12-mile hike, partially through prickly pear covered terrain, back to the main camp for the night.

* * *

For Captain Lewis, one of his last dangerous encounters occurred as a result of warring Native American tribes. The Corps had numerous interactions with Native Americans during its two-year journey, and Sacagawea is widely credited and praised for helping with both language translation and the diplomatic efforts required in these meetings. Despite the distrust and wars various tribes had with one another, the Corps of Discovery safely traded and interacted with most of the Natives they met. One exception occurred near the end of the journey, on July 26–27, 1806. Lewis, along with George "Drewyer" Drouillard and brothers Joseph and Reubin Fields, took a side-trip to the Great Falls, following a route recommended to them by the Shoshone the previous summer. On July 26, while following the Marias River, Lewis's group encountered a party of at least eight Piegan Indians (one of three Blackfeet tribes) on horseback. Lewis and one of the Fields brothers, while displaying a peace flag, slowly approached the group. Although both parties were skittish of each other, they eventually met, communicated, and camped together that night on the banks of the river. "[W]ith the assistance of Drewyer I [Lewis] had much conversation with these people in the course of the evening. I learned from them that they were a part of a large band which lay encamped at present near the foot of the rocky mountains on the main branch of Maria's river one ½ days march from our present encampment."[19] Unfortunately, during their communication, Lewis told them he had promised guns to various tribes the Corps had previously met on their journey. Lewis did not know many of these tribes were longtime enemies of the

Piegan Blackfeet. This unfortunate comment changed things dramatically.

Early the next morning, the Piegans snuck over to try and steal guns and horses from Lewis and his men before they were awake. Reubin Fields awoke and chased the man who took his gun. After catching him, Reubin wrestled the weapon back and stabbed the Piegan with a knife. Lewis later noted in his journal that Fields had seen "the fellow ran about 15 steps and fell dead."[20] The commotion made by the fighting woke Lewis. He reached for his rifle, but found it gone. When he saw a Piegan escaping with his rifle, Lewis drew a pistol and demanded the thief immediately put down the firearm, which he straight away did. At this point, all the Piegan ran to drive off the horses. Lewis "pursued them so closely that they could not take twelve of their own horses but continued to drive one of mine with some others; at the distance of three hundred paces they entered one of those steep nitches in the bluff with the horses before them."[21] Lewis then threatened to shoot, which he did, hitting one of the Piegan in the belly. The same man shot back at Lewis, likely with a North West trade musket. "[H]e overshot me, being bearheaded I felt the wind of his bullet very distinctly."[22]

* * *

The last, and one of the most serious times Meriwether Lewis's life faced peril took place on the return trip home. In the afternoon of Monday, August 11, 1806, near where the Yellowstone River meets the Missouri (in modern day North Dakota), Lewis decided to hunt some elk the group had seen grazing on the willow-covered sandbar island in the middle of a river. He grabbed his rifle and asked fellow expedition member Pierre Cruzatte to take as a second. Cruzatte was "an experienced riverman and a fur trader. He owned a violin and often entertained the party at night with his playing."[23] But he only had one eye, which in this instance proved to be critical. Especially because Lewis had on elk-colored buckskins at the time.

According to Lewis's journal, here's what happened next:

> "...we fired on the Elk I killed one and he wounded another, we reloaded our guns and took different routs

through the thick willows in pursuit of the Elk; I was in the act of firing on the Elk a second time when a ball struck my left thye about an inch below my hip joint, missing the bone it passed through the left thye and cut the thickness of the bullet across the hinder part of the right thye; the stroke was very severe; I instantly supposed that Cruzatte had shot me in mistake for an Elk as I was dressed in brown leather and he cannot see very well..."[24]

After being shot, Lewis immediately yelled to Cruzatte not to fire again. In fact, he yelled several times for help from Cruzatte, but had no answer. For a while Lewis wondered if maybe he had been shot by a Native, and rushed as quickly as he could with his injured leg back to the pirogue and his waiting men. But when his men searched the area, they found only Cruzatte. Later, when Lewis discovered the musket ball still in his trousers, he immediately recognized it as being from a US Army Model 1803—the same type of gun used by Cruzatte, and not a weapon Native Americans were likely to have. Cruzatte later admitted his fault. He had mistakenly assumed Lewis to be an elk in the thick brush on the riverbank.

Upon determining the group faced no further danger of attack, Lewis then cleaned and dressed his wounds. He packed the holes to encourage regrowth of flesh from the inside. When he experienced a high fever, he used a poultice of Peruvian barks on the wound. Captain Clark, although not present the day of the shooting, saw and described the injury succinctly in his journal the following day: "I examined the wound and found it a very bad flesh wound the ball had passed through the fleshey part of his left thy below the hip bone and cut the cheek of the right buttock for 3 inches in length and the debth of the ball."[25]

With this description, it is clear Lewis narrowly avoided three possible outcomes that could have led to death or severe disability. If the bullet had nicked an artery, he could have died quickly. Secondly, if the ball had shattered his hip joint, he could have had a slow, painful death. And lastly, if the shot had hit the sciatic nerve, Lewis likely would have been permanently crippled. Retired physician David J. Peck confirmed how fortunate Meriweather Lewis had been in this incident:

> "If Pierre Cruzatte was fifty yards away from Lewis when he shot him, that as little as one fiftieth of an inch change in his aim would have resulted in the bullet's, going an inch deeper and very possibly wounding Lewis's sciatic nerve, leaving him with a worthless left leg and very painful wound. If Cruzatte had been seventy-five yards away, only one seventy-fifth of an inch change in his muzzle's position could have produced a crippled Captain Lewis. That is less than a twitch in Cruzatte's arm that supported his rifle."[26]

Although Lewis avoided any of these potentially deadly outcomes, he still endured a great deal of pain. Early on he could not bear to be moved. For much of the first week he remained lying on his stomach in the boat as the Corps continued its journey. "[H]e had to position his body, on land or in the boat, so that he put no pressure on his wounded buttocks. That essentially means he was prone, face down, or bent over a bundle or keg for the month after the shooting."[27] Eleven days after being shot (on August 22), Lewis finally walked a little again; however, he had to rest after overtaxing his abilities. It took an additional two weeks (until September 9) for him to feel considerably healed and able to walk without significant pain.

* * *

Meriwether Lewis's return to society after the expedition proved short-lived. He traveled to Washington DC to meet with President Jefferson and report on the Corps' findings. Lewis promised to put together a written report from his journals, but he never submitted it. Jefferson appointed Lewis as Governor of the Louisiana Territory in 1808, but his skills in leading the Expedition did not translate well to a career as a governor over a hornets' nest of bickering and backbiting settlers, fur traders, and others.

Two pressures weighed greatly on Lewis, including the need to get his journals on the expedition finalized, and a lawsuit from the government based on a false accusation of personally profiting from fulfilling his political duties. The accusation, made by his lieutenant governor, William Bates, led to financial problems for

Lewis when the federal government refused reimbursements to him until the court case was settled. "Feeling the pressure of these political [issues]... caused Lewis to apparently sink into a deep depression,"[28] something he had experienced from time to time during his life. Unfortunately, while traveling to Washington in October 1809, Meriwether Lewis died of a gunshot wound in Grinder's Stand, Tennessee. Most historians believe he died by suicide. Neither Jefferson nor Clark were surprised by the cause of death.

Lewis's death at 35 only highlights the many instances during the cross-country Expedition when his life was preserved. In considering the many other explorers and mountain men who tried unsuccessfully—some even dying in the process—to accomplish what Lewis and Clark were able to do, the question arises: why Meriwether Lewis? What did he contribute that others could not supply? The answer to these questions lies in the legacy of the Corps of Discovery.

It is important to note that there would have been no Lewis *and Clark* if it had not been for Lewis. Meriwether Lewis had served under William Clark during the Northwest Campaigns in the early 1790s in Kentucky, Indiana, and Ohio. Clark commanded the Chosen Rifle Company, a group of sharpshooters, and earned high regard from his men. Twenty-one-year-old ensign Lewis was transferred to the Chosen Rifle Company following a drunken altercation with a lieutenant. During their brief time serving together, Lewis and Clark became close friends. Although they had different ranks and notable discrepancies in their personalities and temperaments, they were only four years apart in age (Clark being the eldest).

Clark resigned his commission in the military in 1796. But after being asked to head the exploration of the Louisiana Territory, Lewis immediately wrote to Clark asking him to be his "co-captain." When Clark agreed, the military reinstated him with a rank of first lieutenant; but Lewis ignored the difference in rank and treated Clark as his partner and co-captain in every regard throughout the expedition. The differences and strengths of Lewis and Clark served to balance each other. Lewis's tendency toward aloofness and his need for solitude juxtaposed with Clark's easygoing people skills. Meriwether's passion and brilliance for scientific study were balanced by William's consistent and methodical management abilities. While Clark's duties focused on map-making and management of supplies, Lewis attended to President Jefferson's instructions to catalog plants, animals, and other resources observed during the journey. The complementary friendship served them well.

One of Meriwether Lewis's primary accomplishments on the Expedition involved significant contributions to science, particularly in biology, botany, and zoology. "Before the trip is completed, Captain Lewis, especially, and the others, will describe 122 animals and 178 plants that had previously not been recorded for science, unknown to the Euro-American world."[29] In fact, Lewis wrote about and sketched so many new plants that a new genus was named after him (Lewisia). Five new species of fish, six new species of reptiles (including the Western garter snake and the Western rattlesnake), five new species of birds (including the Lewis's woodpecker), and at least six new species of mammals (including the grizzly bear and the white-tailed jack rabbit) had been discovered and documented by Captain Lewis in his journals during the journey. Over a hundred other types of animals were also seen and meticulously reported on by Lewis. No other explorer had both the understanding of natural sciences and the keen eye for detail that Meriwether Lewis demonstrated. The details recorded in his journals were exactly what President Jefferson had asked and hoped for, and were Lewis's unique contribution to our modern understanding of American Western ecology.

In addition to recording details of plant and animal life seen on the trek, Lewis also documented groundbreaking ethnographic information. Prior to the expedition, almost nothing had been known about Native American tribes living west of Fort Mandan. The Corps members were likely the first white men to engage with tribes living in the North Dakota area, including the Northern Shoshoni, Flatheads, Nez Perce, Cayuse, Yakima, and Walla Walla. Taking pains to observe how the Natives were governed, the languages they spoke, their traditions, and day-to-day activities, Lewis's notes (although not completely accurate) "as a whole... were so astonishingly accurate and complete that they provided a basic document for western ethnologists."[30] The effort to collect information on native social behavior and customs included new maps of the territory reflecting Native lands. The maps, mostly made by Clark, were used extensively in the following decades as the American settlers pushed west.

Of course, geographically Lewis and Clark were the first explorers to verify no navigable water passage existed from the Missouri River to the Pacific Ocean. The Corps had worked with various Native American tribes to glean knowledge of the land and were directed to a road through the Bitterroot Mountains used by local Indians. On August 12, 1805, Captain Lewis and three other Corps members used this road and found the head of the Missouri River, crossing the Continental Divide at Lemhi Pass. "Here Meriwether Lewis ...stood in awe of the never-ending mountain ridges rising before him [to the west] and realized the huge challenge ahead. It was a heart-sinking moment for him."[31] The experience felt disappointing because of the original directions he'd been given by President Jefferson:

> "The object of your mission is to explore the Missouri river, & such principal stream of it, as, by its course & communication with the water of the Pacific ocean may offer the most direct & practicable water communication across this continent, for the purposes of commerce."[32]

Lewis must have recognized that in some regards the mission of the Corps of Discovery would be considered a failure; without a Northwest Passage, the object of the mission would not be met and Jefferson's goals for commerce would be impeded. Despite this sobering realization, the next day Captain Lewis met up with a band of Shoshone and returned with them across the pass to rendezvous with the rest of the expedition members. On August 26, 1805 the entire team crossed Lemhi Pass as they left their boats behind and continued their journey west on horseback, following the headwaters of the Columbia River in search of the Pacific Ocean. The fact that Lewis and Clark carried on in the face of both failure and the arduous journey before them is a testament to their resilience, diligence, and spirit of discovery. What other explorer would have persisted after recognizing inevitable failure? Surely Meriwether Lewis stands in a class alone for persevering.

If Captain Lewis were to be categorized among the nineteenth century explorers, he would likely be considered one of the best in terms of his leadership capabilities. Neither Zebulon Pike nor John C. Frémont, two other prominent American explorers, exhibited leadership skills to the capacity of Lewis and Clark. The same is true with Robert Stuart. In contrast, many historians have reviewed and analyzed Lewis and Clark's leadership skills. For example, Stephen Ambrose noted of Lewis's talents that "[t]he most important was his ability as a leader of men. He was born to leadership, and reared for it, studied it in his army career, then exercised it on the expedition."[33] In particular, Lewis exhibited a talent for demonstrating servant leadership. He wasn't afraid to take on menial tasks. When the Corps reached the Great Falls on the Missouri River, for instance, they encountered a significant challenge with the need to portage their boats and supplies around the waterfalls. The team tirelessly shuttled back and forth, transporting provisions and tools from downstream to the river above. The time-consuming and arduous process took several days to complete because of the hilly terrain of the area. On the second day of the portage, Lewis noted in his journal: "to myself I assign the duty of cook…. I collected my wood and water, boiled a large quantity of excellent dried buffalo meat, and made each man a large suet [sweet] dumpling by way of a treat."[34] Being willing to take on humble tasks, like cooking, and working shoulder-to-shoulder with his men earned Lewis deep respect from his team.

* * *

The Lewis and Clark expedition accomplished more than a journey of territorial exploration; it serves as evidence of remarkable determination, leadership, and the American spirit of adventure. "Their successful traverse of uncharted territories laid the foundation for westward expansion and opened the door to further exploration and settlement."[35] Meriwether Lewis's essential participation in the expedition ultimately led to its success and the historical impact on the nation. However, Lewis's untimely death nearly led to the disappearance of the expedition from history. His inability to complete his journal, and the report promised to President Jefferson, led to a significant delay in making public the many findings of the Corps of Discovery. "Clark took the information gathered on the expedition and gave it to Nicholas Biddle, who eventually penned a report of the expedition in 1814 [nearly a decade after the fact]. By the time Biddle's report was published, the country's attention had shifted to the War of 1812."[36] Even worse, the expedition's original journals were filed away at the American Philosophical Society in Philadelphia—as though the American public had once again "long Since given out by the people of the U.S. Generaly and almost forgotten" them.[37]

For much of the century that followed, Lewis and Clark all but disappeared from the history books. Prior to 1904, no scholarly review of the Lewis and Clark journals or scientific findings had ever been published. Although a few historians began to research and write about the Lewis and Clark expedition in the early twentieth century, true interest blossomed in the 1960s when author Donald Jackson published his book *Letters of the Lewis and Clark Expedition*. After the book came out, Jackson continued to press for a thorough analysis of the journals and documents associated with the 1804–1806 trek. When the project finally came about, Jackson served as a project coordinator and authored the detailed historical account for the National Endowment for the Humanities. As Lewis and Clark's work finally emerged, the public readily consumed the history. Americans, with their passion for cowboys, Western movies and TV shows, and national parks and trails, deeply enjoyed the legacy of the Corps of Discovery. They viewed Lewis's significant role in the exploration and expansion of the United States as an example of traditional American values: bravery, fortitude, hard work. Meriwether Lewis's lasting impact on American history had finally come to life.

Chapter 5: Clara Barton

Clara Barton's influence for good has blessed the lives of so many and changed the course of history so powerfully that to consider her loss at an earlier age is to contemplate a devastating increase of human suffering. Her's is a story of overcoming extreme fear by finding courage in serving others. "[I]n the earlier years of my life I remember nothing but fear," Clara once wrote.[1] Despite her fear (and maybe to dispel it), Clara Barton found ways to teach and serve others. She risked her life over and over again to help the wounded soldiers of the Civil War, and exemplified bravery in convincing the US Congress to sign the treaty that would establish the American Red Cross. In being brave and serving others, Barton has been called "America's greatest humanitarian."[2]

Born on Christmas Day in 1821 in Oxford Massachusetts, Clarissa Harlowe Barton was the youngest daughter of Captain Stephen and Sarah Stone Barton. As the fifth child, Clara, as she became known, was more than a decade younger than her four older siblings. At age five Clara suddenly became frightfully ill. Her parents sent a man on horseback to summon the doctor. When the doctor arrived, many of the Barton's neighbors waited in the yard to hear the diagnosis. "Shortly the verbal bulletin went out: 'A sudden, unaccountable and probably fatal attack of bloody dysentery and convulsions.'"[3] The entire neighborhood immediately assumed Clara would likely die. Miraculously, though, she pulled through.

Clara's timidity in childhood caused her parents to be greatly concerned. The age difference with her siblings seemed to have a strong impact on her personality and the innate timidity she often felt. They protected her, but were rarely her playmates. Her debilitating shyness made it difficult for her to make any friends outside of family members. At age eight, her parents sent her to a boarding school, hoping it would force her out of her shell. But, when Clara arrived at the school, she felt so overwhelmed and afraid that she stopped eating and became lethargic. On the doctor's recommendation, her parents soon brought her home, where her older siblings helped educate her. Overall, her older brothers and sisters greatly influenced Clara's upbringing, teaching her everything from horseback riding to arithmetic. In essence, she had at least "six surrogate parents."[4]

On one occasion, however, two male cousins persuaded Clara to sneak out at night to learn how to ice skate—something her father had strictly forbidden. Sadly, the lure of the moonlight shining on the pond in the wee hours of a Sunday morning nearly ended in catastrophe. Clara later wrote in her personal memoir: "Swifter and swifter we went, until at length we reached a spot where the ice had been cracked and was full of sharp edges. These threw me and the speed with which we were progressing, and the distance before we could quite come to a stop, gave terrific opportunity for cuts and wounded knees. The opportunity was not lost. There was more blood flowing than any of us had ever seen."[5] At first, she tried to hide the "frightful" injury, but after several days of limping the problem was discovered, and the doctor brought in. She spent the next three weeks with her knee elevated as the deep wound healed. It is likely a miracle she did not damage an artery in the accident. A severe injury to an artery could potentially cause a person to bleed to death in as little as three minutes.

* * *

Clara's childhood lessons prepared her well for her future as a nurse and working with the military. Her mother influenced her temperament: independence, thrift, and a bit of eccentricity came from Sarah. From her father, Stephen, Clara learned management skills and, from the many stories he told of his military career, the importance of being prepared and keeping supplies on hand. As for being a nurse, Clara learned from hands-on experience. While working on a ridge-pole of a barn, Clara's older brother David fell. Although able to get up and move around, he likely suffered a severe concussion. He soon experienced a terrible headache and fever. Clara later recalled, "[F]rom the first days and nights of illness, I remained near his side. The fever ran on and over all the traditional turning points, seven, fourteen, twenty-one days. I could not be taken away from him except by compulsion, and he was unhappy until my return. I learned to take all directions for his medicines from his physician (who had eminent counsel) and to administer them like a genuine nurse."[6] She was only 11-years-old at the time.

At age 15 Clara's parents pushed her to become a teacher. They hoped her timidity and social anxieties would diminish as she worked in the classroom. In 1839 she began her first teaching job and found she had a talent for it. Her anxieties diminished when she helped her students learn. After six years as a teacher, she started a school for the children of her brother's mill workers. Later, in 1852, Clara established the first free public school in Bordentown, New Jersey. The school saw great success and significant enrollment increases in its first two years; but when the school board decided to hire a new principal, the job went to a man and Clara left in protest. She deeply disliked being treated as inferior when her work matched what her male colleagues provided.

As the Civil War began in the spring of 1861, 39-year-old Clara worked as a patent officer for the federal government in Washington. The 21st Massachusetts regiment had been under attack while on their way south and were housed at the capitol. "Some of these recruits were boys from Miss Barton's own town who had been her pupils, and all were dear to her because they were offering their lives for the Union."[7] She began volunteering as a nurse to care for the injured, feeding groups in the Senate Chamber, reading newspapers and letters to patients, and in one instance purchased a cemetery plot for a deceased soldier. Soon afterward, during the Peninsula Campaign, thousands of injured soldiers were brought to the capitol on hospital ships for medical care. Clara would take basic medical supplies, coffee, and anything else she could find that would help to relieve the suffering soldiers—but supplies were difficult to come by. Seeing the need for resources, she petitioned newspapers in Worcester,

Massachusetts to run a notice for financial donations and other various necessities. So many items were sent in response to the ad that Barton had to rent a large warehouse to store all the provisions that arrived. She used her talents for organization and administration to manage and use these supplies to care for those in need. Eventually, enough donations arrived to fill three warehouses.

While tending the wounded pouring into Washington, Clara could see how many men suffered as they waited for medical care and transport to hospitals. "[H]er whole nature revolted at the sight of the untold suffering and countless deaths which were resulting from delay in caring for the injured."[8] Clara recognized the need for prompt medical care. She wanted to be "between the bullet and the hospital"[9]; the greatest impact for good could be made in that time frame, even if it occurred on an active battlefield. But her biggest challenge involved obtaining accurate information about when and where a battle would take place—and then getting permission from the military to allow her to be there. Clara mustered her courage and worked to make connections with military leaders who could help make her vision come true. Luckily, she found several willing to champion her efforts.

General Daniel H. Rucker, head of the Quartermaster Depot in Washington became one such champion. When she first visited Rucker's office to request permission and supplies to go to the front, she sat in the corner trembling with fear as numerous orderlies bustled about, working to keep the Union army supplied. When Rucker finally looked up and crossly asked her what she wanted, Clara burst into tears. Caught off guard, Rucker immediately softened his demeanor and tone. He invited Clara to come closer to his desk and asked what she needed. "She steadied herself and leaped at the opening he offered."[10] After explaining her desire to go to the front, and that she had three warehouses full of supplies to take to the soldiers, Rucker promptly provided her with a pass, permission to travel on any military boat or train, and an army wagon to help transport her provisions. He even went to the Surgeon General's office to have her pass fully authorized. Throughout the remainder of the war, Rucker remained a faithful supporter of Clara Barton's work.

Clara finally had the opportunity in the fall of 1862 to go to an active battlefield. Despite her fears, she felt driven to help the wounded. The Battle of Antietam represented the first time she realized her vision for the care of injured soldiers. General Rucker shared privileged information with her on September 13 that a great battle would soon take place. Clara resolved to be on site and ready with provisions, rather than arriving a day or two after the fighting ended. With her supplies loaded in three Army wagons, Clara headed out with a small team of assistants. She took only a few personal items tied in a handkerchief. Her wagon soon joined a slow-moving convoy of military vehicles headed toward Harper's Ferry. She passed weary soldiers walking along the roadside. On September 15, Clara's team came upon the South Mountain battlefield, and she ministered to the injured men there. Once again, she saw the need to be on the scene earlier to provide needed care and save lives. But she knew an additional battle lay ahead, and she determined to "follow the cannon."[11]

In an effort to break free from the slow-moving wagon train, Clara had her team pull over to the side of the road prematurely. They rested and waited until the wee hours of the morning when the military would be camped for the night. With the road empty of other vehicles, Clara's team gained ten miles, placing their wagon immediately behind the artillery being transported to the battle front. The result of this effort put her at Antietam before the first shots fired.

On arriving, Clara's team discovered a field hospital set up in the farmhouse of Joseph Poffenberger. Following a pathway through the corn field, she found the barn where surgeons worked. Here she met up with Dr. James L. Dunn, whom she had encountered previously at Culpeper while caring for wounded men. Dunn, a tall, blue-eyed Pennsylvanian, expressed his surprise at seeing her and gave thanks for the supplies she had brought. After having previously cared for the injured at the recent battles of Harper's Ferry and South Mountain, Dunn's team of surgeons had run out of the most basic of medical supplies and had been using corn husks for bandages. Clara immediately went to work distributing supplies, providing food and drink for the wounded, and helping to clean the make-shift facilities. When

Dunn lamented the inability to continue operating when darkness fell, Clara produced four boxes of lanterns to light up the house and barn. Later at Antietam, she went onto the battlefield to help the injured at the peril of her life, sharing the following experience:

> "A man lying upon the ground asked for a drink; I stopped to give it, and, having raised him with my right hand, was holding him. Just at this moment a bullet sped its free and easy way between us, tearing a hole in my sleeve and found its way into his body. He fell back dead. There was no more to be done for him and I left him to his rest. I have never mended that hole in my sleeve."[12]

Clara stayed at Antietam several days after the end of the battle. Only when she knew every wounded soldier would receive the care they needed, and after all her supplies were depleted, did she finally return home to the capital. By this time, she was physically, mentally, and emotionally exhausted and had to be transported back to Washington while suffering from a fever.

While the Battle of Antietam had the greatest number of casualties of any single-day conflict in the war, Clara Barton witnessed numerous other bloodstained dates. Just a few months later, in mid-December 1862, Clara helped at the Battle of Fredericksburg. Once again, she arrived on the scene before the first shots fired. Initially she watched from the portico on the second floor of Chatham House (identified by the military as Lacey House). She later wrote, "For two long hours the shot and shell hurled through the roofs and leveled the spires of Fredericksburg."[13] On the second day of action, during the peak of the battle, Clara received a message requesting her help across the Rappahannock River where many of the injured were being treated in a local church. Despite the likelihood of danger, she immediately left Lacey House to cross the river. While en route, her life became endangered:

> "An officer stepped to my side to assist me over the debris at the end of the bridge. While our hands were raised in the act of stepping down, a piece of an exploding shell hissed through between us, just below our arms, carrying away a

portion of both the skirts of his coat and my dress, rolling along the ground a few rods from us like a harmless pebble into the water. The next instant a solid shot thundered over our heads, a noble steed bounded in air and with his gallant rider rolled in the dirt not 30 feet in the rear. Leaving the kind-hearted officer, I passed on alone to the hospital. In less than a half hour he was bro[ough]t to me dead."[14]

Clara spent the rest of the day and night helping care for the wounded in the Fredericksburg Baptist church and a number of neighboring buildings used for medical purposes. A reporter from the *New York Tribune* noticed her frequent movement between buildings and expected she would soon be shot or injured. In fact, Union General Marsena Patrick, while riding through town on horseback, actually stopped and argued with her about putting herself in such grave danger; but Clara's determination and independence won out. She continued to help in whatever way she could no matter how much risk it required. One of Clara's assistants, Cornie Welles, recalled, "One shell shattered the door of the room in which Miss Barton was attending to wounded men. True to her mission, she did not flinch, but continued her duties as usual."[15] Although she struggled with fear, she found courage in providing service to those in need.

When the Union Army had to retreat back across the Rappahannock River, Clara returned to Lacey House, which had become nearly overridden with wounded soldiers. The head surgeon estimated there were consistently 200 injured men being cared for there, with a continual flow of new patients arriving while others were removed, either to receive care elsewhere or to be buried. But when the house became too full, six canvas tents were set up on the grounds to provide additional beds. For several weeks, Lacey House and its surroundings served as an awful setting of agony and death. Unfortunately, winter weather compounded the suffering. Frigid temperatures and fog plagued the battlefield, and Clara worked to keep patients warm with blankets, fires, heated bricks, and hot drinks. She also used some 130 gallons of confiscated liquor to help relieve the suffering. The liquor had been passed on to her by Surgeon General Albert Hammond, who trusted she would make better use of it than anyone else in the military. When Hammond visited Lacey House three days after the Battle of Fredericksburg ended, he found 33 severely injured soldiers "measurably drunk"[16] from a strong hot toddy Clara had served. As a result, they slept more comfortably through the night—a temporary respite from the desperate situation around them.

The last few weeks of 1862 were spent tending to the remaining wounded in Fredericksburg who were sent off by train and boat to hospitals in the north for further care. On Christmas Day (Clara's 41st birthday), she noted seeing off Irish-born Sgt. Thomas Plunkett, who had lost both of his arms (right arm just below the shoulder, and left arm at the forearm) from an exploding shell while trying to raise the fallen US flag carried by the 21st Massachusetts regiment. When he had held the flag aloft, the fight for Fredericksburg was at its height, and his actions attracted enemy fire. After being injured, Plunkett walked until he fainted from loss of blood, after which stretcher bearers brought him to Lacey House where Clara cared for him, touched by his bravery. Although the surgeons had deemed Plunkett's case hopeless, and had left him lying on the floor while they saw to others, Clara sutured and bandaged his arms. When he departed on Christmas Day, she joined the 21st regiment to escort him to Falmouth Station and to salute him goodbye. "She later used her influence with Senator Wilson to get Plunkett a furlough and secure for him a substantial pension."[17] In March 1866, President Andrew Johnson awarded Thomas Plunkett the Medal of Honor for his bravery at Fredericksburg.

Less than a week later, on New Year's Eve, Clara returned home, shoeless and bedraggled, to her apartment in Washington. Absent for over a month, she had again reached physical and emotional exhaustion. The extensive suffering she witnessed in Fredericksburg weighed heavily and she wept uncontrollably, overpowered by grief. The next morning, New Year's Day 1863, President Abraham Lincoln issued the Emancipation Proclamation, promising freedom and justice to Black Americans, and forever changed the course of American history.

* * *

The early months of 1863 were notably quieter for Clara as she recovered from the Battle of Fredericksburg. The Union Army's strategy suffered from a severe coastal storm dropping heavy rain on Virginia. The downpour disrupted General Burnside's offensive plans and led to what became known as the "Mud March." Clara attempted to follow Burnside's troops but got bogged down in Falmouth (just north of Fredericksburg) by the heavy rain. After returning home again, her information on military movements indicated the war would shift further south. Clara's brother David had been appointed a captain in the Quartermaster Corps and received orders to report to Hilton Head, South Carolina; she went with him. The first three months there were quiet, and she questioned if she should have sought out a more active battle front.

When on July 10 the Union attacked a small Confederate fort called Battery Wagner, located on Morris Island in the Charleston Harbor, Clara's skills were needed. A week later, on July 18, ten Union regiments successfully scaled the parapet and entered Fort Wagner, but were soon driven out and forced to retreat. Heavy casualties resulted from the battle. "By then, Barton had joined the troops massing on the island, bringing with her an ambulance, horses, driver, and saddle horse, but few supplies."[18] She did her best to help feed and care for the wounded until they could be transported on ships to hospitals farther north. For weeks she served while the Union ships continued to shell Battery Wagner and Fort Sumter, and the Confederates returned fire. Even the hospital where she worked often experienced shelling. Clara described the situation in a letter to her cousin:

> "Frequent shells burst at night within ¼ of a mile of my tent, and no hour of the night that the cannon did not thunder in our ears. [A]lthough one may care very little for these things and they become like an every day tale still they wear a little upon the rest even of our hardiest soldiers because you cannot forget the fact that possibly each shot as it falls upon your ears has sent some poor fellow to the earth w[r]ithing in agony."[19]

After about four weeks assisting at the hospital on Morris Island, Clara became severely ill with acute dysentery and had to return to Hilton Head Island. Leander Poor, one of Clara's companions and cousins, worried Clara would not survive the high fever and dehydration from diarrhea. Moreover, Clara herself admitted in writing the severity of her condition. For the first time she suffered with extreme weakness and diminished sight, likely caused (at least in part) by pushing herself to exhaustion. When she recovered enough to help again, military leaders refused to give permission. Although she continued to send supplies to various army hospitals, and to an outbreak of smallpox in St. Helena, Clara spent the remainder of the year at home in Washington.

By the spring of 1864, Clara had sunk into depression. In her journal she wrote entries describing her lack of desire to get out of bed, feelings of discouragement, and refusing to answer the door to visitors. Thoughts of suicide brought her down: "I cannot raise my spirits. [T]he old temptation to go from all the world. I think it will come [to] that some day."[20] By the end of March she considered returning to her former post in the patent office and abandoning her nursing work altogether. But she could not find peace with that decision. Not until the last days of April did she pull out of her state of hopelessness. Her spirits were boosted by visits with family members who came to town, as well as the arrival of her beloved 21st Massachusetts regiment, who wanted her to serve with them again.

Clara immediately wrote the Secretary of War, Edwin McMasters Stanton for a pass to join the army on the battlefront. When she received a positive response from Stanton, her sense of purpose returned. In the correspondence, Stanton praised her for past service and granted her permission to go to the front lines to continue her work. Within two weeks Clara gathered supplies and set forth to help the wounded after the Battles of the Wilderness and Spotsylvania Court House near Fredericksburg. Once again, she found the conditions of the wounded deplorable and worked tirelessly for weeks on end while witnessing unimaginable suffering. In addition to battlefield wounds, summer neared, and the military became plagued with "cases of diarrhea and dysentery, malarial fevers, typhoid fever, and other disorders. Behind the statistics were scenes of human misery: wards reeking of vomit and pus and bloody excrement, men crying out in delirium, doctors and nurses struggling to save lives."[21] Working day after day in such conditions likely posed significant risks, but Clara persevered in an effort to help save lives.

One of the malaria patients Clara began tending was her own brother, Stephen, who had been arrested and imprisoned for allegedly trading cotton to the South. In June 1864, General Benjamin F. Butler appointed her as the "lady in charge" of the triage hospitals at the front of the Army of the James. Butler ordered Stephen Barton transferred to the triage hospital and Clara's care; Stephen arrived shaking with fever and chills, and could neither sit up nor walk on his own. As the war carried on, Clara spent long days tending to a never-ending stream of wounded men, and long nights looking after her brother.

At this point, Clara's fame as the "angel of the battlefield" (a nickname given her by Dr. Dunn) had spread across the nation. In a letter to his wife, Stephen wrote, "[N]o day since I have been here that I have not been introduced to officers, many of them high in rank, who call to pay their respects to Clara, not a few of them having received her care and attention when wounded, and on the field of battle."[22] In December 1864 Stephen traveled alone to Washington, still suffering from symptoms of malaria. Clara followed a month later, moving home to help him and other family members. Lamentably, Stephen died March 10, 1865; Clara's favorite nephew Irving passed away a month later. Despite being in mourning for her beloved family members, she felt relieved and grateful when the war effectively ended. The Confederacy surrendered to the Union's General Ulysses S. Grant at Appomattox Court House in Virginia on April 9, 1865.

* * *

The loss of Clara Barton's life, either in her youth or on the battlefield, would have resulted in human anguish likely too costly to imagine. Conversely, the preservation of her life led to the immediate comfort to generations of wounded, worried, and distressed individuals. By the end of the war Clara had already affected thousands of soldiers' lives (and by extension, their loved ones), but her humanitarian work had just begun. At age 43, she had much to give and a deep desire to continue to ease the pain and burdens of others. While her mental and emotional health took its toll from the traumas of the front lines, her healing would take some time. Her greatest accomplishments were still ahead of her: the establishment of the Missing Soldiers Office and the founding of the American Red Cross.

* * *

Shortly before the end of the war, prisoner exchanges between the Union and Confederacy resumed.[23] "A result of the resumed exchanges was thousands of emaciated and desperately ill former Union prisoners from infamous camps like Andersonville and Belle Isle began arriving at a designated drop-off point known as Camp Parole, near Annapolis, Maryland."[24] Clara's ailing nephew, Irving Vassall, heard of the difficulties government officials had in Annapolis in trying to help relatives of soldiers who sought their missing loved ones. Thus far in the war, the government had not been issuing death or missing notices, and thousands of families were left in the dark as to the fate of their servicemen. Some of these families had written to Clara Barton directly, seeking her help in finding information. These letters, and the news shared by Irving, pulled deeply on Clara's heart. In February 1865 she wrote directly to President Abraham Lincoln to get government permission to seek out information:

> "To his Excellency Abraham Lincoln President of the United States
> "Sir, I most respectfully solicit your authority and endorsement to allow me to act temporarily as general correspondent at Annapolis Maryland, having in view the reception and answering of letters from the friends of our prisoners now being exchanged.
> "It will be my object also to obtain and furnish all possible information in regard to those that have died during their confinement."[25]

Within a month, President Lincoln gave his permission for Clara to work with Major General Ethan A. Hitchcock, the Commissary General of Prisoners, to create a list of soldiers who had died in Southern prisons and then notify their families. She immediately went to work establishing what she called the Missing Soldiers Office, which she initially ran out of a tent on the grounds of St. John's College in Annapolis where Camp Parole operated. Clara placed a notice in newspapers to inform people of their ability to write to the office for information. Within a week over 360 letters had been received. Within months, thousands of letters arrived—sometimes more than 100 arriving each day.

At Camp Parole, more prisoners arrived by ship daily and "[a]s the weakened men struggled from the ships, Barton noted that inconsistent record-keeping made it almost impossible to know who had been left behind in the graveyards at the prisons. In lieu of official reports, Barton turned to the best source of information she had on-hand: the soldiers themselves."[26] She sought out the newly arriving prisoners and asked them to share their experiences, particularly the names of their friends who had not survived.

After three months of receiving letters, Clara published her first "Roll of Missing Men," a list of 1,533 names. The list, tacked up in military barracks and post offices across the country, indicated that a soldier was being sought by a friend or family member; the published list asked for anyone with knowledge of these individuals' whereabouts to send information to the Missing Soldiers Office. Over the next three years, several additional lists were released, eventually totaling more than 6,600 names. On average, Clara Barton and her team located information for about one in thirty of the names on the list.

Private Dorance Atwater, however, helped to improve Clara's success rate as she searched for missing soldiers. As a shy, paroled prisoner, Atwater saw the first "Roll of Missing Men" posted. While serving as a clerk to the surgeon's office in the infamous Andersonville Prison in Georgia, Atwater had secretly copied a list of over 12,000 names, date and cause of death, and burial locations of soldiers who died while imprisoned there. He had successfully smuggled his copy of the list out of the prison and brought it with him to Camp Parole, where he gave it to government officials. When Atwater saw Clara's list, he knew the smuggled Andersonville copy he had made would likely be of great help to her. Atwater contacted Barton and shared with her the existence of his document. Clara immediately recognized that with this information "they could identify [nearly 13,000] graves with proper head markers and notify the families of exactly where their 'loved ones' were buried."[27] She was thrilled by the possibility of helping so many.

After petitioning military and government leaders, President Johnson's secretary of war, Edwin Stanton, reached out to Clara with his approval for an expedition to Andersonville. By late July 1865 the excursion had begun, and the identification of the graves took about a month using Atwater's information. While assisting at Andersonville, Clara wrote to Secretary Stanton suggesting the grounds of the prison be made into a national cemetery. In 1970 this suggestion finally became a reality.

Most of the funds required for running the Missing Soldiers Office originally came out of Clara's own savings. In 1866 she temporarily closed the office because her savings ran out. When Congress finally reimbursed her and awarded some additional funds, the office re-opened for an additional year or so.[28] Later, in her testimony to Congress regarding the work of the Missing Soldiers Office, Clara Barton noted she and her staff "had received 63,182 inquiries, written 41,855 letters, mailed 58,693 printed circulars, distributed 99,057 copies of her printed rolls, and identified 22,000 men."[29] Despite her efforts, over 40,000 Civil War soldiers remain missing today.

Clara's efforts finding missing soldiers has had a lasting impact: widows and their children were able to apply for pension benefits and receive financial security; family members found closure in knowing how their sons, brothers, and husbands died; some deserters were able to come out of hiding and resume living their lives; and even today, a searchable database of Clara's "Roll of Missing Men" allows historians and researchers to better understand the magnitude, devastation, and sacrifices of the Civil War.

* * *

While the Civil War blazed, the first Geneva Convention for the Amelioration of the Condition of the Wounded in Armies in the Field was held in Geneva, Switzerland in August 1864. The establishment of the International Committee of the Red Cross occurred during the convention; its primary goal focused on delivering neutral aid to those injured in times of war. Burdened with work on the battlefronts of Virginia, Clara Barton remained unaware of the newly formed International Red Cross. However, after her haunting pilgrimage to the Andersonville Prison, her health, both mental and physical, declined. She spent some time on the speaking circuit trying to rebuild her savings, but the travel took its toll. Recognizing her celebrity interfered with her health, Clara's doctors recommended a trip to Europe to rest and recover. In her diary, she reflected about her 48-years of life, her health, and work. While on the steamer en route to visit friends in Geneva, Switzerland in September 1869 she wrote:

> "Is my life really worth while? I give all of my time and strength to the public that seems unappreciative. In obscurity I might have had health, at least personal comfort. I might have married and had a home, a family of children; I might have taken up painting or literature, in each of which my friends say I have ability. In either of such life's work I might have achieved success. As it is, even while serving the public, I am alone in the world, buffeted about and nobody seems to care for me unless to use me for some purpose."[30]

While in Switzerland, Clara met two individuals who would have a profound impact on her life. Initially, she met Dr. Louis Appia, a Swiss military surgeon and one of the founding members of the International Red Cross. Clara found the formation of this unique charitable organization intriguing and felt its work would be much needed in the world. Appia and Clara had many similar viewpoints about caring for wounded soldiers and living a life of service. "Appia saw in Barton a kindred soul and encouraged her to take news of their endeavors home with her to America."[31]

Later, after the Franco-Prussian War began in July 1870, Clara went to Germany to be of help; while there she met Princess

Louise, Grand Duchess of Baden, daughter of King William of Prussia. Princess Louise urged Clara to support the Red Cross's relief efforts on the battlefield and helped provide financial support. Together, they worked to procure supplies for military hospitals and other resources to civilians impacted by the war. Clara's experience proved to be invaluable to the International Red Cross, especially on the frontlines where both France and Germany requested neutral aid for their wounded. She formulated the strategies the organization would use to provide supplies to military hospitals, to mitigate the aftereffects of war, and to distribute relief funds to those in need. The Iron Cross in Prussia and the Golden Cross of Baden were both awarded to Clara as an expression of gratitude for her work on behalf of wounded soldiers. Her work and contribution to humankind had finally received some recognition.

The additional time on grisly battlefields, however, were hard on Clara's mental health. In late 1873 she returned to the United States still suffering. Finally, in 1876 she checked herself into a sanitorium in Dansville, New York in the hopes she would be able to regain her health. Although a resident of the sanitorium for ten years, Clara didn't sit idly by. She used this time to write letters in an effort to convince political leaders of the need for an American Red Cross. The challenge seemed monumental because it meant convincing two-thirds of the Senate to be willing to ratify the Geneva Convention Treaty. Initially, some were doubtful about the request—because there would not likely be another Civil War or need for neutral aid on a battlefield in North America. To make her argument more persuasive, she broadened the mission of the Red Cross to include giving aid to those impacted by natural disasters. Although President Rutherford B. Hayes decided not to support it, Clara convinced his successor, Chester A. Arthur. On May 21, 1881, the American Red Cross was formally organized with Clara Barton serving as its first president. She led the organization for over 20 years, solidifying its place as the most well-known and trusted charity in the US. Since its formation, it is estimated that the American Red Cross has blessed the lives of nearly 10 million people.

* * *

For a woman who began her life living in fear, Clara Barton learned to manage her anxieties and depression by working and serving others. She survived life-threatening illnesses, battlefront near-misses, and conquered thoughts of suicide. In doing so she lived to accomplish much and relieve the suffering of many. Later in life she contemplated her achievements in her journal: "I wonder whether or not any woman thinks her life a success? Oh, well, I guess it was intended that I should do the work I am doing, forget myself and live for others, so I might as well make the best of it and try to be happy."[32] Not only did she make the best of it by forgetting herself, but she blessed the lives of millions of others with her choice.

Chapter 6:

Benjamin Franklin

In the fall of 1745, Prussian science hobbyist Ewald von Kleist filled a glass medicine bottle with water and firmly corked the top. The cork had a nail hammered through it, reaching down into the clear liquid. The nail head, after coming into contact with an electrostatic machine, gradually developed a charge through friction, generating static electricity. Von Kleist soon noticed a line of light, like fire, hovered all around the nail, which lasted for about a minute after he removed the bottle from the electrical machine and paced around the room holding it in his hand. Curious about the fire-like glow, von Kleist touched the nail with a finger and received an immense electrical shock that traveled up his arm and into his shoulder. It was a jolt that would shake the world.

Although wary about touching the medicine bottle again, von Kleist wrote a number of letters to various European scientists and academics about his experience. Four months later, Leiden University's professor of physics Pieter van Musschenbroek duplicated and refined von Kleist's experiment. Although neither von Kleist nor van Musschenbroek understood the significance of their experiments at the time, what came to be known as a Leyden jar proved that an electric charge could be stored for future use: it became the forerunner of the battery.

Within a short time, van Musschenbroek's experiments were made known to other European scientists, as well as the Royal Society in London. Royal Society member Peter Collinson, in addition to being interested in advancements in science, served as the first book purchasing agent for the Library Company of Philadelphia—and became a faithful correspondent of Benjamin Franklin.

* * *

Benjamin Franklin is arguably one of the most famous Americans in the history of the nation. His creativity, curiosity, and penchant for inventing led him to unforeseen vistas, both geographical and theoretical. He was born January 17, 1706, to a candlemaker from Boston, Massachusetts. Josiah Franklin fathered 17 children (from two wives), and Benjamin held the position of the youngest sibling. As parents, Josiah and Abiah were actively engaged in their children's lives, making certain they were well educated and attended church services on a regular basis. Abiah ensured Benjamin had plenty of creative play time, while Josiah sought to nurture his mind through conversation and engaging him in the family business. Benjamin did not enjoy the process of candle making—cutting wicks, melting wax, and helping to sell wares—so Josiah sought out other professional opportunities for his bright son to try.

Eventually, 12-year-old Benjamin began an apprenticeship under his brother James, who had recently returned from London with equipment to open a printing shop. Despite the family relationship, James's temper made for unpleasant working conditions. Still, under James's tutelage, Benjamin learned how to set type, to write both journalism and prose, and to market and sell a product. One of the best perks of the job included his access to books. He would often read late into the night to finish a book before having to return it the next morning. His late-night reading served as way to extend his education and learn more of the world. In 1721, James began publishing *The New England Courant*, an irreverent newspaper that did not shy away from criticizing local government officials or clergy members. "*The Courant* would be remembered by history mainly because it contained the first published prose of Benjamin Franklin."[1] Two years later, at only 17, Benjamin took over publishing *The Courant* while James served a prison sentence after being convicted of contempt charges related to a particularly offensive article he had published. Taking advantage of the lack of supervision, and his brother's signature of release on his apprenticeship papers,[2] Benjamin ran away to Philadelphia.

Philadelphia proved to be to Benjamin's liking. He quickly found a job, again working for a printer. He obtained lodging with the Read family, whose daughter Deborah would eventually become Benjamin's wife. Less than a year later, though, Benjamin set sail for London in hopes of purchasing his own printing press and going into business for himself. What he initially planned to be a relatively short stay in England was extended when a letter of credit promised to Benjamin by Pennsylvania's Governor William Keith failed to appear. Franklin had no choice but to find employment to support himself. For the next two years he worked for two different printing companies in London, refining his skills. But he also continued his program of self-education through reading, attending plays, and joining in debate and discussion at local coffeehouses. Finally, in 1726, at age 20, a penniless Benjamin returned to Philadelphia with a business partner, Thomas Denham, and a plan to open a mercantile.

Benjamin's return home brought new experiences. "Mr. Denham took a store in Water-street, where we opened our goods; I attended the business diligently, studied accounts, and grew, in a little time, expert at selling. We lodged and boarded together; he counseled me as a father, having sincere regard for me,"[3] Franklin wrote of this time. After only working together for four months, in the spring of 1727 both Denham and Benjamin took ill. Benjamin's doctor diagnosed him with pleurisy, a term then used to describe a variety of respiratory infections that include chest pain. He became so ill he felt the pleurisy "very nearly carried me off."[4] After much suffering his constitution won out and he began to slowly recover. Denham, on the other hand, suffered greatly from the disease; he died after a drawn-out battle with infection.

Pleurisy is an inflammation of the lining of the lungs (known as pleura). Although often mild, pleurisy can progress to causing collapsed lungs, heart disease, or other chest problems. In Benjamin's case it appears his pleurisy may have been viral. Viral infections, such as influenza, are the most common cause of pleurisy. Whatever the cause, Benjamin had chronic issues with the disease for the rest of his life. At age 34, for example, he had a reoccurrence that included an abscess developing on his left lung. When the abscess ruptured Benjamin nearly suffocated to death on the quantity of the discharge. "This condition has always been a grave one, because it can set off a cascade of inflammation, fluid exudation into the airspaces, and a respiratory distress syndrome that is both mechanical and hormonal."[5] Miraculously, Benjamin survived a second time, although his recovery took four months, causing him to miss meetings both at work and at the Library Company. Eventually, pleurisy played a contributing factor in Benjamin Franklin's passing in 1790.

* * *

After the death of Denham, 21-year-old Benjamin once again found himself unemployed. With his previous job as a journeyman printer, however, he quickly received an offer from an old employer. Because of his experience with Governor William Keith's deceit and the loss of Thomas Denham, Benjamin decided that to achieve professional success, he would have to rely solely on his own efforts. His success came when he and co-worker Hugh Meredith borrowed money to open their own printing shop in 1728. The next year they began printing their own newspaper, *The Pennsylvania Gazette*. By the time Benjamin reached his twenty-fourth birthday, his business had been named by the Pennsylvania Assembly as the official government printer.

During this time Benjamin also found success in his personal life. In September 1830 he and Deborah Read entered into a common-law marriage.[6] By all accounts Deborah was an intelligent, reliable woman. She managed all of Benjamin's business affairs for years while he worked abroad as a diplomat; he even trusted her enough to give her power of attorney. Deborah's willingness to manage the businesses and their home life gave Benjamin the ability to experiment with electricity and to spend years in public service both at home and abroad. Together the couple had two children: Franky, who died of smallpox at age four, and Sarah ("Sally"). Deborah also helped to raise William Franklin, an illegitimate son born in 1730 to Benjamin before his marriage.

The 1730s proved to be very profitable for Benjamin Franklin. *The Pennsylvania Gazette* became the most widely read newspaper in the colonies by 1732. With news articles about both local and foreign events, he interspersed comics, maps, and letters to the editor. Many articles he wrote himself using pseudonyms.

Additionally, his *Poor Richard's Almanack* garnered sales of nearly 10,000 copies annually. Soon Benjamin branched out to printing Bibles and even a novel written by Samuel Richardson. In addition to the printing company, Benjamin received an appointment from the crown to be postmaster for the colonies. This position provided extra income and supplied a convenient distribution channel for his publications. In essence, it gave Franklin a vertical monopoly as a media magnate. By the mid-1740s Benjamin had become one of the wealthiest men in the colonies. "He also had built a network of profitable partnerships and franchises from Newport and New York to Charleston and Antigua. Money flowed in, much of which he invested, quite wisely, in Philadelphia property."[7]

By 1745, with his business ventures on firm footing, Benjamin's attention began to turn elsewhere. His tendency toward curiosity grew. Fourteen years prior, he had established the Library Company of Philadelphia, the first successful lending library in the colonies. In an effort to grow the collection of books at the Library Company, Benjamin contracted Peter Collinson, an English import-export merchant to locate and ship copies of new or important older books across the Atlantic. Finding similar interests in science, natural history, and plants, Benjamin and Collinson soon became friends and regular correspondents. As a member of the British Royal Society, Collinson became one of the first to learn about the invention of van Musschenbroek's Leyden jar. And knowing how remarkable Benjamin Franklin would find it, Collinson shipped him one of the glass tubes, along with a pamphlet describing its use.

Two years prior to receiving Collinson's Leyden jar, Benjamin Franklin had learned a little about electricity while on a visit to Boston. During that time, Dr. Archibald Spencer of Scotland had delivered a series of "lectures" on medicine, light, and electricity. Although licensed as a medical doctor, Spencer spent the majority of his time as a traveling showman whose demonstrations were more for entertainment than scientific purposes. He used static electricity to charge a married couple, who then felt a strong spark on kissing. Additionally, Spencer made bits of metal fly from one table to another, and he made sparks flash from a boy suspended in flight position from the ceiling by silk cords. Benjamin, who had paid the advertised £6 fee to attend the May 1743 seminar, wrote of being greatly "suprize'd and pleas'd"[8] by the spectacle. Later, when Dr. Spencer came to Philadelphia to deliver his lectures, Franklin helped by running ads in *The Pennsylvania Gazette* and sold tickets. In time Dr. Spencer became a mentor to Benjamin and eventually sold his electrical tools and apparatus to Benjamin for his research.

With this equipment, Benjamin immersed himself into experimenting with electricity. Through various tests, Benjamin determined that electricity consisted of a common element he called "electric fire," claiming that it flowed like a liquid, and that it had the ability to jump between charged objects. Benjamin also correctly concluded that lightning was simply a massive flash of electricity. During his experiments, he coined various electricity-related terms still used today, including "charging," "discharging," "conductor," and "battery."

Unfortunately, the experiments did not always go as Franklin planned and on at least two occasions he put his own life in danger. In December 1750, while attempting to use electricity to kill a turkey for Christmas dinner, he electrocuted himself for the first time. He described the accident in a letter written on Christmas day to his brother John Franklin:

> "Two nights ago being about to kill a Turkey by the Shock from two large Glass Jarrs containing as much electrical fire as forty common Phials, I inadvertently took the whole thro' my own Arms and Body, . . . the flash was very great and the crack as loud as a Pistol; . . . I had a Numbness in my Arms and the back of my Neck, which Continued till the Next Morning but wore off. Nothing Remains now of this Shock but a Soreness in my breast Bone . . . . I am Ashamed to have been Guilty of so Notorious A Blunder."[9]

Benjamin's guests present during the electrocution incident reported hearing a loud crack, like a pistol shot, and seeing a bright flash of light. They also noted the jolt knocked Benjamin senseless. Franklin elaborated on how the electrocution felt:

"I know not how well to describe—a universal blow through my whole body from head to foot, which seemed within as well as without; after which the first thing I took notice of was a violent, quick shaking of my body, which, gradually remitting, my sense as gradually returned, and I then thought the bottles must be discharged, but could not conceive how, till at last I perceived the chain in my hand, and recollected what I had been about to do. That part of my hand and fingers which held the chain was left white, as though the blood had been driven out, and remained so eight or ten minutes after, feeling like dead flesh; and I had a numbness in my arms and the back of my neck, which continued till the next morning, but wore off. Nothing remains now of this shock but a soreness in my breast bone, which feels as if I had been bruised. I did not fall but suppose I should have been knocked down if I had received the stroke in my head. The whole was over in less than a minute."[10]

When the human body experiences electrocution, the electrical current can cause a variety of physiological reactions, ranging from minor tingling sensations to severe burns, muscle contractions, and even cardiac arrest. The severity of these effects depends on the voltage, current, and duration of the exposure. Benjamin's description of his electrocution as stunning and debilitating likely indicates he felt several thousand volts of electricity. This incident could have been life-threatening, as high-voltage electrical shocks of 2,500 or more typically are fatal. He was fortunate to survive without severe harm.

The experience with electrocution may have ultimately saved Benjamin's life. Eighteen months later, Benjamin conducted his famous kite in the thunderstorm experiment. In preparing to prove his hypothesis, Benjamin made a kite out of a silk handkerchief attached to a light cedar frame. He attached a wire to the top of the kite to help attract lightning, while jute string provided tension from the ground. Because of the turkey experiment, "he was concerned that if he were to hold the end of the kite string directly, he might very well be killed as the electricity passed through him."[11] To protect himself, Benjamin tied the end of the jute string to a key; from that he attached a piece of silk ribbon, which he could then hold onto to guide the kite. Since dry silk is an excellent electrical insulator, Benjamin conducted the experiment safely during the rainstorm as he stood inside a shed near his home. When the static electricity from the storm clouds traveled down the jute to the key, he then touched it to a Leyden jar and captured the electricity for storage. History had been made. But it only happened because Benjamin survived his previous brush with death.

* * *

In 2006 the Constitution Center in Philadelphia held an exhibit to celebrate the 300th anniversary of Benjamin Franklin's birth. Officials appropriately named the exhibit "In Search of a Better World." More than any other man of his generation, Franklin certainly made the world a better place than it had been previously. If Franklin had died earlier of pleurisy, or if he had died from being electrocuted in his experiments with electricity, the world today might be a very different place. Franklin's impressive spectrum of talents included those of a writer, scientist, inventor, statesman, diplomat, printer, publisher and political philosopher. Consequently, the impact of his life reaches into the far corners of the earth with his achievements in science, public service, and improvements made to everyday life.

Franklin's achievements in science began after his retirement. In 1748, at age 42, he turned over the operation of the printing business to his foreman David Hall, with a contract that awarded Franklin 50% of the profits over the next 18 years, at which time Hall would become the owner. The income from this arrangement provided more than enough to give him "leisure to read, study, make experiments, and converse at large with such ingenious and worthy men as are pleased to honor me with their friendship."[12] For the most part, Franklin's scientific pursuits were based on fascination and the joy of discovery, rather than a desire to make more money. In fact, he refused to patent most of his inventions because he wanted others to freely benefit from them. Although initially driven by the power of his curiosity, he ultimately worked to try and determine how to make things useful. Moreover, for many years he lamented how there was no real use for knowing that lightning and static electricity could be stored in a Leyden jar.

Human understanding of electricity prior to Benjamin Franklin had not advanced for several thousand years. Early in his experimentation, he made a breakthrough in determining static electricity is not *created*, but simply *collected* from another source through friction, and that it moved from source to source with fluidity. One of the more popular "party trick" experiments Franklin used to demonstrate how electricity flowed, involved having a group of people stand in a circle holding hands. Franklin would use friction to add charge to a Leyden jar, then joined the circle. On one side, he would join hands with another participant's hand; with his other hand he would hold the Leyden jar. He then instructed the person on the other side of the Leyden jar to touch the nail, making a full connection. Instantly, each person in the circle would simultaneously feel a jolt of high voltage, low amperage static charge. The trick never failed to entertain, but also helped Franklin better understand the properties of electricity.

Prior to Benjamin Franklin, scientists had thought electricity involved two types of fluids that could be created individually. "Franklin's discovery that the generation of a positive charge was accompanied by the generation of an equal negative charge became known as the conservation of charge and the single-fluid theory of electricity."[13] He simply related the concept to bookkeeping and the need to balance credits and debits. Practical application and analysis, such as this, helped him succeed over and over again in his experiments.

Franklin's unique accomplishments stemmed from his background, understanding of mechanics, deep level of curiosity, and his interest in conducting utilitarian experiments. These traits were more beneficial to him in the discovery of electricity than a background in mathematics or theoretical knowledge. And "by being removed so far from the European centres of experimentation and discussion of electrical events, Franklin was able to view his own observation with a freshness not encumbered by the earlier notions of others."[14] The end result: some researchers consider the single-fluid theory of electricity to be as great a discovery as vaccines, the molecular structure of DNA, or even Isaac Newton's discovery of gravity and planetary movement.

One of the long-lasting impacts of Benjamin Franklin's studies of electricity is the development of the lightning rod. Early on he noticed numerous parallels between lightning and electricity. Initially, Franklin proposed to test the theory of lightning as a form of electricity by placing a sentry box—a phone booth like structure used to shelter a soldier on guard—up near a steeple, in which a person (standing on a grounded floor) could measure the electricity conducted through an iron rod protruding upward. Franklin himself never conducted the experiment, but instead proved the theory using his unique kite-key test. However, scientists in France, after hearing of Franklin's theory, used the sentry box experiment successfully. From this knowledge, Franklin reasoned that buildings and lives could be saved if iron rods, connected by a wire that ran to the ground, were placed on top of buildings to draw out the static electricity from storm clouds, thereby preventing the damage of lightning strikes. There ensued some debate as to whether the lightning rod should have a pointed or blunt top, but ultimately the invention proved effective whether it was pointed or not.

John Adams described the notability that resulted from the invention: "Nothing, perhaps, that ever occurred upon this earth was so well calculated to give any man an extensive and universal celebrity as the discovery of the efficacy of iron points and the invention of lightning rods."[15] The National Lightning Safety Institute estimates that even with lightning rods, annual damages from lightning in the United States alone costs $6 to $7 billion. Calculating the collective damage that has been prevented worldwide since the invention of the lightning rod would be significantly higher, not to mention the potential loss of life that many have occurred without it.

* * *

After becoming famous for his experiments with electricity and lightning, Franklin shifted his focus to experimenting with issues related to public affairs. In 1753, at the age of 47, he had been appointed deputy postmaster-general for the colonies. He traveled up and down the coast on horseback and by carriage setting up communications and logistics to ensure efficient delivery of the post. Poor road conditions and long distances made the work both difficult and dangerous. But these tours of the colonies, as well as his time spent living in London, gave Franklin a unique perspective: he viewed the colonies as a united, cohesive unit rather than as individual entities.

In addition to serving as postmaster-general, Franklin participated in the Pennsylvania Assembly, which struggled with managing and financing frontier issues. William Penn's sons, the proprietary owners of the colony of Pennsylvania and titleholders of massive tracts of land, rejected the need to pay taxes to help support a militia to protect the western border. Franklin clashed with the Penns on these issues. Eventually, the Pennsylvania Assembly sent him to London on a mission[16] to petition Parliament for a change to the proprietary ownership of the colony. Ultimately, the roles of Postmaster and Representative of the Assembly placed Franklin in a distinctive position of prominence and influence.

Benjamin Franklin wanted Pennsylvania to become a Crown colony—one that would garner representation in the Houses of Parliament. But in the 1760s very little support existed among the British aristocracy for such a change. Instead, Franklin found his attention focused on a completely new issue: taxes. In 1765, the British passed the Stamp Act, which required a tax stamp on many common items used by the colonists, including almanacs, cards, newspapers, books, and legal documents. For the first time Parliament imposed an internal tax on the colonists, and it angered them:

> "The Stamp Act crisis sparked a radical transformation in American affairs. A new group of colonial leaders, who bristled at being subservient to England, were coming to the fore, especially in Virginia and Massachusetts. Even though most Americans harbored few separatist or nationalist sentiments until 1775, the clash between imperial control and colonial rights was erupting on a variety of fronts."[17]

Insulated in London, Franklin did not at first understand the depth of anger colonists had in reaction to the Stamp Act. However, after reports that a mob approached his own home in Philadelphia with the intent to burn it down (Deborah, with the help of friends and family, stood her ground against the crowd, and they eventually moved on), Franklin went to work lobbying to get the act repealed. While he lobbied British politicians, he simultaneously encouraged colonists to boycott any item included in the Stamp Act. And he went to work writing. Franklin published (sometimes anonymously) essays and scalding satire to try and force people to see the absurdity of enforcing military rule on British citizens. He also designed a political cartoon that reflected back to what happened historically when a Roman general had oppressed his people. Franklin's cartoon clearly criticized government policies; the short-sighted British regulations ran the risk of alienating the American Colonies—and it got people talking. Eventually, in February 1766, shortly after his sixtieth birthday, Franklin had the opportunity to testify before Parliament about the negative impact of the Stamp Act. Although he had never developed the skill of public speaking, he elegantly made a logical and persuasive case, withstanding several hours of questioning. Parliament repealed the act within a month.

In December 1774, while Franklin still lived in London, Deborah died from a stroke. Now a widower, Franklin remained abroad for the rest of the winter, trying to prevent Parliament from oppressing colonists. By the time he returned to Philadelphia in May 1775, the first battles of the Revolutionary War had taken place and delegates for the Second Continental Congress were already beginning to gather. The Pennsylvania Assembly unanimously nominated Franklin to be their representative. Although he was, at age 69, by far the oldest attendee, his life experience made him uniquely qualified. With celebrity born from electricity experiments, and proficiency as a diplomat and ambassador, Benjamin Franklin now possessed a unique set of credentials that would enable him to change history. No other individual from the colonies had the name recognition, experience as a statesman, mature temperament, or philosophical background that would be required over the next eight years to ensure the move for independence succeeded. Throughout 1775 and 1776, as the Second Continental Congress worked to unite the colonies and fight the war, Franklin's expertise was called on again and again. His achievements included the following:

- The Continental Congress immediately appointed Franklin as the postmaster-general to ensure the safe delivery of mail between colonies. "British postal officials would be loath to deliver letters for practicing rebels; already the mails were being regularly opened. And already colonial governments were making separate provisions for delivery."[18] Franklin easily put a new system in place and then donated the entirety of his £1000 salary to help wounded soldiers.

- He helped draft the first Articles of Confederation that would serve as a constitution should the war be won. His draft provided for a strong central government and a unicameral (single-chamber) congress.

- Assigned by Congress, Franklin took on the task of establishing a system of paper currency. His former printing business had held the Pennsylvania, New Jersey, and Delaware contracts for printing paper money for over 30 years. The back of each of the Continental dollars featured an image of a leaf, the fine veining of which counterfeiters were never able to accurately reproduce.

- With his background in science, Franklin helped the Continental Army collect lead for munitions, devise a way to manufacture gunpowder, and gather other needed provisions to supply Washington's men. "The job was immense, being hardly less than creating an army from scratch—or, what was worse, from a motley collection of militias jealous of their rights and confirmed in their ignorance."[19]

- As part of Pennsylvania's defense committee, Franklin "oversaw construction of a secret system of underwater obstructions to prevent enemy warships from navigating the Delaware River."[20]

- Franklin also served on a committee sent to Montreal, Canada to determine if a union could be formed to create a cohesive alliance against Britain. The journey, which took place in May 1776, took a toll on the 70-year-old; he wondered if it would lead to his death. "I begin to apprehend that I have undertaken a fatigue that at my time of life may prove too much for me," he wrote while in Saratoga, New York. "So I sit down to write to a few friends by way of farewell."[21] Ultimately Franklin survived, but he did not persuade Canada to become an ally. Canada deferred, primarily due to the lack of funding the Continental Congress could provide.

- Shortly after returning from Canada, Franklin participated in a five-person committee tasked with drafting a declaration of separation from Great Britain. Franklin's 50 years of publishing and writing would help to create one of history's most influential documents. Jefferson, who possessed a talent for lyrical phrasing, wrote the initial draft for the committee. Franklin, home ill with gout and recovering from the trip to Montreal, helped to provide some edits to Jefferson's work. One of the more notable changes Franklin made to the document modified the phrase, "We hold these truths to be sacred and undeniable" to "We hold these truths to be self-evident." Jefferson's use of the word *sacred* "was an assertion of religion. Franklin's edit turned it instead into an assertion of rationality."[22] Eventually a draft of the document was presented to the Continental Congress, which severely critiqued and further edited the wording. After cutting the length nearly in half, the Continental Congress officially approved the Declaration of Independence on July 4, 1776. Later, when Franklin reflected on the moment, he described the signing of the Declaration as "a miracle in human affairs."[23]

* * *

In the fall of 1776 Benjamin Franklin received his most important assignment that would greatly influence the course of the American Revolution. A congressional committee chose him to serve as an envoy to Paris in an effort to secure financial assistance and form a military alliance with the French government. Despite being elderly and in poor health, the committee felt his international experience and time spent as an agent of the colonies made him the most qualified of the patriots. The assessment not only proved to be fully accurate, but understated Franklin's capabilities. "Of all the representatives sent abroad to secure aid from friendly nations, no one has equaled Benjamin Franklin in ability, tact, common sense, diplomacy, and international reputation."[24] Franklin spent eight years in Paris, where he played French interests against those of the British in an effort to forward America's agenda. As news of American military successes began to reach France, he obtained extensive financial and military support from King Louis XVI. His accomplishments in Paris during the war "display a dexterity that would make him the greatest American diplomat of all times."[25]

Benjamin Franklin's personal influence on the American Revolution is equaled only by that of George Washington. While Washington fought militarily on American shores for independence, Franklin fought a public relations battle on the international front to both finance the war and to legitimize America as a new nation in the eyes of European nations. Although Postmaster General was the only federal office he ever held, of all the Founding Fathers, only Benjamin Franklin's signature appears on all four of the key documents that solidify the birth of the United States of America: The Declaration of Independence (1776), Treaty of Alliance with France (1778), Treaty of Paris (1783), and the Constitution of the United States (1787). One can only imagine how the course of American history might have changed had Franklin died before becoming one of the Founding Fathers.

* * *

Throughout his career as an agent and a diplomat, Franklin relied heavily on his writing abilities to help sway public opinion and persuade those in power. Some historians consider Franklin to be the greatest writer of his generation; the quantity of his writings certainly qualifies as prolific. He began writing as a teenager working for his brother, James, and practiced by developing specific exercises used to expand his skills in prose and structure. In time, he felt confident enough to "submit" his writing to the *Courant*:

> "[B]eing still a Boy, and suspecting that my Brother would object to printing any Thing of mine in his Paper if he knew it to be mine, I contriv'd to disguise my Hand, and writing an anonymous Paper I put it in at Night under the Door of the Printing-House. It was found in the Morning and communicated to his Writing Friends when they call'd in as usual. They read it, commented on it in my Hearing, and I had the exquisite Pleasure, of finding it met with their Approbation, and that in their different Guesses at the Author none were named but Men of some Character among us for Learning and Ingenuity."[26]

After a while Franklin's writing abilities matured and flourished. Although the vast majority of his work is journalistic, he had the skill to write poetry and fiction. "Franklin's works also can be compared to those of the great eighteenth-century English prose writers."[27] In 1732, 26-year-old Franklin achieved great success when he began writing and publishing *Poor Richard's Almanack*. Published for 25 years, the almanac had a strong cultural impact that forever changed the format and style from humdrum to humorous. Later, in 1771, 65-year-old Franklin began writing his memoirs, a project that took nearly 20 years. The resulting autobiography received widespread popularity and became the first book written by an American taken seriously in Europe. Franklin's autobiography has been described as "a book for all times and all cultures, as basic and universal in its appeal as *Cinderella* or the Twenty-Third Psalm."[28] Overall, the body of Franklin's works served to galvanize what would eventually be identified as the core characteristics of American identity: self-improvement, common sense, freedom, and morality. No other American author of his generation so deeply impacted both national culture and international mores through the written word.

* * *

Benjamin Franklin was endlessly curious. That curiosity led him to create innovative inventions and make new discoveries that would have a long-term impact on everyday living for people around the world. Aside from his discovery of electricity, Franklin crossed the Atlantic Ocean eight times and mapped the Gulf Stream by taking temperature measurements. Franklin's map is still used by scientists today. In 1784, Franklin invented "double spectacles" or bifocals in an effort to improve his own eyesight. He came up with the idea of using bucket brigades for fire safety in building codes. His Library Company of Philadelphia is one of the earliest libraries in the colonies. In an effort to reach books on the high shelves in his personal library, he created the long arm (essentially a long stick with a claw device at the end). Later, in his travels as postmaster, Franklin wondered how far he had been traveling. To measure the distance, he created an odometer to attach to his carriage wheel. Lastly, one of Franklin's older brothers, John, suffered greatly from kidney stones and had to use a catheter. When John expressed the desire for a catheter that would be easier to insert, Franklin invented one with a flexible tube. By the end of his life, his curiosity had reached broadly and deeply in widely-varied directions.

* * *

In early April 1890, at age 84, Benjamin Franklin took to his bed. He suffered from a fever and chest pains resulting from another bout of pleurisy. At one point in the last ten days of his life, he rose briefly to have his daughter Sally remake the bed so he "might die in a decent manner."[29] When she responded with the hope that he would recover and live a longer life, Franklin replied, "I hope not." On April 17 an abscess in one of his lungs burst, making it difficult to breathe and impossible to talk. At 11 p.m. that same night, Benjamin Franklin passed away.

In his will, Franklin set aside funds for Boston and Philadelphia. He hoped the £1000 given to each of the cities would grow significantly through compound interest. The trust funds were to be invested for 100 years before it could be used to benefit those learning a trade. When the cities received the final balances after 200 years, the combined bequest had grown to $6.5

million. Boston ultimately used the money to fund the Franklin Institute of Boston; Philadelphia's funds continue to grow and are designated to help high school graduates who wish to pursue careers in trade. Benjamin Franklin continues to change history, even today.

Chapter 7:
Winston Churchill

After a decade of being distrusted by both the National Labor and Conservative political parties in Great Britain, Sir Winston Churchill found himself anxiously concerned by the rise of Adolf Hitler. With the aid of friends and government officials, Churchill began gathering intelligence on Nazi party movements on the continent. The late 1930s brought great turmoil to Europe, including an Italian invasion of Ethiopia and the Spanish Civil War, but Churchill maintained German aggressiveness was the greatest security risk facing the British. It wasn't until March 1939, after the failure of Neville Chamberlain and the Munich Agreement, that Churchill emerged as England's spokesperson and wartime leader. Churchill's time had come.

"In a sense, the whole of Churchill's previous career had been a preparation for wartime leadership."[1] But his preparation had extended beyond vocational training. He had sensed the future importance of the role he would play on the world's stage. In July 1891, at the young age of 16, Churchill told his close friend Murland Evans:

> "I tell you London will be in danger – London will be attacked and I shall be very prominent in the defence of London. I see further ahead than you do. I see into the future. This country will be subjected somehow, to a tremendous invasion, by what means I do not know, but I tell you I shall be in command of the defences of London and I shall save London and England from disaster."[2]

How Churchill knew this at such a young age is a mystery. Not known to be actively engaged in religious practices, he characterized himself as agnostic much of his life. Still, Churchill acknowledged many times how his life had been extended or preserved by a higher power. "I could not help feeling thankful that I had been preserved," he wrote after escaping from prison in South Africa in 1899.[3]

But this event did not mark the first or only time his life had been miraculously extended.

* * *

Winston Leonard Spencer Churchill was the oldest son of Lord Randolph Churchill and Jeannette "Jennie" Jerome, a wealthy American debutante. Winston recalled his childhood at Blenheim Palace in Woodstock, Oxfordshire as one of neglect and sadness. His parents were often too busy with their social lives to engage with him. Only his nanny, Mrs. Everest, made him feel loved and valued. After being sent to St. George's boarding school in Ascot, nine-year-old Winston felt even more unhappy and lonely. Soon, Mrs. Everest discovered the physical abuse Winston suffered at St. George's when he was flogged for misbehavior. To their credit, Lord and Lady Churchill immediately removed Winston when they learned of the cruelty. On recommendation from their practitioner and close friend Dr. Robson Roose, in 1884 they moved Winston to a new boarding school in Hove, near Brighton—more than 100 miles away from home.

The new school served as an improvement for Winston's circumstances, although he still longed to spend more time with his parents. Located on the edge of a wooded area where Winston could ride his horse. The picturesque seaside town of Hove had much to offer young boys with a bent for the outdoors. Winston also had the opportunity to study more subjects of interest to him, including French, drawing, and history. And Bertie Roose, son of Dr. Roose, became a close friend.

Sadly, while living at Hove, Winston caught pneumonia. "I very nearly died from an attack of double pneumonia," Winston later wrote in his autobiography.[4] For five days in March 1886 he clung to life. Dr. Roose faithfully tended Winston while continuously writing updates to Lord and Lady Churchill, who were given only limited time in the sick room.

Sunday, March 14: "Temp. 104.3, right lung generally involved, left lung of course feeling its extra work. . ... This report may appear grave yet it merely indicates the approach of the crisis."[5]

Monday, March 15: "'We are still fighting the battle for your boy. Your boy on his perilous path is holding his own well."

Tuesday, March 16: "'We have had very anxious night. The left lung still uninvolved. The delirium I hope may soon cease. Your boy is making a wonderful fight."[6]

Early on in Winston's bout with pneumonia, Dr. Roose indicated that by keeping his temperature under 105 degrees Fahrenheit (40.6 degrees Celsius), the crisis would pass within four days. "The 'crisis' was the turning point of the disease in pre-antibiotic days, after which the patient either improved or deteriorated."[7] Dr. Roose aimed to do this by using alcohol as a stimulant (both orally and rectally), and watching closely over the patient.

Dr. Roose's predictions were as accurate as his care was meticulous. By the fourth day of Winston's illness, March 17, the severity had declined. At seven a.m. that day, the doctor reported that the boy had slept well the previous night and no longer experienced delirium. Roose felt so confident in the progress of his patient that, for the first time in four days, he left Hove to go to check on his practice in London. Winston remained in the care of Roose's colleague, Dr. Joseph Rutter. Although the fear of relapse concerned both Roose and Winston's parents, continued rest and treatment helped to avert the possibility. Winston convalesced for several months. "By November he came top of the school in gymnastics, and felt fitter than before the illness."[8] But the pneumonia had weakened his lungs permanently. He experienced four more bouts of pneumonia before his death in 1965.

How dangerous was pneumonia in 1886? Pneumonia commonly affected both children and adults during this time period. In fact, Lord Randolph Churchill, Winston's father, passed away in 1895 of bronchial pneumonia. But among children, the disease proved particularly vicious. "Between the ages of 5 and 14 years, pneumonia accounted for almost 10 percent of all childhood deaths in the late nineteenth century."[9] Without antibiotics or the financial resources to pay for medical care, most of those who caught pneumonia struggled to stay alive. Winston counted himself as one of the lucky ones who survived.

* * *

"Are you desirous of a reputation for courage? You must risk your life," Churchill wrote in his novel, *Savrola*.[10] These sentences weren't written simply to forward a fictional plot. With the goal to eventually enter politics, Churchill knew being a war hero would help his cause. He believed participating in war "was the swift road to promotion and advancement in every arm. It was the glittering gateway to distinction."[11]

In January 1895, now 21, Churchill had joined the 4th Hussars as a subaltern.[12] During the five winter months of leave, he and fellow Hussar Reginald Barnes used their aristocratic connections to obtain permission to join with the Spaniards in a fight to quell Cuban rebels. In early November that year they sailed to New York before making their way to Havana. Once in Cuba, they met up with a Spanish general and were sent to Santa Clara. "The journey [to Santa Clara] was quite practicable," Churchill later wrote. "The trains were armoured; . . . when firing broke out, as was usual, you had only to lie down on the floor of the carriage to arrive safely."[13]

Eventually, the pair joined up with a convoy seeking to secure the jungle lands. On Churchill's 21st birthday, he heard his first shots of war. A bullet struck a horse between its ribs, killing it while Churchill stood nearby. Winston determined the bullet that killed the chestnut had come within a foot of his own head. Several days later, while sleeping in a hammock a "bullet ripped through the thatch of our hut, another wounded an orderly just outside."[14] The next few days Churchill and Barnes experienced more gunfire and participated in an attack on the Cuban rebels. But by the end of December, after a month of service, they were on their way back to England safe and uninjured.

Now with actual war experience, 23-year-old Churchill continued to both seek out battle opportunities and to write. In fact, he wrote *Savrola* primarily in India where he served as a

Hinge Points in History

second lieutenant and war correspondent. While in India in August 1897 he took part in the Malakand campaign. Malakand was Churchill's first experience being under fire as part of the British Army. He wrote about the battle in several columns for *The Daily Telegraph*, receiving £5 per column. Churchill later received the India Medal with the clasp *Malakand 1897* for participating in the battle.

Despite receiving the Indian Medal and legitimately being a war hero, Churchill continued to search for chances to serve on the battlefront. By this time, Great Britain had begun defending territories in Africa. In 1898 he joined with the British–Egyptian expeditionary forces to fight against the Sudanese Army; simultaneously he worked as a news correspondent. By early August Churchill arrived in Cairo on his way to meet up with British Commander in chief Major General Sir Herbert Kitchener's forces (20,000 strong). Kitchener had been tasked with overthrowing Sudan's leader, who commanded 60,000 men. Winston's southbound regimental journey of 1,400 miles included transportation by train, steamer, horses, and military railway. At one point, Churchill got separated from his convoy and lost his way in the desert. "He wandered for 70 miles before finding it again through the use of 'the glorious constellation of Orion. Never did the giant look more splendid,' he later wrote. It had directed him towards the Nile, and probably saved his life."[15] Less than a month later, Churchill participated in a cavalry charge at the Battle of Omdurman. Once again, he experienced bullets whistling dangerously close by, but he remained safe and uninjured.

Major General Kitchener's forces were able to successfully overthrow the Dervish Army at the Battle of Omdurman. The British-Egyptian army had superior training, equipment, and discipline. But one of the consequences of the victory gave Kitchener the ability to immediately dispense with the 21st Lancers cavalry regiment, in which Churchill served. Once back in England, Winston's income as a correspondent ended. Despite his family's wealth, he resolved to support himself financially by winning a polo tournament in India, writing his third book (*The River War*), giving speeches, and trying to get elected to

Parliament. He succeeded with all but the latter, losing the election for a seat in Oldham by a narrow margin in July 1899. Luckily for him, by this time a new war had cropped up in South Africa. Churchill used his notoriety to secure a lucrative job as a war correspondent for *The Morning Post* and caught a ship headed to Cape Town.

In November 1899, 24-year-old Churchill arrived in South Africa, where Boer (Dutch) settlers were fighting off British rule over the Orange Free State. Prior to Churchill's arrival, the British infantry had been forced to surrender to the Boers. With General Penn Symonds killed in battle, the remaining British forces were pushed back to the town of Ladysmith. Due to the thin spread of British troops, an armored train helped patrol central Natal, where the skirmishes had occurred.

"Eager for trouble,"[16] Churchill gained permission to ride on the armored locomotive patrol on November 15, 1899. The train, under the command of 37-year-old Captain Aylmer Haldane, departed Estcourt carrying 150 soldiers and a naval gun. The train had been authorized to patrol the track going approximately ten miles to the north, as far as Frere; however, Churchill convinced Captain Haldane to continue on several miles farther north to Chieveley. Churchill's persuasiveness proved poor judgment. The Boer forces obstructed the train tracks and attacked the derailed train with a "hailstorm"[17] of bullets.

> "Churchill directed unblocking the line and freeing the locomotive, displaying great bravery by completely disregarding hostile fire. He placed the wounded on board, and it escaped to Estcourt. Courageously, he then left the locomotive to rejoin Haldane and the doomed defenders. En route, he was taken prisoner by a Boer trooper."[18]

Churchill, Haldane, and others were taken to a secure facility in Pretoria. "I consider myself unfortunate in having been captured so early in the operations . . .," Churchill immediately wrote in a letter to his friend, the Prince of Wales. "I could not help feeling thankful that I had been preserved," he admitted.[19]

Despite his gratitude at being alive, Churchill deeply disliked incarceration. As soon as they arrived in Pretoria, Churchill,

Haldane and a third man began plotting an escape. The three planned to go over the iron lattice-work fence on a dark night with little moonlight, but the plan went awry when Churchill made it over the fence without the others. After waiting in the bushes for a while, Churchill soon realized he would be alone in the escape. "Having waited as long as he could, Churchill walked through the Boer capital at night . . . He had to cross 300 miles of enemy territory with no map, compass, food, money, firearm, or knowledge of Afrikaans."[20] He later told one of his nephews that during this escape he "prayed very earnestly."[21]

His prayers must have worked. "Orion shone brightly,"[22] Churchill recalled later as he related once again using the stars to help guide his journey. After making his way back to the train tracks, he managed to surreptitiously board a train and hide among sacks of coal. Unfortunately, the train left the station going the wrong direction and Churchill had to jump off as it sped down the tracks. After roughly rolling down a ravine, he waited until dusk in a nearby thicket of trees. That night he wandered until hunger pains forced him to knock on a hut door to ask for help. Fortunately, a British mining engineer opened the door. The engineer, along with a few other Britons in the area, willingly came to Winston's aid. They stowed Churchill in a dark mine for three days to hide him from the door-to-door manhunt that had been launched on discovery of his escape. Eventually, his accomplices concealed him in the bottom of a railway car headed to Lourenço Marques (modern-day Maputo), which he reached only days before Christmas.

After connecting with the British consulate in Lourenço Marques, Churchill took a boat back to Durban. At the docks, a crowd of well-wishers welcomed him. His escape had been the bright spot in what had thus far been a war of setbacks and losses. Taking advantage of the opportunity, Winston delivered some impromptu remarks to the crowd:

> "It is for the people of South Africa, for those of the Cape Colony, and those in Natal to say whether or not the British flag is going to be hauled down in this country. When I see around me such a crowd as this, such determination and such enthusiasm, I am satisfied that, no matter what the

difficulties, no matter what the dangers and what the force they may bring against us, we shall be successful in the end."[23]

* * *

In his escape from prison Churchill had perfectly exemplified determination and enthusiasm in the face of danger, although his motivation for serving in Natal appeared to have been more self-serving than that of patriotism. But what if Churchill had not survived his bout with pneumonia, or had been killed on one of the many battlefronts he had purposefully sought out? How might the vacuum of his death have had an impact on Great Britain's future, particularly in World War II?

Despite Churchill's efforts to establish himself as a war hero beloved by Britain, his political career remained challenging. In 1900 he once again ran for office in Oldham, this time winning by the same narrow margin by which he had previously lost. Winston modeled his political career and speaking style after his father, who had been famous across the country. As a Tory, Winston excelled in giving speeches and helped negotiate peace with the Boers. But when he came to blows with his own party over tariffs, Churchill joined the Liberals in 1904.

Over the next ten years he served in a variety of offices as he rose to political prominence. He worked on prison reforms, imposed work-hour restrictions on mining operations, and obtained a promotion to the office of home secretary. But when he came at odds with rioting labor unions, he once again switched political parties. With this decision, politicians on both sides of the aisle felt Churchill couldn't be trusted. By 1915 he removed himself from government office and went back to the military, serving primarily in administrative positions.

"[I]n 1931 the National Government was formed, Churchill, though a supporter, had no hand in its establishment or place in its councils. He had arrived at a point where, for all his abilities, he was distrusted by every party."[24] At this time he began to worry about Hitler's rising power in Germany. Although he did his best to bring attention to the potential threat to Europe, particularly the growing size of the Luftwaffe, few others in the British government seemed to share his concern. Unable to gain access to top secret government intelligence on Germany, Churchill set up a report gathering system based at his home, Chartwell. When Neville Chamberlain was elected prime minister in May 1937, Winston's exclusion from the inner circles of government deepened. Chamberlain ignored Churchill despite the fact his intelligence on Germany frequently proved more accurate. By 1939 Churchill began to speak publicly about the dangers of Germany's actions and he criticized the Munich Agreement, which sacrificed Czechoslovakia to Germany, as "a total and unmitigated defeat."[25]

* * *

Many of Winston's leadership successes in World War II came from fifty years of experience, both in the military and serving in government positions. His month in Cuba taught him to keep a cool head when under fire. His time in Sudan and serving in the Boer War left him with an understanding both of the frailties of military brass, and how to communicate with them. The experiences he had serving as Secretary of State for Air, First Lord of the Admiralty, and as Minister of Munitions prepared him to better understand the capabilities and limitations of the British forces. The vital insights gained from these experiences provided Churchill with more accurate life and death decision-making abilities necessary in a time of national crisis.

But what if Churchill had not had such vital preparation? What would have happened in World War II if Churchill had not been at the helm? Leadership required during a time of crisis such as Great Britain experienced at the start of World War II is rarely found in any time period. A mere look at Churchill's contemporary European leaders confirms this point. France's prime minister Paul Reynaud stood staunchly opposed to German actions, but lacked the persuasive power needed to inspire his colleagues and his commander in chief, General Weygand, to fight. Norway's King Haakon, who refused to surrender his rule to the Germans, had not recognized the danger posed to his country or had the vision required to prepare. Belgium's King Leopold III ordered an outright surrender to Germany without even consulting his own government. Even the efforts of Churchill's predecessor, Chamberlain, lacked the moral strength to stand up to Adolf Hitler and Benito Mussolini.

Scholars have long tried to understand what makes a good leader. What most have discovered is that the "best" leadership skills depend on the circumstances of the moment—both the difficulty of the task at hand and the abilities of the people being led. In the case of Winston Churchill, he was the right man for the moment. Lists of the greatest leaders of the twentieth century consistently place Churchill at or near the top. Although Churchill certainly was not the perfect statesman, it was not perfection that would bring Britain through WWII. As President Dwight D. Eisenhower wrote of him, "I have known finer and greater characters, wiser philosophers, more understanding personalities, but no greater man."[26] Churchill's greatest strengths as a leader in WWII include his energy and work ethic, his power of articulation, and his wisdom and perceptiveness.

* * *

With the call to lead the country as prime minister on May 10, 1940, at age 65 Churchill had finally reached his life's purpose. "I felt...that all my past life had been but a preparation for this hour and for this trial."[27] Without delay he called a cabinet and extended enough magnanimity to include Chamberlain. But Churchill's leadership style varied greatly from Chamberlain's. "Under Chamberlain, even the advent of war had not altered the pace of work, according to John Colville; but Churchill was a dynamo."[28] Churchill regularly worked 18-hour days. Although not apt to rise early, he often worked from both his bed and bathtub, reviewing documents, dictating letters and memos. His staff of personal secretaries were kept on hand until late into the night, only leaving when Churchill finally retired around 11:30 or midnight. "When he wanted something done, everything else had to be dropped," noted General Alan Brooke.[29] And Churchill always wanted to be on site and see things first-hand. He frequently walked out into the streets of London, seeing the latest damage from German air assaults and encouraging the people. He went on 19 grueling (sometimes dangerous) journeys overseas in an effort to build and maintain alliances. King George VI's intervention finally convinced Winston that his presence at Normandy on D-Day was unnecessary. But he showed up six days later anyway.

* * *

One of the most notable leadership strengths Churchill brought to the position of prime minister involved his ability to compose "magnificent wartime oratory."[30] Winston had spent years learning to both write and deliver inspirational speeches. He did not employ speech writers but spent a great deal of time composing drafts and rehearsing. "He wrote speeches like psalms, setting out his notes in a distinctive 'Psalm form'. The phrased passages helped him to maintain the right cadence in his delivery, and he made use of rhythm and dramatic pauses."[31] Although Churchill had struggled with a lisp in his early years, by the time he became prime minister he had embraced it, believing it gave him a unique voice for the radio. He even had his dentures fashioned to preserve his lisp.

But more importantly, Churchill understood how to craft a persuasive speech. He knew to begin with an honest, even stark, assessment of the situation. After this, Churchill would transition into a reason to be optimistic—something based in truth and reality. Then he would end strongly with a call to action written with rhetorical bravado to inspire determination and embolden his listeners:

> "We shall go on to the end, we shall fight in France, we shall fight on the seas and oceans, we shall fight with growing confidence and growing strength in the air, we shall defend our Island, whatever the cost may be, we shall fight on the beaches, we shall fight on the landing grounds, we shall fight in the fields and in the streets, we shall fight in the hills; we shall never surrender."[32]

Very few public speakers, even experienced ones, master the ability to persuade like Winston Churchill could. As journalist Edward R. Murrow wrote, "He mobilized the English language and sent it into battle to steady his fellow countrymen and hearten those Europeans upon whom the long dark night of tyranny had descended."[33]

* * *

Winston Churchill is often criticized for his poor judgement. He doubted votes for women, supported Edward VIII in the abdication debacle, underestimated enemies, appointed people who failed to perform, could be ethnocentric, and failed to retire after a stroke in 1953 (just to name a few). But Churchill wasn't necessarily bothered by these failures. He willingly made mistakes, and he tried to experiment, grow, and trust himself. "I should have made nothing if I had not made mistakes," he once told his wife, Clementine.[34]

But when it came to managing the British government during WWII, Churchill arrived at the post as a remarkably well-qualified and knowledgeable leader. Prior to the war starting, he had been one of the lone voices promoting rearmament (the practice of equipping a military with needed weapons and related supplies) and a draft. Additionally, as part of the process of putting together his cabinet, he appointed himself as the Minister of Defense, causing some to question his judgment. But Winston recalled from his earlier days as Munitions Minister when a communication gap seemed to exist between the military and government officials. By making himself Minister of Defense, he ensured no such gap would occur during his tenure.

Other key decisions showing Churchill's superior judgement in WWII include:

- His leadership during Dunkirk, the Battle of Britain, and the Blitz.

- He knew from the outset that Great Britain would have to draw the United States into the war if Germany was to be beat.

- Despite Stalin's wishes, Churchill resisted rushing the invasion of northern France. He believed the second front in Europe required detailed planning and training.

- He knew the inherent need to cloak Allied strategy in a web of deceit to mislead the enemy.

- And finally, "When it came to all three of the mortal threats posed to Western civilization, by the Prussian militarists in 1914, the Nazis in the 1930s and 1940s and Soviet Communism after the Second World War, Churchill's judgement stood far above that of" those who criticized him.[35]

* * *

Beyond his leadership capabilities, one of the unique ways in which Churchill had a significant impact on World War II stemmed from using his past experiences in planning for D-Day. Churchill clearly remembered the failed marine invasion of Gallipoli during World War I. British troops had been stuck on the beaches without protection from the Germans or equipment or vehicles to move inland. An unfortunate repeat of this failure occurred when the Allies tried to take the French port of Dieppe in August 1942. To avoid this same failure on D-Day, Churchill demanded a team of engineers, scientists, and military officers design a port system that would allow Allied ships to safely anchor and unload equipment needed for the massive operation. "They must float up and down with the tide. The anchor problem must be mastered. Let me have the best solution worked out," Churchill instructed. "Don't argue the matter. The difficulties will argue for themselves."[36]

The resulting solution became the Mulberry Harbour, an easy-to-assemble temporary port. It consisted of artificial breakwater barriers made of sunken ships and huge steel and concrete chambers. These chambers were filled with air to make them float until they were towed into place. Churchill first witnessed the concept of the Mulberry Harbour being demonstrated in a bathtub on the Queen Mary while crossing the Atlantic in 1943. "Churchill's scientific adviser, Professor John Bernal, floated paper boats in the prime minister's bathtub, agitating the water to simulate waves, then used a loofah, or sponge, to demonstrate the pacifying effect of breakwaters."[37] With this demonstration, Churchill felt satisfied. The barriers would solve the problem and help increase the likelihood of a successful invasion. Two Mulberry Harbours were used successfully during the D-day invasion, one of which was nicknamed Port Winston.

Additionally, in June 1940 Churchill authorized the new Special Operations Executive (SOE) arm of the British forces to wage a covert war. The SOE agents were tasked with espionage, sabotage, and subversion behind enemy lines and to give aid to resistance movements where possible. Churchill instructed them specifically to "Set Europe ablaze!"[38] And Churchill's Secret Army successfully pulled off operations in Europe, Asia, and the middle East. Even women were included in SOE. Some disguised as nurses while doing their work, they were the only women considered to be in a combat role during the Second World War.

* * *

It is difficult to imagine the tremendous impact an early death of Churchill would have had on World War II. After Germany's invasion of the Low Countries in May 1940 proved Chamberlain's policies had failed, he immediately resigned. When discussing his replacement with King George VI, Chamberlain noted Lord Edward Halifax seemed the logical choice; but surprisingly, instead he recommended Winston Churchill. If Churchill had been out of the picture, Halifax may well have taken Chamberlain's place. Halifax, as a close friend and colleague, had gone along with Chamberlain's policy of appeasement toward Adolf Hitler. With this position of weakness "prime minister" Halifax would likely never have been able to rally or galvanize British resolve to fight off the Germans. England could have been invaded.

Many historians and armchair generals have imagined what the potential German invasion (Operation Sea Lion, as the Germans called it) and occupation may have looked like. After the Dunkirk evacuation in July 1940, the British military found themselves in dire straits. Without Churchill at the helm of the government giving his people backbone, this would have been a prime opportunity for Germany to advance. Author Kenneth Macksey envisioned a German land invasion to be swift and thorough. He hypothesized Germany would have been in full control of England by August 1940. Conversely, other historians do not see a setting where Germany could have invaded. Although the possibility of Germany invading British soil—and being able to take over the government—is highly debatable, even an unsuccessful attempt would have led to serious ramifications. About 44,000 Britons were killed in the Blitz alone; many more lives could have been lost if Germany had attempted a land invasion. In a worst-case scenario, the United Kingdom could have come to an end.

Other possible impacts the early death of Winston Churchill may have caused include:

- An estimated 40–50 million people died during World War II. Without Churchill's ability to build a coalition between the Allies, many more lives would likely have been lost (including an increase in the Holocaust), and the geopolitical landscape of Europe might be significantly altered.

- When the war reached its height in 1944, Churchill stated that the "United Nations is the only hope of the world."[39] Without Churchill's collaborative support and persuasive capabilities, the UN likely would not have been established until the 1950s.

- Churchill set the tone when the scale of the Nazi atrocities against the Jews became apparent. He described it as "probably the greatest and most horrible crime ever committed in the whole history of the world."[40] Without this perception, particularly in naming it a "crime," extensive prosecution of war crimes for the Holocaust may not have occurred.

- History is what historians say happened. Churchill wrote and published more books (primarily about history) than Shakespeare and Dickens combined. His works have greatly influenced the interpretation of events and people, particularly the years between 1850 and 1950. Without these books, our collective understanding of some significant world events would likely be greatly altered.

- Churchill coined the term "iron curtain" in a speech denouncing Soviet expansion on March 5, 1946. Without his willingness to speak up, especially during his second term as prime minister in the early 1950s, the USSR may have been more emboldened, and the Cold War could have led to more physical aggression.

* * *

Winston Churchill passed away in January 1964 at the age of 90 after suffering a stroke. His death occurred on the 70th anniversary of his own father's passing, a seeming homage paid to the man he admired most in life. After three days lying in state at Westminster Hall, Churchill's funeral held at St. Paul's Cathedral became only the third ever for a person not of the royal family. His body was finally laid to rest near his birthplace at Blenheim Palace.

Churchill's remarkable life seemed to be the stuff fiction is made of. His legacy of leadership sparked a new era of Western individualism and achievement, strategic national defense, and economic growth. Surprisingly, in 2008, a poll of British citizens revealed nearly one in four believed Winston Churchill to be fictional character.[41] Despite Great Britain's fading national memory, his impact has been tangible and lasting. More than fifty years after his passing his life and leadership is still studied and deeply admired.

Chapter 8:
Brigham Young

After the return to Kirtland, Ohio from Zion's Camp in February 1835, Joseph Smith, first prophet of the Church of Jesus Christ of Latter-day Saints (more commonly known as Mormons), called a special leadership conference. The goal of the meeting sought to re-establish a "foundation of the apostles and prophets"[1] as described in the New Testament by formally organizing a modern-day Quorum of the Twelve Apostles. Smith delegated the selection of the Twelve to three men who had assisted with and financially supported the translation process of the Book of Mormon. With the help of fasting and prayer, 12 men were chosen; after Lyman Johnson, Brigham Young became the second man appointed, and the third oldest of the group. A week after being chosen as an apostle, Oliver Cowdery ordained Brigham to the office. Collectively the new apostles received a promise from the Lord: "Your lives shall be in great jeopardy; but the promise of God is, that you shall be delivered."[2] This profound promise found fulfillment on at least three occasions in the life of Brigham Young, including bouts with yellow fever, scarlet fever, and another unknown prairie disease that left him emaciated.

Born June 1, 1801 in Vermont to farmer John and Abigail "Nabby" Howe Young, Brigham was the ninth of eleven children. The family moved to upstate New York during his toddler years, and over time he lived in two homes in the Finger Lakes district. As a young adult he apprenticed as a carpenter and glazier. At age 23 he married Miriam Angeline Works (as the first of 56 wives), had a daughter, and received baptism into the Methodist faith before eventually moving to Mendon, New York in 1830.

In Mendon Brigham met Heber C. Kimball, a member of the Church of Jesus Christ of Latter-day Saints. After a thorough investigation of the Book of Mormon and a face-to-face meeting with Joseph Smith, Brigham Young accepted baptism on April 9, 1832. From the beginning, he took his baptismal covenant seriously—he was fully committed. His dedication to his faith is seen when he volunteered to serve in the Zion's Camp march, which aimed to help the expelled Missouri Saints, and when he lent his time and skills as a master glazier to build the gothic arched windows in the Kirtland Temple. He became an ardent missionary for the Church, traveling to Canada, England, and other countryside areas around Kirtland and Nauvoo. In 1846, he supported President James K. Polk's order for military to be stationed in the American Southwest and he helped recruit and lead the 2,000-mile Mormon Battalion march to San Diego.

Despite his dedication, Brigham's vigorous approach to life and his faith often placed him in dangerous situations. Most people envision Brigham as a robust, healthy man. And, at 5' 10", 190 pounds he was, for the most part. He lived an arduous, active life, working with his hands for a living, and crossing the American plains. But during these travels he often encountered the bugs and viruses that caused him serious health issues.

One of Brigham's first brushes with death came in 1839. The winter season had been particularly challenging for the Saints and for Brigham. Members of the Church had been forced out of Missouri by an extermination order from Governor Boggs during the early months of the year and took refuge in Iowa and Illinois. The Young family left Missouri on February 14, 1839, abandoning most of their personal belongings and furniture. Brigham's journal entry commenting on the event only garnered a few short sentences. "I left Missouri with my family, leaving my landed property and nearly all my household goods, and went to Illinois, to a little town called Atlas, Pike County, where I tarried a few weeks; then moved to Quincy."[3]

The Youngs stayed for a short time in Quincy, Illinois, while Joseph Smith searched for a new headquarters for the outcast, beleaguered Saints. Brigham, as a member of the Quorum of the Twelve assisted by providing him counsel. Soon afterward, the Youngs took up residence in a room in an old military barrack in Montrose, Iowa on the western bank of the Mississippi River. By late May, summer had begun to bloom. Unbeknownst to Brigham, an epidemic of yellow fever had just begun. Yellow fever is a viral disease caused by a particular type of mosquito native to Africa and South America. Symptoms of yellow fever include fever, chills, vomiting, headache, kidney problems, and fatigue; and like malaria, it can lead to death. Medical professionals of the day recorded the existence of the yellow fever epidemic occurring in "the towns on the Mississippi River, the Lake Shore, and the interior of Louisiana and Mississippi."[4] And Brigham himself mentions in a letter penned in July that many of the Saints in Commerce (Nauvoo) and Montrose were taken ill with the "ague," or "chills and fever."[5] In the same letter he mentions he had been caring for others until he took ill himself.[6]

On July 22, 1839, "a day of God's power," Joseph Smith, also ill, apparently rose from his bed to go from home to home giving priesthood blessings of healing, including one to Brigham Young. In his journal Brigham recorded, "Joseph arose from his bed of sickness, and the power of God rested upon him. He commenced in his own house and dooryard, commanding the sick, in the name of Jesus Christ, to arise and be made whole, and they were healed according to his word. . . He walked into the cabin where I was lying sick, and commanded me, in the name of Jesus Christ, to arise and be made whole. I arose and was healed, and followed him and the brethren of the Twelve."[7]

Despite feeling significantly better, Brigham's health still lacked vigor. He wrote in his journal, "During my further stay in Montrose I attended meetings and administered to the sick when I was well myself."[8] At 38-years-old, his full health took time to recover. Eight weeks later, on September 14, 1839, his departure for a mission in England arrived, but Brigham's journal entry notes his entire family remained so ill they could not care for each other. His second wife Mary Ann (his first wife having died in 1832) had given birth ten days prior to a daughter, Alice. Still recovering from this birth, Mary Ann had chills and a fever. Brigham himself felt so poorly that he was "unable to go thirty rods to the river without assistance."[9] But he determined to serve the Lord and departed as scheduled. He later wrote, "[I]f I had known that every one of [my family] would have been in the grave when I returned it would not have diverted me from my mission one hour."[10]

Brigham headed east with an ailing Heber C. Kimball (and others), hoping to arrive in Great Britain the following spring. They departed by ship on March 9. By the time they reached their destination on April 6, Brigham's health had declined further, mainly due to being "sick nearly all the way [across the Atlantic] and confined to [his] berth."[11] So emaciated from seasickness, his cousin Willard Richards failed to recognize Brigham at the dock. In time, Brigham's health improved and he served successfully over the next year, traversing much of the countryside, visiting London, and all the while preaching the gospel and overseeing Church administrative needs. Other than being seasick on the oceanic journeys to and from England, he does not mention in his journal ever being ill. As for his family, although Mary Ann and the children sacrificed dearly during Brigham's absence, they all survived to be reunited.

Two years after returning home from his mission to England, Brigham had another near-death experience. Now age 41 and living in "Nauvoo, the Beautiful," he took ill in November 1842 by suddenly falling unconscious (a "fit of apoplexy" he called it).[12] Although the next morning he felt somewhat better, when the evening came Brigham again suffered with a high fever—the "most violent fever" he ever experienced, he recalled later in life.[13] Joseph Smith and Willard Richards administered to him, promising he would live and recover; however, the severity of the illness would not be lessened. After the blessing, Joseph sat at Brigham's bedside for six hours and gave instructions to his caregivers as to what to do.[14] A day or so after the fever began, the skin on Brigham's body severely exfoliated. Smith advised Brigham to stay in bed on his back and not scrub at the skin, which felt itchy. Brigham followed the advice and spent the next 18 days abed flat on his back. The cabin where the Youngs lived lacked adequate insulation against the winter weather, and those who cared for Brigham had to bundle up while his fever burned.[15]

Modern day doctors suspect he likely suffered from a combination of scarlet fever and a secondary infection. Scarlet fever frequently occurred as a deadly ailment in the mid-nineteenth century. "From 1840 until 1883, scarlet fever became one of the most common infectious childhood diseases to cause death in most of the major metropolitan centers of Europe and the United States, with case fatality rates that reached or exceeded 30% in some areas–eclipsing even measles, diphtheria, and pertussis."[16]

Midway through December, Brigham's fever finally broke. By this time, he had grown so weak he reported not being able to close his eyes. On December 15, 1842, Brigham's wife MaryAnn sat him up in a chair. While upright, his chin drooped, blocking his windpipe, and his breathing stopped. Recognizing his distress, Mary Ann first threw a bucket of water in his face, then a handful of camphor, both an effort to shock him into breathing again. When these attempts failed, she held his nose and blew air into his mouth, succeeding in getting Brigham to breathe again. Mary Ann may have learned to use this mouth-to-mouth technique from Brigham himself. Many years earlier Brigham had used it to help resuscitate a drowned child. He had likely shared the story with her. His life saved once more, Brigham needed another month to feel confident he had made significant progress on the path to recovery. He remained unable to leave his home until January 18, 1843, almost three months later, when he attended a dinner at the Smith home.[17]

After the martyrdom of Joseph Smith and his brother, Hyrum, Brigham Young had another year of poor health on the frontier beginning in August 1846. The stress of leading the Church, especially when the Saints were expelled from Nauvoo, took its toll on Brigham's health. By February 1847 he had declined even more. John D. Lee, a bodyguard and close friend, recorded in his journal that Brigham had "taken very unwell, being much distressed in the stomach and bowels. Fainted away, apparently dead for several moments, and it was with much ado that he could be kept from falling asleep to await the resurrection morn."[18] Brigham himself recorded that he had become so emaciated from the illness that he could wrap his greatcoat around himself twice.[19]

Brigham shared this experience with several others, firmly believing he had died for a time: "I know I went to the world of spirits." While in the "spirit world" Brigham spoke with Joseph and Hyrum Smith. After returning to life, Brigham Young dreamt about and later recorded what he had seen. "In my dream I went to see Joseph," he wrote. Joseph sat by a large window looking "perfectly natural." Brigham shook Joseph's hand, kissed his cheeks, and asked him why they could not be together as before. Joseph arose from his chair and spoke to Brigham saying, "It is all right. . . You will have to do things without me a while and then we shall be together again." Brigham then took the opportunity to ask Joseph for counsel. "Be sure to tell the people to keep the spirit of the Lord," Joseph advised. Brigham then turned and saw Joseph in the light, "but where I had to go was as midnight darkness." Because Joseph insisted, Brigham "went back in the darkness" and awoke and later told his wife, "It is hard coming back to life again."[20]

* * *

Two months later, Brigham had recovered enough to lead the advance party that would lay the trail for future companies of Saints that would follow. The group "consisted of 143 men, 3 women [Clara Decker, Brigham's plural wife; Harriet Decker, Lorenzo's wife; Ellen Sanders, Heber's plural wife], and 2 children—148 souls. They had a boat, a cannon, 70 wagons and carriages, 93 horses, 52 mules, 66 oxen, 19 cows, 17 dogs, and some chickens."[21] Additionally, they took some of the latest scientific instruments (two sextants, two barometers, two artificial horizons, and a telescope) recently brought from England by Elder John Taylor. Although the first week of travel included numerous spurts and stops, by the second week the group was organized and well on their way. Brigham had implemented a strict, military-like protocol over the group in an effort to protect them during the journey. The route they followed had been planned and mapped by Joseph Smith as early as 1832, but "by the end of December 1845, the leaders of the church had a wealth of information on the American Far West. They had some of the most recent journals, guides, and maps of those who had visited the far west regions [especially John C. Fremont's] and they were using these materials in selecting locations for settlements."[22] In fact, Heber C. Kimball noted in his journal that hanging in the Nauvoo temple there were at least five large maps of the United States, which were used by leaders to help plan the eventual removal to the Rocky Mountains. Their intended destination, the desert shrubland of the Salt Lake Valley in the Great Basin, had been singled out several years prior to be the future center place of Zion.

Now 45-years-old, Brigham had been thorough in planning the journey, but his own health continued to plague him. As early as April 20, in a letter from the trail to Mary Ann, he mentions feeling improved, but having to rest because, "I found myself complet[el]y tired out."[23] But he carried on with his usual resilience and vigor, feigned though it might be at times. Unfortunately, for the entire camp, by the end of June many were suffering from a tick-borne "mountain fever," which included symptoms of fever, headache, and joint and back pain. "Brigham's attack began the morning of 12 July, and he was forced to discontinue his trek at noon. By evening he was 'very sick,' 'raving and insensible.'"[24] Coming on the tails of his previously undiagnosed illness, the mountain fever likely easily overpowered him. Although over the next few days he appeared to be improving, on July 17 he became bedridden once more. This time all activities in the camp were put on hold and a prayer meeting held because "Brigham appeared to his brethren to be 'nigh unto death.'"[25] The company did not resume their journey for another three days, giving their leader time to rest. Eventually, when they moved forward, he traveled in a bed arranged in the back of a carriage. He rested in the carriage for at least two more weeks. From this bed Brigham first viewed the Salt Lake Valley on July 28, 1847, reportedly remarking, "This is the right place, drive on." After a slow convalescence Brigham eventually regained his health enough to continue to oversee the westward migration of the Saints.

* * *

After reaching the Great Basin, Brigham spent the next thirty years helping to develop "Mormon Country," which was frequently "at odds with the United States [g]overnment and its officials both in Utah and in Washington,"[26] especially over the issue of the Church's encouragement of plural marriage. During this time, he advanced into his senior years. In his 50s he walked with a spry step and even danced gracefully; Sir Richard Burton, who visited the Saints and 59-year-old Brigham in August 1860, noted, "he looks about forty-five."[27] As he approached the later decades of his life, he more frequently experienced upper-respiratory illnesses, consistently suffered from rheumatism, and gradually put on weight (reportedly at 5'10" he weighed 200 lbs.). By 1870, he began traveling to Southern Utah more frequently for warmer weather, but it took him longer to get back on his feet after an illness. In the winter of 1869–1870 he experienced a bout of mumps, and in 1874 he started to suffer from urological blockages that would plague him for the rest of his life. Despite this, he remained optimistic, remarking in an 1876 sermon, "As to my health, I feel many times that I could not live an hour longer, but I mean to live just as long as I can. I know not how soon the messenger will call for me, but I calculate to die in harness."[28] True to his word, Brigham remained active up to his death on August 29, 1877 of "cholera morbus" (most likely appendicitis).

* * *

An early death of Brigham Young could have had significant negative impacts on the development of the American West, guiding the Mormon pioneers to Utah and establishing a successful settlement in the harsh frontier, as well as the development and leadership of The Church of Jesus Christ of Latter-day Saints. As a pivotal leader who succeeded Joseph Smith, Brigham played a crucial role in stabilizing the Church during a period of great turmoil following Smith's assassination. The impact of his leadership on the future of the Western frontier and its population has been significantly greater than any other pioneer or colonizer in American history. Loss of his life to disease or other dangers would have left a vacuum in religious, geopolitical, and economic development in the region.

A succession crisis in the Latter-day Saint movement emerged less than a week following the assassination of Joseph Smith on June 27, 1844. On August 3, Sidney Rigdon arrived in Nauvoo and some looked to him for leadership. "He had been with the Church almost from the beginning. For the past eleven years, he had served as Joseph Smith's First Counselor in the First Presidency, the Church's highest quorum."[29] The next day, while preaching to the Saints, Rigdon claimed he held the priesthood keys of the dispensation and would be the "guardian" of the Church. Members of the Quorum of the Twelve Apostles who were in Nauvoo (Richards, Taylor, Parley P. Pratt, and George A. Smith) tried to meet with Rigdon that day, but their efforts were chiefly ignored. It wasn't until Tuesday, August 6 that Brigham Young and four more Apostles—Elders Kimball, Orson Pratt, Wight, and Woodruff—arrived in Nauvoo via river boat. "When we landed in the City," Wilford Woodruff wrote in his diary, "there was a deep gloom [that] seemed to rest over the City of Nauvoo which we never experi[en]ced before."[30] Despite the melancholy and uncertainty, the nine apostles present in Nauvoo met twice the next day, mainly to be brought up-to-date so they could better understand the various claims being made to the twin offices of Church President and trustee-in-trust. The apostles ended their meeting with a plan to hold a general assembly the following Tuesday, August 13 at 10 a.m., during which Rigdon and Brigham would speak, and then the Saints could ratify a vote on the succeeding leadership of the Church. But the issue came to a resolution more quickly than anticipated.

On Thursday, August 8, Sidney Rigdon held an informal worship session in an outdoor grove where the Saints commonly met. A large multitude gathered, with reports of many having to stand due to lack of seating. Brigham, forgetting he had another meeting with the Twelve, saw the Rigdon meeting in progress and decided to attend. Because of windy conditions, Rigdon spoke from a wagon bed instead of from the pulpit. His speech lasted an hour and a half, and just as he came to a conclusion and prepared to call for a vote on the leadership succession, Brigham stood forward and, in an effort to stall the vote, announced a solemn assembly (important meeting held for matters of doctrine and instruction) for 2:00 p.m. the same day.

That afternoon the meeting began late, but over 6,000 church members were in attendance. Brigham spoke to the people, his remarks contrasting sharply with Rigdon's. Biographer M. R. Werner described what Brigham said:

> "Brigham Young did not once mention himself as the possible head of the Church or as successor to Joseph Smith. He merely contended that the Twelve Apostles, as ordained by God through the dead Prophet, Joseph Smith, were the heads of the Church, and that no man could alter that eternal position. This position of the Twelve Apostles as immediately in line of succession to the Prophet had always been recognized."[31]

Brigham wrote his own account of giving the speech: "I arose and spocke to the people. my hart was swolen with composion toards them and by the power of the Holy Gost even the spirit of the prophets I was enabled to comfort the harts of the saints."[32]

Maybe "the spirit of the prophets" felt by Brigham was more literal than he realized, but over 100 of those in attendance later testified that the "mantle of Joseph" came upon Brigham. Some believed Brigham's voice sounded like Joseph Smith's. Others said his mannerisms were reminiscent of Smith's. A few even felt Brigham's 5'10" stature appeared to be equal to Joseph Smith's height of 6'2". Of the many "mantle of Joseph" experiences shared, 57 are firsthand accounts, such as the one shared by Caroline Barnes Crosby: "[A]s soon as the twelve apostles with bro brigham young at their head took the stand it was shown conclusively where the power rested. it was the first time that I ever thought he [Brigham] resembled bro joseph but almost every one exclaimed that the mantle of joseph had fallen on brigham."[33] So many of those present at the meeting felt similarly to Crosby that the succession crisis had ended. The Church of Jesus Christ of Latter-day Saints would move forward, led by the Quorum of the Twelve Apostles.

Although a few small schisms of the faith occurred at this time, Brigham kept the main body of the Mormon Church faithful to his leadership. His ability to help the members pivot in a time of great difficulty ultimately led to their mass exodus from Nauvoo to the Great Basin. After several years of the Church being led by the Quorum of the Twelve Apostles, the group once again established a First Presidency (in late December 1847), with Brigham at its head. He became the longest serving President of the Church (29 years and 8 months). Under his tenure, membership grew from about 17,000 to 125,000.[34] As of 2023, membership for the Church surpassed 17.25 million worldwide, with annual humanitarian aid totaling over $1.3 billion in 191 countries and territories around the world.[35]

* * *

One of the achievements for which Brigham Young is most famous is the colonization of the American West. With the initial trek to the Salt Lake Valley completed, Brigham returned to Winter Quarters, Nebraska to help plan the safe exodus of the remaining Church members. The primary goal of the Twelve Apostles focused on helping the poor and weary Saints to be able to gather. In December 1847, Church congregations both near and far received a detailed letter of instructions for emigration. The letter urged as many members as possible to be ready to depart by spring thaw 1848.

The following May about 2,000 Saints were ready for the journey. With groups organized in companies with leaders over hundreds, fifties, and tens, they departed Winter Quarters and headed west. Brigham wrote of the departure in his journal: "On the 26th I started on my journey to the mountains, leaving my houses, mills and the temporary furniture I had acquired during our sojourn there [Winter Quarters]. This was the fifth time I had left my home and property since I embraced the gospel of Jesus Christ."[36] This time, with women, children, and elderly requiring extra care, the crossing took longer. Brigham again experienced illness during the expedition, but recovered enough to enter the Salt Lake Valley in good health and spirits. In total the trek took 122 days, with the first wagon train arriving September 20. Additional wagon trains trailed into the valley over the next four days, with approximately 3,000 Saints migrating by the end of the year.

With the arrival of the first group of Saints in the Great Basin, Brigham's work of colonization began. City blocks, each containing eight lots, were distributed free of cost using a lottery system. Lots for farming and animals were also divvied out to heads of households (including females), but were located further west in the valley. The work of building commenced, with

Brigham urging the Saints to be self-sufficient. With an average of an additional 3,000 immigrants arriving annually, the pioneers were able to adapt with industry, innovation, and hard work. Brigham managed the many Saints arriving by setting up the Perpetual Emigration Fund (PEF) Company in 1849. Essentially, the PEF provided immigrants with loans for the travel costs required to get to Salt Lake; once arrived, they would work to help repay the money, which was used again on a revolving basis. "The sum of five thousand dollars, subscribed in cash and ox-teams, was raised that year and Bishop Edward Hunter was appointed to 'carry the funds back to the states, buy cattle, take oversight of the property, and bring the poor to this place.'"[37] Although the PEF helped many destitute Church members left behind in the Midwest, it also helped Saints immigrate from Europe and elsewhere.

As the fund began to work, with immigrants arriving in the fall, they were put to work for the winter on public projects, such as the building of the Salt Lake Tabernacle. Then, the following spring, the families would be sent to settle various colonies within the territory. Using this method, Brigham "supervised the overland trek of 60,000 to 70,000 pioneers to the Salt Lake Valley from Illinois and other staging points, such as Iowa and Missouri, founded 350 to 400 settlements in Utah, Arizona, California, Idaho, Nevada and Wyoming, and established a system of land distribution later ratified by Congress."[38] Later, during a national depression in 1873, the Church cancelled half of the indebtedness to the Perpetual Emigrating Fund, easing the burden on the poorest Saints. Ultimately, with his eye on caring for the poor and helping gather the Saints to "Zion," the impact of Brigham Young's leadership deeply influenced geopolitical structures of the American West for generations.

* * *

One historian has placed Brigham Young with William Penn, Eli Whitney, Thomas Edison, Andrew Carnegie, E. H. Harriman, and J. P. Morgan as being "among the major protagonists in America's economic progress."[39] Aiming for independence, self-sufficiency, and self-respect, Brigham encouraged Mormon settlements to establish mills, factories, and tanneries, and to produce all the necessities needed for daily living, including flour, lumber, paper, leather, cloth, hats, gunpowder, salt, and other essentials. He also urged the Saints to be united and to share one another's burdens to help ease the economic troubles so many felt, while being as independent as possible from outside influences.

These principles of self-sufficiency and unity, Brigham believed, would establish a moral foundation for the exchange of goods and labor. Still, he exercised caution when in pursuit of profit because it frequently resulted in the enrichment of only a select few. With this in mind, he supported the formation of cooperatives. A cooperative agreement formed between producers and merchants would protect local residents from being taken advantage of by outside businesses but would also help to care for the poor in a community. "The cooperative's employees received pay in scrip, redeemable at the enterprise's various departments."[40] Formed by local entrepreneurs, including Brigham Young, Zion's Cooperative Mercantile Institution (ZCMI) served as an example of how the cooperative could benefit its employees and a network of other cooperative establishments. ZCMI sold household goods, clothing, and other basic necessities. The cooperative strategy proved successful for many years. During times of economic decline, these cooperatives generally survived and even prospered.

Since church and state were thoroughly entangled with each other in Utah Territory, the principle of tithing observed by the Saints became a sizeable factor Brigham could employ to help the local economy. The Bible teaches that faithful believers should pay a tithe (tenth) of their income to the Lord. Mormon tithing donations, whether given as cash, goods, or labor, were utilized to support those in need and to further the kingdom of God. All types of contributions were turned towards both religious and community development, including the construction of public buildings and temples. "The Department of Public Works worked in tandem with the tithing office to absorb and put to use the constant influx of both skilled and unskilled laborers coming into the valley."[41] This management of tithing-in-kind helped to build a skilled workforce that ultimately ensured even the poor could find an income to put food on their table.

Another key element Brigham used to help build the economy of the Utah Territory included promoting new technologies. As the United States expanded and more people journeyed westward, Salt Lake City found itself located on the primary route between the East and West Coasts. In 1861when the first transcontinental telegraph wire reached completion, it immediately revolutionized communications in Salt Lake City. Brigham wanted this technology to also be available in the settlements located both north and south. He advocated that the Church build its own adjunct line, named Deseret Telegraph, to link to these other communities. Construction on Deseret Telegraph began in 1866 and Brigham requested that each settlement train at least one person (including women) in the art of telegraphy. Sixteen-year-old Eliza Luella Stewart, for example, became the first telegraph operator at the Pipe Spring office in Southern Utah, which opened in 1871.

A few years later, Brigham promoted the construction of the transcontinental railroad. For many years he could see the potential rail travel could offer Utah. When approached by the Union and Central Pacific rail companies to help finish the last section of the transcontinental line, he wasted no time. After signing the contracts, Brigham sent 5,000 workers to help complete the final 350 miles of rail. On May 10, 1869, the final rail tie, a golden spike, was set in place at Promontory Summit in northern Utah, officially completing the transcontinental railroad. Less than a week later workers began constructing an extension to Salt Lake City. The completion of these rail lines benefitted immigrants, the transportation of commodities, and even the postal service, all of which helped to boost and expand the economy of the West for years to come. "Whatever effect its religious tenets have had, or may have in the future, there can be no question that Mormonism has contributed to America's economic progress."[42]

* * *

A broad-shouldered man with both strong opinions and compelling presence, Brigham Young is often thought of more as a caricature than a force in history. Whenever his name is mentioned, stories of folklore are sure to follow. Moreover, many are quick to dismiss his work and life as that of a religious fanatic. His own self-assessment, though, is less mythological and more pragmatic: "When I think of myself, I think just this: I have grit in me, and I will do my duty anyhow."[43] Despite facing life-threatening illnesses and journeys, Brigham used grit and determination to survive and carry forward a work he deeply believed in. In spite of his imperfections, he made a positive impact on history and the world.

Chapter 9:
Queen Victoria

The Princess Charlotte of Wales, the only legitimate granddaughter—or grandchild—of King George III, was expected to rule Great Britain, bringing youth and vitality to the throne. The strong-willed princess first turned down an arranged engagement to William, future King of the Netherlands. But in 1816, at age 19, Charlotte married prince Leopold of Saxe-Coburg-Saalfeld. The prince and princess were well-loved and viewed as the future of the nation. However, the happy couple soon experienced tragedy. On November 6, 1817, Charlotte gave birth to a stillborn son. Within hours, she herself hemorrhaged[1] and died. Her death preceded both her father and grandfather, and set in motion a race among her uncles to produce a legitimate heir to the throne.

Princess Charlotte's father, who became King George IV, remained married to her mother, Caroline. But the marriage existed in name only and the couple lived apart. And at the time of Charlotte's death, 49-year-old Caroline likely had become too old to produce another child. But King George III had several other sons, three of whom were unmarried. Prince Edward,[2] Duke of Kent and Strathearn, was the fourth son in the royal family. Although aged 50 and unmarried at the time of Charlotte's unfortunate death, Edward had been in a long-term relationship with a mistress, Julie de St. Laurent. However, seeing the possibility of fathering the future regnant, Edward broke off the relationship and proposed marriage to a German widow with two children (Charlotte's sister-in-law). Princess Victoria of Saxe-Coburg-Saalfeld could not speak English, but the fact that she already had children made her an attractive option; the children were proof of her fertility. She accepted his proposal. Edward and Victoria married in 1818 and they were soon pregnant with what would be their only child: Alexandrina Victoria. The little princess was born on May 24, 1819 at Kensington Palace in London. When news reached her maternal grandmother back in Coburg, she rejoiced, saying, "Another Charlotte!"[3]

At her birth, Victoria became fourth in line to the throne. Her father took great pride in his daughter, telling his friends to look at her well because she would be Queen of the United Kingdom. But hopefully the Duke took a good look himself—he, too, died before his precious daughter reached her first birthday. In January 1820 he came down with a severe cold. On the 20th of the month fever and delirium developed, leading doctors to use bleeding and leeches as their primary form of treatment for his pneumonia. After a few days, Edward realized he was dying and rushed to put a will in place. In it, baby Drina, as Victoria had been nicknamed, would remain in the care of her mother. The Duke died early the following morning. Victoria was only eight months old.

* * *

Despite poor sanitation and medical care of the day, Queen Victoria lived a relatively healthy life. She enjoyed robust health through most of her days. Although only 60" tall, she gave birth to nine hale and hearty children during a time when mortality rates for both mothers and babies were significantly higher (with Princess Charlotte's death being the terrifyingly all too real example). Only once in her teenage years did Victoria suffer from a serious illness. For three weeks in October 1835, while visiting Ramsgate, on the coastline of Kent, she lay bedridden, her journal silent. "Her journal, begun when she was thirteen, [is] where she registered day by day the small succession of her doings and her sentiments."[4] For her to not record in her journal at all during the three weeks of her illness is a strong indication of how sick she truly was.

When Victoria first felt poorly, her mother and John Conroy did not believe she genuinely suffered from an illness. Conroy served as comptroller to the Duchess of Kent's household and executor of her deceased husband's will. As such, he had great influence over Victoria's mother. Together, Conroy and the Duchess imposed what became known as the "Kensington System" on Victoria to keep her safe—after the deaths of her father and grandfather in 1820, she became the heir-apparent to her uncle, King William IV. The System also protected Victoria's reputation from scandal and rumors. The Kensington System involved ensuring Victoria never took the stairs without being accompanied; her simple diet consisted of plain roast mutton; and she was not allowed to spend time with other adults without her mother or governess present. Although extremely restrictive of the young princess, the Kensington System effectively achieved its goal of making Victoria "the Nation's Hope."[5] But Conroy wanted more than this: he wanted Victoria to sign a paper that would make him her private secretary and chief advisor. In other words, he wanted the power to influence her once she became queen.

On October 7, immediately preceding her illness, Victoria's favorite Uncle Leopold (Princess Charlotte's widower) left Ramsgate. The annual seaside holiday came as a gift from her uncle. For several weeks, Victoria had greatly enjoyed spending time with Leopold, whom she considered to be a loving father figure. His departure, however, meant a return to the restrictive Kensington System; she felt abandoned, under pressure, and depleted. On the way home from seeing her uncle off at the docks, Victoria "collapsed, and was apparently very ill."[6] When the carriage arrived at Albion House, she went immediately to bed with a sore throat. At first her mother felt the situation warranted a visit from Dr. James Clark, the family medical advisor who resided in London. The Duchess sent for Dr. Clark, but John Conroy convinced her that Victoria's stubborn behavior came from being a temperamental teenager, not from illness. As a result, Clark returned to London without the chance to evaluate the princess.

By October 9, however, even Conroy had to admit Victoria had become seriously ill. Her symptoms included a severe fever, no appetite, and difficulty sleeping. Dr. Clark received another summons, but on arrival Conroy only allowed him a brief visit with the patient. Lousie Lehzen, Victoria's devoted governess and baroness in her own right, recorded that even she did not have the opportunity to provide the doctor a detailed report of the "dangerous symptoms of the illness," but instead forced into silence by Conroy and the Duchess.[7] Once again, Clark returned home believing the princess's symptoms to be more exaggeration than genuine. At this point Victoria's fever spiked and she experienced disorientation. "The fever 'rose dreadfully', recorded Lehzen, 'and delirium set in'."[8] The princess appeared to have typhoid fever, a bacterial infection usually contracted from poor sanitary conditions. Ironically, the same disease would eventually take the life of Victoria's beloved husband, Albert, 26 years later (in 1861). But somehow the princess miraculously survived.

With Victoria fighting for her life and too weak to argue, the debate over Conroy's position as personal secretary/chief advisor intensified. Conroy and the Duchess tried to get Victoria to sign paperwork that would both approve the arrangement and make the Duchess the regent (guardian) over the future queen until age 21. Despite her weakened state, Victoria mustered all her willpower and held firm in the face of intimidations and threats. "But Victoria, as she later wrote, 'resisted in spite of my illness, and their harshness'. She was determined to defy her mother's drive for power."[9] The only support Victoria received came from her governess Lehzen. As a result of this experience, Victoria's relationship with her mother greatly deteriorated. Indeed, the resentment the princess felt toward Conroy led to his dismissal when Victoria ascended to the throne at age 18.

Finally, "[a]s Victoria's illness entered a second week, it dawned on her mother that this could actually be serious."[10] Perhaps the Duchess saw similarities between Victoria's illness and that of the duke, her deceased husband. Whatever the reason, on October 14 Lehzen noted in her journal the Duchess's worry over Victoria had increased. "The Duchess could contain her terror no longer."[11] Dr. Clark and local Dr. Plenderleath were called in to provide urgent care. Soon afterward, Victoria's condition stabilized. She received doses of quinine, typically used as a muscle relaxant. The prescribed medication likely had little impact on the bacteria in her system, but the presence of two doctors to oversee cleanliness in the sickroom in all probability had a beneficial effect that led to Victoria's recovery. At any rate, by October 31, 1835 she had resumed writing in her journal, noting her hair had begun falling out and she had become too weak to walk. She had inexplicably survived the ordeal, but never forgot it.

* * *

Victoria was not the only one with a severe dislike of Sir John Conroy. King William IV intensely disliked both his sister-in-law and Conroy. Despite ill health, the King vowed not to die until after Victoria had turned 18 so she would be able to take the throne without having to be under the control of a regent (likely to be the Duchess under the influence of Conroy). Fortunately, the king kept his vow. But less than two weeks after Victoria's eighteenth birthday, it became clear his health was deteriorating. Victoria knew her time had come. She began studying Jean-Louis de Lolme's *The Constitution of England* and *The Letters of Madame de Sévigné*.[12] Baron Stockmar, an old family doctor and political advisor from Coburg, began relaying information daily from Prime Minister Lord Melbourn. The entire household remained on high alert.

King William died at 2:20 a.m. on June 20, 1837. His death came less than a month after Victoria's eighteenth birthday. The Lord Chamberlain,[13] Lord Coyngham, and the Archbishop of Canterbury, William Howley, immediately left Windsor to inform the new queen of the death of her uncle. In the early hours of the morning, her mother woke her and told of the visitors waiting in the sitting room. "Victoria wrote in her journal, 'I got out of bed and went into my sitting room (only in my dressing-gown) and *alone*, and saw them.'"[14] Coyngham and Howley knelt as soon as she entered the room, and immediately she knew. She had ascended to the throne.

As queen, and now without the bullying of Sir John Conroy in her life, danger took on a different guise. Nineteenth century Europe is called the Age of Assassination by some historians because of the dangers faced by so many leaders in the region. "In the late nineteenth century alone, assassins tried to kill nearly every major European ruler and head of state, including Emperor Franz Joseph of Austria, the Kaisers Wilhelm I, Friedrich III and Wilhelm II of Germany, the Tsars Alexander II, Alexander III and Nicholas II of Russia, the kings Victor Emmanuel II, Umberto I and Victor Emmanuel III of Italy, and various presidents of France, as well as numerous prominent politicians."[15] For some unknown reason Queen Victoria's name is missing from this list. During her lengthy time on the throne, she endured seven different assassination attempts. Prince Albert, Victoria's husband, and two of their sons, Edward VII and George V, also faced similar threats, but not nearly as many as the Queen.

The first assassination attempt on Queen Victoria's life took place four months after her marriage to Prince Albert in 1840. She was already pregnant with her first child. Before her marriage, Victoria had been in the habit of riding on horseback through St. James and Hyde Park for exercise. However, in her condition, she and Prince Albert instead took regular daily open carriage rides to get fresh air and greet crowds gathered to see them. The evening of June 10 was no exception, the weather perfect for an outing in the park. At around 6 p.m. the couple's carriage departed Buckingham Palace and they were soon headed up Constitution Hill toward Hyde Park. "[T]wo outriders, the Prince and the Queen in a droshky, a very low carriage that rendered the royal couple sitting alone fully visible to all. Two pair of horses pulled the carriage; riders sat upon the horses on the left side, responsive to Albert's commands. Two equerries followed behind."[16] Within moments, the unthinkable happened.

Prior to heading to Constitution Hill, 18-year-old Edward Oxford had spent several months preparing for his moment in the spotlight. In early May he'd purchased two pistols and had practiced shooting in the garden of his rented Lambeth home, a stone's throw from the Bethlem Royal Hospital, also known as Bedlam. Oxford practiced his marksmanship at several different shooting ranges, including the well-known William Green's 'pistol repository and shooting gallery' in the West End of London. On June 3 he purchased percussion caps, a quarter pound of gunpowder, and two dozen bullets for his pistols. A week later he would use them.

In addition to purchasing pistols and practicing shooting, Oxford also prepared some unusual documents. In his rented rooms, he kept a locked box that stored a curious collection of papers associated with a secret society called Young England, a pseudo-military revolutionary group of over 400 members intending to overthrow the British government. Among the documents were the rules and regulations of the society, a manifesto signed by secretary "A.W. Smith," and a few letters addressed to himself, which had never been postmarked. All of the papers were written in Oxford's handwriting. A uniform of sorts and a cap were also found in the box. The paperwork of the secret society turned out to be entirely falsified. Although a product of Oxford's imagination, it likely drew inspiration from his favorite pastime: reading.

Oxford, by all accounts, read voraciously. He loved adventurous plotlines, sea tales, and the rags-to-riches trope. In fact, he longed to become a national hero—to become someone of importance. One of Oxford's favorite novellas had been *The Bravo of Venice*, a German work by Heinrich Zschokke. In the novella, an obscure young man rises to become the King of Assassins (despite the fact that he hasn't actually ever killed anyone). At the climax of the story is a scene where the Bravo points a gun, which is loaded with powder (but not bullets) into the face of his leader, the ruler of Venice. Moreover, in the story there is a secret society the shades of which are remarkably similar to Oxford's own made-up Young England.

On June 10 Oxford placed himself at Constitution Hill a full two hours prior to the scheduled time Victoria and Albert were to drive by. He didn't want to accidentally miss out by being late—especially on this date: the anniversary of his father's death. As the royal carriage neared, Oxford acted as though he were the Bravo and took aim with his dueling pistol. "Albert saw a 'little mean looking man' six paces away from him, holding something that the Prince couldn't quite make out: it was Oxford, pointing his pistol at the two, and in a dueler's stance, firing a shot with a thunderous report that riveted the attention of all. Victoria, according to the Prince, was looking the other way."[17] Albert immediately grabbed Victoria to check for injuries. Although startled by the noise, she laughed and declared herself fine. The carriage continued forward and Oxford now pulled out his second pistol, proclaiming, "I have got another here."[18] Albert prepared to leap out of the carriage at Oxford, but Victoria grabbed at her husband and pulled him down with her to the floor of the droshky. Her thoughts immediately turned to God: "If it please Providence, I shall escape."[19] Victoria later wrote:

> "I saw him aim at me with another pistol. I ducked my head, and another shot, equally loud, instantly followed; we looked round and saw that the man had been quickly surrounded and seized. Albert directly ordered the postillion to drive on as if nothing had happened, to Mama's house. Just before the second shot was fired and as the man took aim, or rather more while he fired, dear Albert turned towards me, squeezing my hand, exclaiming 'My God! Don't be alarmed'. I assured him I was not the least frightened, which was the case."[20]

After the second shot fired the whole procession came to a halt as the crowd and authorities came together to catch the would-be assassin. Oxford later wrote, "In an instant several persons seized me by the skirts of the coat, some took hold of my trousers, others twisted their hand into my handkerchief, and all within reach of me had me by the collar."[21] Authorities soon arrested him for high treason.

At first, Oxford loved being the center of attention and willingly spoke to anyone about what he had done. He soon hinted that he had not acted alone and the police searched his room, finding the Young England documents. When the press got wind of the supposed secret society, they wrote numerous articles accusing various politicians and one of Victoria's uncles of being complicit. Oxford's family, however, never believed Young England to be real or that he would be involved in any such organization. His sister had watched over him in the months leading up to the shooting; his schedule and behavior gave no indication of participation in a secret group. He spent most of his time home reading, and would get annoyed when interrupted. Despite the Oxford family's feedback, it took several weeks for the authorities to realize the conspiracy had definitely been falsified.

During the trial of Oxford, two issues took center stage: his sanity and the "ammunition" he had used. At the trial Oxford pled not guilty by reason of insanity. His family history greatly supported the plea. Both his father and his paternal grandfather were well-known for their strange behaviors. His grandfather often believed himself to be the Pope and eventually died in an insane asylum. Oxford's father, Edward Oxford Sr., had severe episodes of mania followed by bouts of depression. During the trial several family members and neighbors testified of Oxford Sr.'s odd habits, including riding his horse into the house on multiple occasions, burning rolls of money, throwing full plates of food out the window, selling all the family furniture without telling his wife, and threatening to commit suicide by overdosing on laudanum. In his hometown, everyone knew that Oxford Sr. abused his wife. On multiple occasions he had threatened to kill her. His wife left him in about 1827, when Edward was around five years old. Two years later Oxford Sr. died.

In addition to the family history of mental illness, Edward Oxford Jr. behaved eccentrically. "Edward had fits of unprovoked, maniacal laughter. [His mother] later admitted that she attempted to cure him of this by beating him."[22] He also suffered from trances, fits of talking animatedly to himself, and bouts of unexplained emotional outbursts. Several former coworkers testified of his "strange ways"[23] during the trial; in fact, Oxford had lost multiple jobs because his behavior had been off-putting to pub patrons where he worked. Additionally, like his father, Oxford had been abusive toward his mother and sister. After buying the pistols used for the assassination attempt, for example, Oxford pointed the guns at their faces when they upset him. The day after buying the pistols, his mother left town after Edward had both aimed the gun at her and punched her in the face. At the conclusion of the trial, the jury had been clearly convinced of his insanity.

The second main issue addressed in the court case focused on whether or not Oxford had shot at the Queen with actual ammunition in the pistols. To miss his mark at only six paces away (according to Prince Albert) seemed remarkable, even considering the poor quality of the pistols. Oxford had been asked numerous times after being arrested if there had been bullets loaded. At first, he confirmed there were: "[I]f the ball had come in contact with your head you would have known it."[24] But after a time, he refused to answer the question. Later, during the trial, Oxford wholly denied that there were bullets loaded when he shot at the Queen. As for the police investigation, they never found any conclusive evidence of real bullets being shot. The authorities scoured the palace wall looking for bullet holes; they even swept up all the dirt and debris at the base of the wall and sifted it for evidence. Although some suspicious marks were found on the wall, no bullets were ever recovered. The prosecution hypothesized that the bullets had cleared the height of the wall and landed somewhere on the palace grounds. That theory lacked evidence as well. Victoria and Albert, however, were absolutely certain real ammunition had been used by Oxford. "'The ball must have passed just above [the Queen's] head,' [Albert] wrote to his grandmother, 'to judge from the place where it was found sticking in an opposite wall.'"[25] Victoria's journal entry agreed: "It seems the pistols were loaded, so our escape is indeed providential."[26]

In the end, the jury struggled with the wording of their verdict. Initially they returned, saying, "We find the prisoner, Edward Oxford, guilty of discharging the contents of the two pistols, but whether or not they were loaded with ball has not been satisfactorily proved to us, he being of unsound state of mind at the time."[27] But this statement alarmed the judge; it meant reasonable doubt existed and Oxford would be acquitted. He would be a free man. After a heated debate between the lawyers and officers of the court, they forced the jury to go back and deliberate again to clarify the verdict. After an hour they returned with, "'Guilty, he being at the time insane.' But by law no one could be simultaneously insane and guilty of a crime."[28] To fix this issue the panel of judges immediately asked the foreman if the jury intended to acquit Oxford on the grounds of insanity. After receiving an affirmative response from the foreman, Judge Denman then rewrote the verdict: "Not guilty on the ground of insanity." With this verdict Oxford would be confined for life in an asylum at the Queen's pleasure.[29]

* * *

Queen Victoria survived an additional six assassination attempts during her reign. In reviewing the details of these near-death experiences, the similarities are eerily comparable to Edward Oxford's initial bid. For example, all of the assassination attempts were made by young men—two of them only age 17 (compared to Oxford at 18). The oldest of them, Robert Pate, was just 30. Secondly, like Oxford, old and broken pistols were the weapon of choice for four of the other attempts made on Queen Victoria's life; however, only one (Roderick Maclean) used a properly loaded gun with actual ammunition. Three of the assassin's shots went wild. On one of John Francis's two attempts to shoot his gun, it misfired. None of the shots harmed[30] the Queen despite being made at close distances.

Thirdly, four additional assassins made attempts on Queen Victoria's life within less than a mile of Oxford's initial choice of location. Two other would-be assassins (John Francis and William Hamilton) revisited Constitution Hill, located just outside of Buckingham Palace. Two others tried their luck by going at the Queen nearby: John William Bean took his shot just outside Buckingham Palace and Arthur O'Connor climbed over the wall to Buckingham and charged at the Queen in the courtyard there.

Next, like Oxford, four additional assassination attempts took place within the first ten years of Victoria's reign.

Lastly, the issue of mental stability remained prevalent in three additional assassins: Bean (a depressed hunchback dwarf) was confined to a lunatic asylum in later years and died of suicide; Pate pled not guilty due to a momentary lapse of a weak mind; and Maclean pled not guilty by reason of insanity.

Most importantly of all, however, is the miraculous similarity of failure in every single attempt on Queen Victoria's life. Considering the number of attempts made by youthful, inexperienced marksmen—four of which were struggling mentally—the Queen had faced a high likelihood of being mortally wounded. She herself recognized the miraculous outcome of each attempt and often attributed it to Providence.

Remarkably, the only assassination attempt made on Queen Victoria's life where she suffered injury occurred on June 27, 1850 near Piccadilly. While leaving her uncle the Duke of Cambridge's home to return to Buckingham Palace, Robert Pate physically assaulted Victoria. A short man, formerly in the military, Pate cracked a brass-plated, iron-tipped cane over her head, crushing the Queen's bonnet. The metal head of the cane gave Victoria a black eye, a large bruise on the right side of her head above her temple, and left her with a red welt on her head "for many years."[31]

* * *

Writer Percy Bysshe Shelley once said the Princess Charlotte of Wales had been "the best and last of her race."[32] But is that true? Queen Victoria likely wondered. In some ways, Victoria spent much of her life being compared to Charlotte. For her birthday in 1845, Leopold gifted Victoria a portrait of Charlotte, describing his deceased wife as a paragon of nobility and exceptional talent, serving as an inspiration for Victoria to emulate. In the letter accompanying the portrait, Leopold wrote, "Grant always to that good and generous Charlotte—who sleeps already with her beautiful little boy so long—an affectionate remembrance, and believe me, she deserves it."[33] Whatever affectionate remembrance Victoria had of Charlotte likely carried tinges of either self-doubt or survivor's guilt. But in spite of their similarities, they would be forever compared.

On her own, Queen Victoria is one of the most well-known royals in history. Her reign of over sixty years remains one of the longest on record for the United Kingdom. The Victorian Era is named after the paradigm of family life, duty, and sacrifice she exemplified. Among eminent leaders, very few have had such a profound influence on their nation or the world as a whole. Still, history is generously littered with 'what-ifs.' What if Victoria's influence had never been exerted? What if she had never ruled? What if Princess Charlotte had not died young? How would the world have been different without the impact of Queen Victoria?

One of the more prominent ways the world would have differed without Queen Victoria is reflected in her moniker as the "Grandmother of Europe." The Princess Charlotte struggled to give birth to her only son, laboring with him for two days. If she and her son had survived, it is unlikely Charlotte would have had many more, if any, children. Her posterity would have had a comparatively limited impact to that of Victoria's. Additionally,

Charlotte's husband Leopold, himself in line for the throne of Belgium, would have been confined to the position of Prince Consort. This would have changed the forces at play in the British and Belgian monarchies. The implications of such a hypothetical situation would certainly have been far-reaching. As it was, Queen Victoria had nine children (five daughters and four sons) whose marriages established royal connections across the European continent. Additionally, she and Prince Albert had 42 grandchildren (22 granddaughters and 20 grandsons), two of which were stillborn; two others died in infancy. Among her children and grandchildren were the leaders of Great Britain, Germany, Russia, Norway, Sweeden, Finland, Greece, Romania, Yugoslavia, Spain, Portugal, and Canada. At the start of World War I, Victoria and Albert's grandchildren sat on the thrones of eight European nations. Victoria provided the "womb of European monarchies,"[34] something Charlotte could not have done.

Despite Victoria's ability to produce progeny, her DNA passed on a dangerous disease: hemophilia. According to the CDC, hemophilia is "an inherited bleeding disorder in which the blood does not clot properly. This can lead to spontaneous bleeding as well as bleeding following injuries or surgery."[35] Hemophilia is caused by the mutation of a gene that provides instructions for clotting factor proteins. It is carried by females in the X chromosome. Research has been unsuccessful in finding any evidence of hemophilia among Victoria's ancestors, including 18 generations on her paternal line and over eight generations of her maternal heritage. "There were no instances of hemophilia in the British Royal Family before Victoria."[36] Although it is impossible to know for sure, some researchers hypothesize the mutated gene began with her; it is suspected she obtained a spontaneous mutation, most likely inherited from one of her parents. Wherever it originated, three of Victoria and Albert's nine children were affected by the gene—two daughters (Beatrice and Alice) were carriers and one son (Prince Leopold, Duke of Albany) was a hemophiliac. The disease also affected their grandchildren. In fact, one of Alice's daughters, Empress Alexandria, gave birth to a son, Alexei Nikolaevich, Tsarevich of

Russia, diagnosed with hemophilia. His disease became one of several catalysts contributing to the fall of the Russian Empire.[37]

* * *

Despite her royal duties, Queen Victoria remained remarkably engaged as a mother. She struggled caring for babies and toddlers but enjoyed her children as they grew and matured into adulthood. "In later years, she would refer to pregnancy and maternity as 'an unhappy condition' and 'the shadow side' of life."[38] Albert had been the glue of the family when their children were young, keeping Victoria connected during years of pregnancy and postpartum depression. As regent, he even handled many of her royal duties when pregnancy and giving birth interfered. After Albert's passing, Victoria seemed to embrace motherhood more fully, as though she knew doing so would please her dear husband. Later, Victoria doted on her grandchildren, and they adored her. "She took a particular delight in her grandchildren, to whom she showed an indulgence which their parents had not always enjoyed, though, even to her grandchildren, she could be, when the occasion demanded it, severe."[39]

One of the major difficulties of Queen Victoria's role as a mother in her later years came from having children and extended family members married into other royal families across Europe. "Around the dining table, the wars made for awkward conversation. Vicky was married to a dovish Prussian prince . . ., Alice to a German prince . . ., Bertie to a Danish princess, and Helena to a German prince born in Denmark."[40] At times, family disagreements could potentially lead to transnational conflict. During the Germany-Austrian war, Victoria's son-in-law fought for Austria, while her brother-in-law took up arms for Prussia. Victoria frequently wielded her pen writing letters urging family members near and far to forgive, be patient, and strive for peace. She became a remarkably effective diplomat, especially when family ties could be tapped to aid with international relations. For example, in late 1870, during the Franco-Prussian war Victoria's sympathies were with Germany, where several of her daughters resided, and because it had been Prince Albert's homeland.

Several years prior to 1870, Otto von Bismarck had been forcefully unifying northern German states, creating the Northern German Confederation. But, convinced of French military superiority, Napoleon III declared war on Prussia in July 1870, in hopes winning would restore his declining popularity at home. Surprisingly, the German forces defeated France.

After the war, tensions between the two nations remained high for many years. In 1875 Queen Victoria became convinced Germany again contemplated war with France. She worried the French armies would overrun Germany this time, placing family members in danger. She busied herself writing letters to keep the peace, including a letter to the Russian Emperor, whose first cousin was married to her daughter, Vicky. She later explained to her daughter: "I wrote a private letter to the Emperor Alexander urging him to do all he could in a pacific sense at Berlin, knowing the anxiety he had to prevent war, and how much he loved his uncle [Vicky's father-in-law] and he him."[41] The letter played a crucial role in preventing another Franco-German war and is considered one of her greatest diplomatic triumphs.

Beyond Queen Victoria's diplomatic abilities, her reign brought about a more modern concept: a constitutional monarchy. Currently, the British monarchy operates within a constitutional framework. While the monarch retains formal authority over the government, referred to as "His/Her Majesty's Government," this authority is limited to compliance within laws passed by Parliament and established precedence. Although the monarch reigns, they do not govern. This had not always been the case. Historically, the British monarchy traces its roots back to Anglo-Saxon England and early medieval Scotland. The first limitations on the rulers began with the Magna Carta, but under Queen Victoria's rule, the power of the monarch further declined. This can in part be attributed to Albert's influence, who on seeing several European royals deposed, firmly believed the monarchy safer if it operated without regard to political leanings. Additionally, the reduction in power primarily took place during Victoria's years grieving in isolation. Throughout this time, she shifted more responsibility to Parliament. Even when she did show up for the opening of Parliament, for example, she usually delegated the duty of reading her speech to the lord chancellor. By "the end of her reign, the Crown was weaker than at any other time in English history. Paradoxically enough, Victoria received the highest eulogiums for assenting to [this] political evolution."[42] And yet, Victoria's strength of personality demonstrated through the years how a constitutional monarch could still reign with influence and power.

* * *

Despite all their similarities in youth, Charlotte and Victoria's deaths were vastly different. Charlotte died after two days of tumultuous labor and a significant loss of blood. Victoria passed away quietly after having felt unwell for several weeks. Only two doctors witnessed Charlotte's passing; Victoria had several of her children at her bedside holding her hand. The differences were reflected greater still in their funerals. The mourning of Princess Charlotte had been symbolized by the color black: eight black horses with tall black plumes pulling the coffin in a black carriage. The service in St. George's chapel at Windsor had been held at night, beginning at 8 p.m. and lasting three hours. "No monarch, no minister, no national hero had ever been so deeply mourned as 'the Beloved Princess.'"[43] At least, not until Queen Victoria's death.

Queen Victoria died on January 22, 1901 on the Isle of Wight at Osbourne House, the family home designed by Prince Albert. She was 81 at her passing. Victoria left detailed, strict instructions about her funeral and burial, particularly that she should be treated as "a soldier's daughter,"[44] a phrase her father had used to describe her when as an infant she wasn't startled by a pellet accidentally shot through the nursery window. Three days after her death, the HMY *Alberta* transported her casket to Portsmouth. A state funeral cortège of boats accompanied the yacht, as well as a German battleship that had accompanied the Emperor.

In Portsmouth, a gun carriage conveyed the white-draped coffin to the railway station for the steam engine journey to London. The train passed by thousands of devoted citizens who knelt in meadows alongside the tracks as they watched in reverence. As the train pulled into Victoria Station, a silent crowd greeted the casket. But her coffin did not remain in London. A gun carriage pulled by eight cream-colored horses helped to transport the coffin to Paddington Station, where it then departed for Windsor. The crowds were there to watch, 10-people deep lining the route. In due course "[s]he was followed by the King of England, and by his brothers, all in uniform, by the German Emperor, by King George I of [Greece], by King Carlos of Portugal, King Leopold II of Belgium, by the crown princes of Germany, Romania, Greece, Denmark, Norway, Sweden and Siam, by the Archduke Franz Ferdinand of Austria-Hungary ..., by the Grand Duke Michael Alexandrovich, and by the Duke of Aosta."[45]

Victoria's funeral was held on February 2, 1801, a cold and blustery day. Upon the casket's arrival in Windsor, it proceeded to St. George's Chapel for a brief service in frigid temperatures. The Queen laid in state for two days under military guard in the Albert Memorial Chapel at Windsor Castle. Afterward, as she had directed, they interred her beside Prince Albert in the Frogmore Mausoleum.

Henry James wrote of the British Empire mourning Queen Victoria as the loss of a "safe and motherly old middle-class Queen, who held the nation warm under the fold of her big, hideous Scotch-plaid shawl."[46] Only the oldest citizens could remember a time another monarch had been on the throne. Her constant presence, stalwart determination to fulfil her duty, and example of decorum had been an anchor during decades of famine, struggle, and technological advancements. Victoria's death marked both the loss of the mother of the nation and the passing of the grandmother of Europe. A fitting tribute, since it was among her own children and grandchildren where Queen Victoria extended her greatest personal influence and experienced her deepest feelings of cherished tenderness.

Queen Victoria's Children

- **Princess Victoria Adelaide Mary Louise** (1840-1901) married Friedrich Wilhelm of Prussia, who became the emperor of Germany. In addition to their son, German Emperor and King of Prussia, William II, who inherited the throne, one of their daughters was Sophia, Queen of the Hellenes (Greece). Another daughter, Margaret, married the (elected) King of Finland.

- **Prince Albert Edward Wettin** (1841-1910) inherited the throne (as King Edward VII) when his mother passed in 1901. He married Princess Alexandra of Denmark. One of his daughters was Maud, Queen of Norway.

- **Princess Alice Maude Mary** (1843-1878) married Prince Ludwig and Hesse who became the Grand Duke Louis XIV. One of their daughters, Alix, married Nicholas II, the last Russian Czar.

- **Prince Alfred Ernest Albert** (1844-1900) married the Grand Duchess Marie, daughter of Tzar Alexander II of Russia. He became the Duke of Saxe-Coburg. One of their daughters was Marie, Queen of Romania.

- **Princess Helena Augusta Victoria** (1846-1923) married Prince Frederick Christian of Schleswig-Holstein.

- **Princess Louise Caroline Alberta** (1848-1939) married John Douglas Sutherland Campbell, a commoner who later became the Duke of Argyll and Governor-General of Canada.

- **Prince Arthur William Patrick** (1850-1942) married Princess Louise Margarete of Prussia. One of their daughters was Margaret, Crown Princess of Sweden.

- **Prince Leopold George Duncan** (1853-1884) married Princess Helena Frederica of Waldeck, Germany.

- **Princess Beatrice Mary Victoria** (1857-1944) married Prince Henry of Battenberg. One of their daughters became Victoria Eugenie, Queen of Spain.

Chapter 10:
Martin Luther King Jr.

Martin Luther King Jr.'s involvement in civil rights began unexpectedly, when in December 1955 Rosa Parks refused to give up her seat on a Montgomery city bus when asked by the driver. The previous year the Supreme Court had ruled segregation unconstitutional in Brown vs. Board of Education, but Montgomery city officials stubbornly maintained segregation rules on buses. When arrested for her determination to keep her seat, the Black community ignited in indignation for Mrs. Parks and her civil rights. Her trial date was set for Monday, December 5. Immediately local Black rights activists, led by outspoken E. D. Nixon, began organizing a bus boycott that would coincide with the trial. But Nixon knew he needed the help of (among others) the dynamic, young, newly hired pastor of the Dexter Avenue Baptist Church. The morning after Mrs. Park's arrest, Nixon called Reverend King asking for his support in the boycott. "Brother Nixon, let me think on it awhile, and call me back," he replied.[1]

Nervous that he might not be able to get Reverend King on board with the boycott, Nixon asked Ralph Abernathy to try and convince King. Abernathy served as an energetic minister at Montgomery's First Baptist Church and had been King's best friend. Ralph immediately called. King agreed to give his support by attending a leadership meeting the next day—but only if he wasn't required to help in any planning. Being a pastor, a member of the local executive board for the National Association for the Advancement of Colored People (NAACP), having recently finished his doctoral thesis, and being the father to an infant daughter likely made life busy for the 26-year-old. In fact, Martin and his wife, Coretta, had recently agreed he should not run for president of the NAACP chapter because of the need to focus more on his congregation. But when Reverend King showed up to the leadership meeting and saw over forty community advisors had assembled to help Mrs. Parks, he knew "something unusual was about to happen."[2]

At the meeting on Saturday, December 3, they formed a committee to help get the word out about the city bus boycott. Reverend King, as part of the group, helped to prepare a message mimeograph in the basement of the church by him and Abernathy. The message read in part, "Don't ride the buses to work to town, to school, or any where on Monday. If you work, take a cab, or share a ride, or walk."[3] Seven thousand copies of the message were delivered throughout the Black community the next day. King recalled vividly the first day of the boycott:

> "My wife and I awoke earlier than usual on Monday morning. We were up and fully dressed by five-thirty. . . . Fortunately, a bus stop was just five feet from our house. We could observe the opening stages from our front window. And so we waited through an interminable half hour. I was in the kitchen drinking my coffee when I heard Coretta cry, 'Martin, Martin, come quickly!' I put down my cup and ran toward the living room. As I approached the front window Coretta pointed joyfully to a slowly moving bus: 'Darling, it's empty!' I could hardly believe what I saw. I knew that the South Jackson line, which ran past our house, carried more Negro passengers than any other line in Montgomery, . . . [but] it was empty of all but two white passengers."[4]

Later that same day, a judge convicted Mrs. Parks of violating the city segregation ordinance and fined her $10, plus $4 in court fees. Because she had cooperated fully with the arrest, her case represented one of the few instances where the defendant faced charges solely for breaking a segregation law. Mrs. Parks appealed the case, but the loss had the effect of galvanizing the community. Local leaders recognized the impact. It was what they had been waiting for; the movement began.

That evening community leaders held a meeting at the Holy Street Church to plan the next steps of the protest. At that gathering the Montgomery Improvement Association (MIA) formed. When it came time to elect a leader, the first nomination named the 'Reverend M. L. King.' Almost immediately the motion was seconded and then unanimously supported by all in attendance. Dr. King later recalled, "The action had caught me unawares. It had happened so quickly that I did not even have time to think it through. It is probable that if I had, I would have declined the nomination."[5] Suddenly he became part of a crusade destined to influence the world.

* * *

Martin Luther King Jr. (originally named Michael King Jr.) was born in Atlanta, Georgia on January 15, 1929. His father had a career as an assertive autocratic preacher, and he deeply hoped his son would join him in the ministry. Despite the fact the Great Depression dominated much of Martin's formative years, his father's position as the preacher at Atlanta's Ebenezer Baptist Church lent enough stability to the family that Martin and his younger brother never really noticed. The King family belonged to the middle-class, living in the Auburn Avenue neighborhood of Victorian-era homes and tree-lined streets. The charismatic Reverend King Sr. and his family were adored by the congregation and community alike; the church was their second home. This protective insulation had the effect of shielding Martin from the racist attitudes of the day. It wasn't until the age of five, when a favorite Caucasian friend could no longer play with Martin, that he noticed racial differences.

As a child, Martin behaved precociously. His interests were wide ranging—from opera to wrestling. Taking after his father's short (5'7"), thick physique, Martin consistently played sports while growing up, including basketball, baseball, and football. From his mother came a love of music and piano lessons. Although he skipped half of the first grade, he proved to be an indifferent student, with particular weaknesses in spelling and grammar. But he loved the vocal use of language to persuade and move an audience. Once, after hearing a visiting preacher speak, Martin told his mother, "Someday I'm going to have me some big words like that."[6] At a young age he worked to develop a broad vocabulary, which he used to get out of trouble or extricate himself from a fight. "I like to get in over my head, then bother people with questions," he once smirked.[7]

Growing up near his maternal grandparents, Martin had a particularly close relationship with his grandmother, Jennie Williams. The Williams lived with the King family for a while during Martin's younger years. Known as "Mama" to her grandchildren, Grandma Williams loved to spend time with them, telling stories and sharing her love of the Bible. "'She was very dear to each of us, but especially to me,' he later wrote. 'I sometimes think that I was [her] favorite grandchild.'"[8] Mama died of a heart attack on May 18, 1941. Her death profoundly impacted 12-year-old Martin. He learned about her passing while at a parade in downtown Atlanta without his parents' permission. He blamed himself for her loss.

> "Grieved by the death of his beloved 'Mama' and remorseful about his transgression, King initially reacted by jumping from a second-floor window of his home. While neither King nor his father later mentioned a suicide attempt in their autobiographical statements, the elder King's account confirms the distress and guilt his son felt: 'He cried off and on for several days afterward, and was unable to sleep at night.'"[9]

Apparently, the youthful Martin felt grief and guilt heavily. On at least one other occasion (at age 12) he again jumped out the second story window of his home. Somehow, he miraculously survived with only minor injuries. The Centre for Suicide Prevention notes that 85% of those who try to kill themselves by jumping from a high place are successful. "Jumping also has the added potential to traumatize those who witness it and endanger the lives of passerby."[10] In an era when suicide remained a taboo subject, very little discussion or documentation exists regarding Martin's two attempts, or the aftermath. He, himself, made no mention of it in his autobiography. It is likely his actions shocked his parents and caused them to take extra vigilance with their son.

* * *

Educationally, Martin Luther King was a late bloomer. He performed well enough to get average grades—and even skipped grades enough to graduate high school at age 15. But his interest in learning wasn't focused. For much of his youth, and even several of his years at Morehouse College in Atlanta, Martin didn't want to become a minister. He considered a career in medicine briefly, then decided to major in sociology as a pre-law student. While at Morehouse he had the chance to study Thoreau's essay *On Civil Disobedience*, and he learned more about Gandhi's peaceful protests. "[T]he only academic intensity he evinced was listening with a transfixed raptness to the weekly addresses of Morehouse president Dr. Benjamin Mays, a nationally prestigious theological scholar."[11] Finally, by 1947, at age 18, he felt the pull of the ministry. Being a minister would give him a framework where he could both help others and employ nonviolent reforms.

With the decision to follow his father into theology, Martin applied and got into Crozer Theological Seminary near Chester, Pennsylvania. As one of only 11 Black students at the seminary, this marked Martin's first experience surrounded by a predominantly white population. At the outset, being in the minority felt awkward for Martin, but he soon found his footing. "It was at Crozer that King strengthened his commitment to the Christian social gospel, developed his initial interest in Gandhian ideas, was first exposed to pacifism, and developed his ideas about nonviolence as a method of social reform."[12] It became a time of intellectual and spiritual growth for him.

Twice during his Crozer years Martin's life was endangered by gun violence. Once, an angry classmate, Lucius Z. Hall Jr., burst into Martin's dorm room with a gun. Hall had mistakenly assumed Martin had pulled a malicious prank on him. Luckily, Marcus Wood, an older student in the room at the time, intervened. Wood saw how terrified Martin was, but noticed he kept a cool head. Wood escorted Hall out of the room and back to his own. Afterward, despite the scare, Martin refused to report Hall for his behavior. King's restraint in the matter earned him greater respect from his classmates. He served as student body president in his third year at Crozer.

A second incident involving a gun occurred near the end of Martin's first year at school. While on a double date at a restaurant near Camden, New Jersey, the white owner of the diner refused to serve the two couples. Initially, the four decided to just stay seated; but the owner returned waving a gun and making verbal threats. When he shot the gun once into the air, Martin and his friends quickly left. They reported the incident to the local police, but the white customers who had witnessed the restaurant owner's rampage refused to testify. The matter had to be dropped.

* * *

Martin Luther King Jr. lived "increasingly in a daily expectation of death"[13] beginning in 1955 with the Montgomery bus boycott. As the leader of the MIA, Martin became the face of the movement, and the King family faced harassment. While living in the parsonage, the obscene and hostile phone calls became so unbearable they left the phone off the hook at night to get sleep. On the evening of Friday, January 27, 1956, Martin answered another threatening phone call: "[expletive], we are tired of you and your mess now. And if you aren't out of this town in three days, we're going to blow your brains out, and blow up your house."[14]

The call unnerved Martin. Unable to sleep, he went to the kitchen to make coffee. While sitting at the kitchen table he thought about his love for and the safety of two-month-old daughter, Yolanda ("Yoki"), and his wife. Was he doing the right thing if it put his family in danger? After pondering what to do, Martin prayed, telling the Lord he felt his actions were fair and just, but his courage was failing him. In that moment he received a confirmation from the Lord:

> "It seemed at that moment that I could hear an inner voice saying to me, 'Martin Luther, stand up for righteousness. Stand up for justice. Stand up for truth. And lo I will be with you, even until the end of the world.' . . . [The Lord] promised never to leave me, never to leave me alone."[15]

This validation from a higher power gave Martin Luther King the resolve to carry on, despite the threats, arrests, and violent acts against him and his family.

Just a few days later, Martin faced a test of his resolve. Three days after the threatening phone call, he left his home to attend an MIA meeting at Abernathy's First Baptist Church. Coretta remained home to tend their daughter. After putting Yoki to bed, she sat in the living room visiting with her friend, Mary Lucy Williams. Suddenly, the two women heard a loud thump on the front porch, followed by footfalls running away. They rushed into a guest bedroom to hide when an unexpectedly large explosion on the front porch shook the house. The front room of the King home filled with smoke, dust, and shards of glass. Deeply shaken, Coretta and Mary Lucy went to collect Yoki, who remained asleep in the rear of the home.

Within moments, neighbors were assembled on the front lawn of the King's home to see what had happened. Someone called the police. Coretta called the church to tell Martin. King immediately dismissed everyone and went home. By the time he arrived, several hundred people were there, including the mayor, the police commissioner, and the fire chief. The windows on the front of the house had been blown out, soot marked the front door, and a shallow hole had been carved out of the concrete front porch.

Within a short time, many who had gathered voiced indignation at the violence. Some felt the bombing stemmed from the firm stance taken by city officials against the boycott, and severe traffic policies the police department had adopted to make boycott supporters want to give up. Martin stepped forward and asked everyone to remain calm since no one had been injured, then sent them all home. After they had dispersed, the Kings left to stay the night at the home of friends. Later, when reflecting on the bombing and how composedly he handled things, he noted, "My religious experience a few nights before had given me the strength to face it."[16]

No suspects were ever arrested in the bombing of the King home in 1956. But this marked only the beginning of the violence against King and his family. "Later that same year, while the boycott was still in effect, someone fired a shotgun at the Kings' home, and they continued to receive death threats and intimidation—including a threatening letter from the Federal Bureau of Investigation."[17] And there were other attacks. In fact, a year after the King home bombing, a similar attempt occurred. On January 27, 1957, someone left a bundle of 12 sticks of dynamite on the porch of the parsonage. The partially burned fuse had somehow fizzled out without setting off the intended explosion. Although Martin and his family had not been home at the time, the attempted murder plot shocked and upset them. Within a month a gang of seven white men were arrested for the second bomb plot; however, an all-white jury decided they were not guilty.

Unfortunately, Martin Luther King's most life-threatening attack had not yet happened. Although he regularly suffered violent outbursts from racist enemies, most were not life-threatening. In December 1957, Martin began writing an autobiographical account of the Montgomery bus boycott. Stanley Levinson, a close friend and advisor, arranged for a publisher to print the manuscript. *Stride Toward Freedom: The Montgomery Story* was released in September the following year. On September 20 King promoted the book in Blumstein's department store in Harlem, New York. While signing a copy of his book, he heard a woman ask his identity. After responding, the next thing he knew he had been stabbed in the chest with a seven-inch letter opener. Surrounded by friends and family, Martin received immediate care. They took him to the hospital with the blade still lodged in his chest. In the meantime, Blumstein's security team handcuffed the perpetrator, a mentally ill Black woman named Izola Curry.

Martin remained conscious throughout the ambulance ride to nearby Harlem Hospital. A team of surgeons took several hours to prepare for the difficult procedure. "Days later, when I was well enough to talk with Dr. Aubre Maynard, the chief of the surgeons who performed the delicate, dangerous operation, I learned the reason for the long delay that preceded surgery. He told me that the razor tip of the instrument had been touching my aorta and that my whole chest had to be opened to extract it."[18] The fact that the weapon had not pierced the aorta—or that Martin had not sneezed or coughed while waiting for surgery—was miraculous. He could have drowned in his own blood. After the ordeal, a small cross-shaped scar remained on his chest for the rest of his life.

* * *

Martin Luther King Jr. and a Hollywood producer once discussed the possibility of making a film about King's life. When the discussion turned to how the film might end, King told the producer, "It ends with me getting killed."[19]

Tragically, he was right.

As the civil rights movement grew, Martin organized and participated in numerous other campaigns, including the 1963 March on Washington for Jobs and Freedom where over 200,000 people converged on the nation's capital. At this event, overlooking the National Mall, King delivered his famous "I Have a Dream" speech. 1963 marked the centennial anniversary of the Emancipation Proclamation, and yet in so many ways Blacks were still restricted and disenfranchised. King later commented, "As television beamed the image of this extraordinary gathering across the border oceans, everyone who believed in man's capacity to better himself had a moment of inspiration and confidence in the future of the human race."[20] The speech marked the climax of Martin's career.

Although King continued to work hard and saw successes over the next five years, he also saw more division among those fighting for civil rights. Many of the younger activists did not feel change was happening fast enough; they felt his nonviolent strategies were not working. Martin's peaceful events gave way to violence more and more often. Near the end of March 1968, King traveled to Memphis, Tennessee to support public works employees who had been on strike there for several weeks. Four days after arriving, King addressed a rally and delivered his "I've Been to the Mountaintop" address, in which he prophetically observed:

> "And then I got to Memphis. And some began to say the threats, or talk about the threats that were out. What would happen to me from some of our sick white brothers? Well, I don't know what will happen now. We've got some difficult

days ahead. But it doesn't matter with me now. Because I've been to the mountaintop. And I don't mind. Like anybody, I would like to live a long life. Longevity has its place. But I'm not concerned about that now. I just want to do God's will. And He's allowed me to go up to the mountain. And I've looked over. And I've seen the promised land."[21]

The next day, Thursday, April 4, 1968, at 6:01 p.m., James Earl Ray fatally shot Dr. King, who stood on the second-floor balcony outside his hotel room at the Lorraine Motel. His best friend, Ralph Abernathy, and the Reverend Jesse Jackson, were both nearby. A fire station stood across the street from the Lorraine Motel, where police officers had been placed to keep King under surveillance. Having witnessed the shooting, officers were on the scene within moments and able to administer first aid. Despite the assistance, King died an hour later at St. Joseph's Hospital while undergoing emergency surgery.

For many in the Black community the killing served as an indication that white America would defend racism by any means required. The thought collectively terrified Blacks and sparked deep emotional reactions nationwide. In the immediate aftermath in Memphis, a demonstration he had planned for the striking sanitation workers transformed into a nonviolent, silent march to honor his memory. Led by Coretta, Ralph Abernathy, and singer Harry Belafonte, those in the procession carried signs reading "Honor King: End Racism." An estimated 30,000–40,000 people participated. After a series of speeches, the crowd sang the African American spiritual "Guide My Feet": "Lord guide my feet, while I run this race. / Lord hold my hand, while I run this race." Soon after, Memphis city officials offered a fair settlement to the sanitation workers, ending the strike. It became Martin Luther King Jr.'s final accomplishment.

President Lyndon B. Johnson declared Sunday, April 7, 1968, a National Day of Mourning in honor of MLK's passing. But Johnson did not attend the funeral in Atlanta two days later, saying he did not want his presence to cause additional unrest. Many found this to be a weak excuse. Despite the President's absence, numerous well-known public figures and celebrities came to show their support: Vice President Hubert Humphries, future President Richard M. Nixon, the Kennedys (Ted, Jacqueline, and Robert, who would himself be assassinated two months later), Supreme Court Justice Thurgood Marshall, and Rev. Jesse Jackson. Although held the day before the Oscars in Los Angeles, many prominent movie stars gave precedence to King's funeral services, including Sammy Davis Jr., Louis Armstrong, Sidney Poitier, Bill Cosby, and Marlon Brando (among others).

Tens of thousands of everyday people traveled to Atlanta to pay their respects to King. The funeral began at Ebenezer Baptist Church, where he had shared preaching duties with his father after moving with his family to Atlanta. Most listened on speakers outside; millions more watched it live on television. After the service, a procession transported King's casket past the Georgia State Capitol building to Morehouse College on a mule-drawn wagon. Over 100,000 mourners joined in the march. Laurence Smith Jr., of South Carolina joined in the march. Although he had never previously been an activist, he had great admiration for Dr. King's work. Smith, already in Atlanta attending a conference, felt more impressed by those who lined the streets in silent vigil than with the big-name figures in the parade.[22] At Morehouse, college president Dr. Mays, whose speeches Martin had deeply admired 20 years earlier, offered the eulogy. That evening King was laid to rest at South-View Cemetery.

The irony of a man who preached nonviolence being violently assassinated led to great turmoil across the nation. Although Memphis and Atlanta were able to keep the peace in the aftermath of King's death, over 120 other cities in the United States experienced sustained violent outbreaks. Smoke from fires in Washington DC hovered over the capitol dome and thousands were arrested for looting, arson, and violence. Eventually, President Johnson brought in Army troops to help maintain the peace in both DC and Baltimore. The military also helped in Chicago by occupying the downtown area and preventing snipers from shooting at firefighters working to put out flames. New York City experienced protests, some violent, others peaceful. In the days following King's death a total of 39 people died from rioting.

* * *

True leadership is won in the trenches. Fortunately, Martin Luther King Jr. had not been in the trenches alone. Numerous others helped to organize, manage, and fund the civil rights movement. Many of these other pioneers contributed significantly to the cause, both during and after King's lifetime. In pondering the numerous times King's life might have ended prematurely, could any of these colleagues have risen up to stand in his place?

Roy Wilkins, 'Senior Statesman' of the civil rights movement, served as a great administrator and executive secretary and director of the NAACP for many years. As a well-educated, strong writer, and nationally recognized leader, Wilkins made a significant impact. But Wilkins remained heavily focused on the legislative aspect of the movement. "[T]he thing which won the Montgomery case was not the walking of the brave people," Wilkins wrote in 1957, "but a decision in the Supreme Court ... secured through the skill of [an] NAACP lawyer."[23] This focus would likely not have given him the ability to win over the hearts and minds of the nation. Wilkins failed to understand what MLK easily recognized: winning over public opinion would help in the battle to change the laws, both locally and nationally.

Whitney Young, Jr. is another peer of Martin Luther King's who may possibly have been able to exert influence if MLK had died earlier. Young had experience and connections in the business community and had talent as a strong orator. King, Young, and others joined together to form the Unity Council to help various civil rights groups collaborate and work together. As the head of the National Urban League throughout the 1960s, Young consulted on racial matters for both Presidents Kennedy and Johnson. But this close relationship with the executive branch of the government limited Young's ability to speak out; he had to take a moderate stance to maintain his connections. Indeed, he readily accepted that compromise. But as a result, he wasn't always trusted by the Black community and the *New York Times* accused him of being an "Oreo cookie."[24]

Ralph Abernathy, Rufus Lewis, and E.D. Nixon all had a hand at the beginning of the Montgomery bus boycott and could very well have been better (or equally) suited to heading up the MIA. Could any of these men have ultimately guided the movement to the national and international levels as King had done? Possibly. But for good reasons these men chose King over themselves. They recognized his educated background and saw the confidence he exuded. Abernathy felt keenly that King was a "man with a special gift from God."[25] And, they knew his recent move to the area meant he would not be perceived as having too close an association with various groups or factions in the city—he could be perceived as neutral. The same could not be said of themselves.

When Abernathy, Lewis, and Nixon pulled Martin Luther King Jr. into the boycott, they had no intention of it leading to anything beyond a brief episode. The call to lead the MIA came as a surprise. Having just landed his first job out of college, King worked to get settled in at his church and in Montgomery. But having completed his PhD in systematic theology fewer than six months prior, King's education set him apart as a leader. In college he had studied about and deeply pondered means of nonviolent resistance, particularly as proffered theoretically by Thoreau and put into practice by Gandhi. When the Montgomery bus boycott began, MLK adapted these philosophies to the needs of the Southern Black community. Prior to this his thoughts had been purely academic. Now, needing something concrete to guide them in real life, King took Gandhian principles and combined them with the Christian values of the Black Church. The end product became resistance based in faith—faith that when their oppressors would see the fearless suffering of the humble masses, change would come about. Moreover, faith that God would support them as they sought for virtuous ends using Christlike means. This lent a sense of morality to the protest that Montgomery's middle-class Blacks connected with and could support.

King's belief in nonviolent resistance stood out as unique at the time. Many in the Black community, including Malcom X and Stokely Carmichael, pushed for more aggressive strategies. Although some of King's own peaceful marches sometimes devolved into violent outbreaks, he persisted in trying to persuade others to remain calm. When in 1963 he led a massive march on Washington DC, he delivered the "I Have a Dream" speech. The march helped to sway public opinion and led to the ratification of the 24th Amendment, which abolished poll taxes, and the Civil Rights Act of 1964, which prohibited racial discrimination in employment and education facilities. These two big accomplishments caught the attention of many around the world. In October 1964 Martin Luther King Jr. won the Nobel Peace Prize for his efforts to improve civil rights using nonviolence. At the time of the announcement, King was a patient in an Atlanta hospital, suffering from exhaustion. When Coretta called him with news of the announcement, he had been sleeping. Coretta remembered that a few minutes after sharing the news and ending the call, Martin called her back asking if he had been dreaming.

One of Dr. King's greatest strengths lay in his ability to communicate his ideas of nonviolent resistance in a clear and motivating manner. "To read the speeches and writings of Martin Luther King is to appreciate the courage of his moral commitment and determination to achieve social justice for his people. It is also to sense the passion of his words and to realize a terrible wrong."[26] Although MLK sometimes had the help of others to draft speeches, with such an extensive educational background, he had a masterful command of language all on his own. His ability to deliver the words, his cadence, timing, and rhythm, also demonstrated rare skill. His talent amounted to more than just a gifted Baptist preacher able to deliver a powerful sermon. Martin Luther King Jr.'s oratorical power seemed to some empowered from on high. In particular, his "I Have a Dream" speech seemed very inspired. "It was as if some cosmic transcendental force came down and occupied his body," lawyer Clarence Jones said. "It was the same body, the same voice, but the voice had something I had never heard before. It was so powerful, it was spellbinding."[27]

* * *

Would the civil rights movement have taken place if Martin Luther King Jr. had passed away from suicide, gun violence in college, or being stabbed? Although difficult to imagine the crusade without his presence, it very likely would still have gone forth; it just would have looked significantly different. Ella Baker, director of the Southern Christian Leadership Council (SCLC), once noted, "The movement made Martin rather than Martin making the movement."[28] And Baker is accurate: Rosa Parks refused to give up her seat before Dr. King ever got involved. There had been boycotts in other cities prior to Montgomery. Even without MLK, the Black community had been primed and ready for change. A symphony of voices came together to make it happen. All this would still have happened without MLK.

However, we cannot discount the elevated influence Martin Luther King Jr. exerted on the civil rights movement. His sincere desire for the country to come together, rather than be divided over violence, is recognized as a distinguished contribution to the nation. Without his voice and his belief in nonviolent resistance, the drive to eliminate segregation and make voting rights fair for all would have been vastly different. In his absence, the civil rights movement would likely have been more radical, divisive, and deadly. Groups such as the Black Muslims, Black Panthers, and Black Power probably would have grown stronger earlier. Because of the polarization these groups caused, the elimination of segregation laws may have been slower to occur. And the passage of other essential pieces of legislation would likely have taken significantly longer and come at greater cost. Notable pieces of legislation passed during the civil rights movement of King's lifetime, which may never have been fully realized, include:

- 24th Amendment to the Constitution – Eliminated poll taxes that infringed on the voting rights of minorities.

- Civil Rights Act of 1964 - A "Magna Carta for the race, a splendid monument for the cause of human rights,"[29] this piece of legislation banned discrimination in employment and public accommodations based on race, color, religion, or national origin.

- Voting Rights Act of 1965 - Restored and protected the right to vote for all people.

- Immigration and Nationality Services Act of 1965 - Equalized immigration from countries around the world, not just European nations.

- Fair Housing Act of 1968 - Banned housing discrimination in both sales and rentals.

King's influence went far beyond civil rights legislation. The reach of his sphere stemmed across the country and the world. MLK's legacy includes influence on civil rights movements in several other countries around the world, including South Africa and Great Britain. Millions of minorities live in better circumstances because of his work. Additionally, Dr. King spoke out and led marches against the Vietnam War, helping to bring attention to the difficulties faced there. His voice helped to change public opinion and placed pressure on Presidents Johnson and Nixon to end the conflict. He also avidly supported Native American rights and helped the Creek in Alabama with their efforts at desegregation. John Echohawk, one of the founders of the Native American Rights Fund, has written about how King inspired the work among Native Americans. Lastly, the federal holiday Martin Luther King Day celebrates the life and ideals of MLK; Japan, Canada, Israel, and the Netherlands each have a holiday named after him, too.

* * *

On December 4, 1964, Martin Luther King Jr. left Atlanta to fly to Oslo to receive the Nobel Peace Prize. Many people asked him what it felt like to win such a prestigious award, but it took him several days to understand how to best express his feelings. He finally settled on a memory of sitting on a plane and seeing through the window the ground crew members working down below. He realized that most people would attribute the successful flight to the pilot, others to the helpful cabin crew. But in reality, the ground crew held a big part in each and every safe arrival. "I thought of the Nobel Peace Prize as a prize, a reward, for the ground crew: fifty thousand Negro people in Montgomery, Alabama, who came to discover that it is better to walk in dignity than to ride in buses."[30] Although his cause is yet unfinished, a ground crew of individuals are still working on King's behalf and looking to him for inspiration to guide them toward the realization of equality.

Chapter 11: Orville Wright

"I want to know why anybody should be inclined to doubt the possibility of a man's flying?" the editor of *The Aeronautical Annual* asked in early 1896.[1] The question posed in a *New York Times* article led into a discussion (complete with illustrations) of strategies Otto Lilienthal of Berlin had been using to master the art of flight by imitating flying squirrels. That same year Lilienthal became the first to make well-documented, repeated, successful glider flights, which were lauded in newspapers around the world.

And studied by two brothers in Dayton, Ohio: Orville and Wilbur Wright.

The Wright brothers had long been inclined to tinkering. In 1889 the two built their own printing press and started a publishing business with two short-lived local newspapers, the *West Side News* and the *Evening Item*. Several years later they opened their own bicycle repair and sales shop. By the time 1896 rolled around, and Lilienthal was experimenting with gliders, the Wright brothers (now in their late 20s) were manufacturing and selling their own brand of bicycle.

Looking back, the year 1896 offered significant advancements in the field of aeronautics. In May, the first unmanned steam-powered model airplane took flight, and a few months later several American flight pioneers met near Lake Michigan to test the latest ideas for gliders. Sadly, on August 9, Herr Otto Lilienthal crashed and broke his neck in a glider accident. He died the next day. The news reports of Lilienthal's death marked the beginning of the Wright brothers' serious interest in flight, and likely motivated Orville's fight to survive a severe bout of typhoid fever late that summer.

* * *

Orville and Wilbur Wright's father, Bishop Milton Wright, had long worried about the dangers of contaminated water. His concerns and warnings to his children were not unfounded. For many years, medical professionals had documented the cause of typhoid fever to be infections leeched into water. Then, in 1880 Karl Joseph Eberth became the first to define the bacillus believed to cause typhoid fever.[2] Within a brief time his discovery was confirmed, and the knowledge spread. "There can be no doubt in the mind of any one as to the mode by which the wells are contaminated. The saturation of the soil with the excreta of patients suffering from enteric fever is now going on in every house where there are no sewer connections to carry off these discharges."[3]

With the understanding of the causes of typhoid fever, public health committees in the United States and Europe worked hard to inform people about the importance of sanitary conditions around water. Still, the disease remained a problem. As is usually the case, putting knowledge into action took time. Sixteen years after Eberth's discovery, deaths by typhoid fever remained endemic. An article published in a January 1896 issue of Washington DC's *Evening Star* included a table of mortality rates of some of the biggest cities in the United States for the four summer months of the previous year. The table shows that in Cleveland (about 200 miles from the Wright's home) 40 people died of typhoid fever. In Chicago, 271 deaths occurred.[4]

Orville Wright's illness, beginning in late August 1896, brought on a fever of 105 and led him to death's door, despite being a healthy and active 25-year-old man. Wilbur and sister Katherine kept faithful vigil at Orville's bedside after sending word to Bishop Wright, who traveled at the time. Their father wrote back, advising, "Put him in the best room for air and comfort. Sponge him off gently and quickly. . .. Let no one use the well water at the store henceforth. Boil the water you all drink."[5]

As experienced by Orville, the primary symptom of typhoid is a high fever. Other symptoms include headaches, rash, vomiting, and sometimes diarrhea; complications such as bowel perforation or hemorrhage can cause death. Orville spent many days in a delirium, on the verge of dying. The family doctor, Levi

Spitler, felt pessimistic about a recovery. Dr. Spitler[6] likely recommended common treatments of the day, including a "mild" diet (liquids such as milk or broth), bed rest, and cold baths to help keep the fever in control. He knew from experience that little more could be done.

Bishop Milton Wright wrote of the progression of Orville's illness in his journal numerous times:

> *"Friday, September 4.* Found Orville very sick with typhoid fever. The temperature at one time, days ago, ran to 105.5 degrees. Temperature is now about 102 or 103 degrees.
>
> *"Saturday, September 5.* Dr. Spitler came at 11:30.
>
> *"Thursday, September 10.* At home, Orville's fever is possibly decreasing a little.
>
> *"Sunday, September 20.* Orville had a little if any fever, but has some delirium, part of the time.
>
> *"Thursday, October 8.* Orville had tapioca today for the first time. He has lived for six weeks on milk, with a little beef broth for a couple of weeks past. He also sat up in bed for the first time in six weeks."[7]

Despite Dr. Spitler's dour predictions, Orville miraculously recovered. Whether this came as the result of Bishop Wright's insistence on clean, boiled water or fervent prayers on his son's behalf, one cannot be sure. Maybe the more interesting point to consider is how the loss of Orville Wright at age 25 might have impacted Wilbur and the eventual invention of the first motor-operated airplane. Orville's illness started the brothers on a trajectory that would change the world.

Even after finally being able to sit up after prone so long, it took several more weeks before Orville could get out of bed. He had grown weak, but at least the fever and delirium were gone. To assuage Orville's boredom, Wilbur began reading aloud to him, including the experimentations of German glider enthusiast Otto Lilienthal. Wilbur had previously read about Lilienthal in an 1894 *McClure's Magazine* article. Photos included in the article generated a great deal of interest in the older brother. Now, after hearing of Lilienthal's unfortunate death, Wilbur and Orville's fascination grew and their study of the possibility of flight began.

Over the next several years Orville and Wilbur consumed every book they could find on aeronautics. "They 'read up on aeronautics as a physician would read his books,' Bishop Wright would attest proudly."[8] But it wasn't until Tuesday, May 30, 1899, that they were ready to move from theory to practice. On this date, Wilbur wrote to the Smithsonian Institute:

> "I am about to begin a systematic study of the subject in preparation for practical work to which I expect to devote what time I can spare from my regular business. I wish to obtain such papers as the Smithsonian Institution has published on this subject, and if possible a list of other works in print in the English language."[9]

Fortunately, the response from the Smithsonian Institution had been thorough. Wilbur received documentation on the works of Sir George Cayley, Chanute, Lilienthal, Leonardo da Vinci, and Langley, enabling them to begin mechanical aeronautical experimentation within months. The following year the brothers went to Kitty Hawk, North Carolina to begin manned experiments with pilot-controlled gliders.

During their time at Kitty Hawk, Orville lived a charmed life seemingly free of peril despite their dangerous pursuit. Once, on September 19, 1900, he crashed into the dunes, but walked away unscathed. Wilbur described the crash in a letter to fellow flight enthusiast Octave Chanute:

> "My brother, after too brief practice with the use of the front rudder, tried to add the use of the wing-twisting [wing-warping] arrangement also, with the result that, while he was correcting a slight rise in one wing, he completely forgot to attend to the front rudder, and the machine reared up and rose some twenty-five feet and sidled off and struck the ground. . . .. We hope to have repairs made in a few days."[10]

After several more months of experimentation, the brothers headed home to Dayton and their bicycle shop. They spent the spring and summer months of 1901 preparing a new plane to take to Kitty Hawk. Finally, by late summer, they traveled back to North Carolina. As new experiments were undertaken, Wilbur and Orville worked steadfastly. Their exhaustion manifested itself one evening when, once again, Orville's and Wilbur's lives were miraculously saved:

> "One night after they had been working late at their shop, Orville returned home ahead of Wilbur. He was in bed when Wilbur came in. A surprising thing was that Wilbur, contrary to his invariable habit, forgot to bolt the front door. Orville, nearly asleep, reminded him of his oversight. Then when Wilbur went back to put on the lock, Orville thought to himself, 'I'll bet he does something else peculiar. He'll blow out the gas in his room.' Why he thought Wilbur would blow out the gas, instead of turning it off, he never could explain. Fearing he would drop off to sleep, he sat up in bed until the light in Wilbur's room was off. Then he went to investigate and found the gas was still turned on. Wilbur had blown out the flame. Except for Orville's presentiment, both could have been asphyxiated."[11]

Two years later, on December 17, 1903, Wilbur won a coin toss and made history. Orville recorded, "Wilbur started the fourth and last flight at just about 12 o'clock. The first few hundred feet were up and down, as before, but . . . [in the end] the distance over the ground was measured to be 852 feet [260 m]; the time of the flight was 59 seconds."[12]

* * *

By 1905 the Wright brothers began the process of refining their flying machine enough to patent and sell it. They spent several years improving and honing the mechanics and demonstrating the abilities of their plane in hopes of opening a business. On December 23, 1907, the United States Army Board of Ordinance and Fortification posted an "Advertisement and Specification for a Heavier-Than-Air Flying Machine."[13] The specifications for the flying machine were based on information from the Wright brothers and what their invention could do and what they could likely deliver. Specifically, the ad required that the machine carry both a pilot and a passenger for 125 miles, fly at a speed of 40 miles per hour, and remain aloft for at least an hour at a time. Additionally, it should be able to land without damage. And the learning curve to train pilots should allow "an intelligent man to become proficient in its use in a reasonable length of time."[14] The Wright brothers set to work, determined to be awarded the Army contract despite additional demands on the French aviation front and constant requests from journalists and publishers for updates on the advancements being made toward flight.

In May 1908, Wilbur Wright left for France to make demonstration flights on behalf of La Compagnie Generale de Navigation Aerienne. On the home front, Orville and employees Charlie Furnas and Charlie Taylor worked to prepare a new aircraft for the US Army flying machine trials scheduled to be held in September in Fort Myer, Virginia. In addition to building the new aircraft, Orville also took over handling correspondence and media requests made about the Wright aviation endeavors. He severely disliked the task. However, his writing abilities were not lacking; he penned an article for *Century* magazine that is considered a masterpiece of aviation writing to this day. He also took time to respond to letters from other engineers, willingly sharing what he and Wilbur had learned in their efforts. However, the practice of sharing may have led to stiffer competition.

Although significantly more advanced than any other engineers that summer, the Wright brothers knew they had to keep moving forward. Many worked hard to catch up—especially the Aerial Experiment Association (AEA) under the guidance of Alexander Graham Bell. Unlike the Wright machine, the AEA invention could take off without a catapult; but it did not stay aloft as long or carry a passenger like the most recent Wright Flyer had accomplished. Still, the competition continued to grow. Orville could feel the heat.

With the new flying machine complete, Orville and the two Charlies headed to Fort Myer in mid-August. The campus of Ft. Myer, first built during the Civil War, included a central parade or drill ground. Surrounded on one end by American colonial red brick buildings with white trim, and Arlington National Cemetery on the other end, the parade grounds would be used for the flight trials. At only 1,000 feet in length, it was on the short side for a runway, but the military personnel and workshop facilities more than made up for this drawback. Orville felt he could make do. The Wright aircraft would be safely housed in a large hot air balloon hangar on site. The parade grounds would be roped off, but spectators were allowed to watch for free.

Although inundated by questions from the press, military, and government officials, Orville and the Charlies set to work ensuring the Flyer would be ready for the demonstrations. At first there were some issues with the engine not producing enough horsepower, but they got it working right with some adjustments to the fuel and by replacing the oil cups. At about 6 p.m. on September 3, with only a very small crowd on hand, Orville made his first short public flight: a turn and a half around the Fort Myer parade grounds. But more demonstrations were still to come. Over the next week Orville began taking longer and longer flights, setting new records almost daily, and even including passengers, aviation experts assembled to evaluate the Flyer.

Friday, September 4: flew for 4 minutes with perfect control.

Wednesday, September 9: flight endurance record of 1 h 02 min 15 s (world's first flight lasting more than an hour); flight endurance record of 6 min 15 s with a passenger (Army Lieutenant Frank P. Lahm) in front of 1,000+ government officials.

Thursday, September 10: flight endurance record of 1 h 05 min 52 s against a stiff wind.

Friday, September 11: flight endurance record of 1 h 10 min 24 s, circling the parade grounds 58 times.

Saturday, September 12: flight endurance record with a passenger (Army Major George O. Squier) of 9 min 6.3 s, watched by 5,000 observers, including the secretary of war.

The next week, on September 17, Orville again flew a demonstration flight in front of a crowd of nearly 3,000 spectators. Although he had taken up passengers on earlier flights, this time he would be accompanied by First Lieutenant Thomas E. Selfridge. Orville suspected Selfridge worked as a spy for the AEA. "I don't trust him an inch," Orville wrote to Wilbur. "He plans to meet me often at dinner where he can pump me."[15] Although the flight began smoothly, after a few circles around the parade grounds two loud thumps were heard (later determined to be the propellor splitting). As Orville reached to turn off the engine, the broken propellor caught on the rigging. The Flyer shimmied violently at an altitude of 75 feet (23 meters), then fell nose-first toward the ground. The aircraft hit the earth with a loud crash, Orville and Selfridge pinned under the wreckage. Luckily, the two Charlies were able to quickly release the moaning Orville from the ruined Flyer. They dragged his injured body clear from the rubble where medical professionals on site looked him over. It took much longer to retrieve Lt. Selfridge who lay unconscious, trapped face down in the debris, with a large gash on his forehead. Eventually both men were taken alive to the hospital, where Lt. Selfridge later died of a fractured skull, having never regained consciousness. Orville, too, was in critical condition. He suffered from a fractured leg and hip, four broken ribs, and a back injury. But, somehow, he survived.

Despite the crash, the world now knew the question of flight had been put to rest.

* * *

Orville Wright's survival of typhoid fever and other accidents in his life seem to indicate a higher power watched over him. Although Wilbur also escaped serious injury testing their machines, and had been protected by Orville's impression about the gas, unfortunately he did not escape typhoid fever. Ironically, Wilbur fell ill on a trip to Boston in April 1912. After being diagnosed with the dreaded disease, he died on May 30 at the Wright family home in Dayton, Ohio. Orville had to carry forward their work alone. The brothers had already secured a patent for their aircraft in the United States (in 1908) and several European countries. A contract with the US government and deals with French investors had secured the financial success of both the Wright Company, which had incorporated on November 22, 1909, and the Wright Brothers Flying School.

After Wilbur's passing, Orville became the president of the Wright Company. But ultimately, he disliked being a businessman. Three years later he sold the company (and the patent) and spent the remainder of his life helping to further develop aviation by serving on the Aeronautical Chamber of Commerce and as a board member for the National Advisory Committee for Aeronautics. Orville also worked hard to defend and protect his and Wilbur's legacy. He personally supervised the preservation of the 1905 Wright Flyer III.

But what would have happened to the development of the aircraft if Orville Wright had actually died in 1896? Certainly, it was not simply a matter of flight—for more than 50 years able inventors had participated in aeronautics through balloons, gliders, and other means. Instead, the question addresses how soon would a manned, controlled, powered, fixed-wing aircraft have been invented and sold, thus enabling broad usage as a mode of transportation. "It is conceded that aerial navigation sooner or later will be the modern mode of transportation," a journalist wrote in 1902.[16] To answer this question requires taking into account both aeronautical knowledge contributed by the Wright brothers and the inspiration they provided to other competitors.

One of the key pieces of knowledge the Wright brothers contributed came from three months of wind tunnel experiments. After their failures during the first year at Kitty Hawk, Orville and Wilbur came to the realization that the tables of air pressure data provided by the Smithsonian (but originally from data provided by Lilienthal and Chanute) were, as Wilbur politely phrased, "somewhat in error."[17] They realized that to discover how to fly they would need to have accurate calculations. So, for three months they worked in a room over the bicycle shop using a homemade wind tunnel to test about 200 airfoils (wing shapes). "We did that work just for the fun we got out of learning new truths," Orville later recalled.[18] Despite the long, tedious process, the results revealed to the brothers correct air pressure data for various wing designs, and how best to build their airplane.

Only one or two others of those involved in the race to invent the airplane used wind tunnels to generate similar data, but "their tests were nothing like those of the brothers, who proceeded entirely on their own and in their own way."[19] The other competitors were relying on inaccurate mathematical calculations being shared through letters or publications on the matter. To remove the Wright brothers from the aeronautical race means the wind tunnel data they generated (and shared with Octave Chanute) would have needed to have been reproduced by someone else. In all likelihood, it would have caused a delay of at least several years.

Additional knowledge the Wrights alone discovered related to propellors. Previous inventors had based propellor design on those from ships. But the Wrights quickly realized the problem required much more thought and new data. The brothers debated each other vigorously about the most efficient shapes and sizes of propellors. From their debate they came to the conclusion that the propellor operated like rotating wings traveling in a spiral course through the air. They then had to determine how to calculate the thrust of a rotating blade. The thrust had to be high enough to overcome drag or the plane would not fly. "The brothers developed a series of quadratic equations from which they designed the propeller. . . Based on their calculations, they used hatchets and drawknives to carefully carve a piece of wood into an eight-foot propeller with a helicoidal twist."[20] When they finally tested the prototype, it worked within 1% of what their mathematical estimations had indicated.[21] "All propellers built heretofore are all wrong," Wilbur wrote to Chanute in 1903.[22]

In addition to the knowledge the Wright brothers contributed, their work served to inspire air ships invented by others. In 1902, Wilbur Wright gave a speech to the Society of Engineers in Chicago, where he described the work and progress he and Orville were making. Some of his remarks were then published in the *Journal of the Western Society of Engineers*, as well as in the *Dayton Daily News* and other newspapers in the United States. They shared their work liberally with aviation enthusiasts and inventors through these publications. Additionally, Wilbur maintained weekly correspondence with Octave Chanute and regularly described in detail their work. Chanute encouraged the Wright brothers' progress, but he also imparted with others and felt an open sharing of knowledge the key to conquering the multifaceted problems of flight. Earlier Chanute had suggested:

> "Success might be much hastened by an association of searchers in this field of inquiry [flight], for no one man is likely to be simultaneously an inventor to imagine new shapes and new motors, a mechanical engineer to design the arrangement of the apparatus, a mathematician to calculate its strength and stresses, a practical mechanic to construct the parts, and a syndicate of capitalists to furnish the needed funds."[23]

Without the Wright brothers sharing of information to Chanute and others, the innovation progress of others would likely have been more drawn-out, and possibly more deadly to those engaged in the process.

Would Wilbur Wright have begun an investigation of aeronautics alone in 1896 if Orville had died? It's hard to say. However, Orville's partnership with his brother was so essential to their work that Wilbur likely would not have moved forward so early. If he had ever begun a study of flight, possibly with another of his brothers, it would probably have been a few years later. Although Wilbur is usually considered the driving force in their partnership, if Orville had passed away Wilbur would have been in mourning and preoccupied by the need to carry forward the cyclery business on his own. His mind just simply would have been elsewhere. Even if he had begun the study of aviation on his own, the amount of research and experimentation would have taken significantly longer. The delay would have meant there would likely not have been a controlled, fixed-winged, powered aircraft developed by 1903, and certainly not one patented and sold by 1908.

During the time frame when the Wrights were working on their plane, the race to get the first powered aircraft aloft had many participants. The primary competitors were Samuel Pierpont

Langley,[24] Glenn H. Curtiss, Clement Ader,[25] Gustave Whitehead,[26] and Alberto Santos Dumont. In considering the age, health, and personal circumstances and accomplishments of these men, it seems unlikely any of them could have stepped up and matched the achievements of the Wright brothers had Orville died. In fact, some of these men were only successful because they were inspired by the Wrights. However, of these men, support for Santos Dumont is vocalized most frequently.

As a Brazilian aviator, Alberto Santos Dumont won a competition in France on October 23, 1906, when his kite-like winged aircraft flew about 200 feet (61 meters) at a height of about 9 feet (2–3 meters) off the ground, then landed safely. The accomplishment won Santos-Dumont a cash prize from the Aero-Club de France and initial recognition of being the first to establish an aviation record. One key difference was that Santos Dumont's plane used landing gear to both take off and land safely. In comparison, the Wrights' plane had at times relied on a catapult system for take-off; they considered the catapult to be safer than landing gear. Still, the Wrights' October 5, 1905 test of the Wright Flyer III proved it could remain airborne for 39 minutes. The Wright Flyer III flew 30 complete circuits of the field and covered over 24 miles (38.6 km), all in front of an audience. And it occurred more than a year prior to Santos Dumont's aviation record.

Although many still debate the Santos Dumont vs. Wright brothers' race, the French Center for the History of Aeronautics and Space later acknowledged documented evidence that the Wrights had been the first. But if Orville Wright had died of typhoid fever, would Santos Dumont have pioneered the fixed-wing airplane instead? Probably not. "During his entire flying career, Santos Dumont never remained airborne in one of his airplanes for more than 15 minutes."[27] And after setting the first aviation record, he only invented one other successful aircraft, the Demoiselle No. 20, which looked similar to a modern ultralight. Additionally, Santos Dumont made his last flights in 1909, likely due to a diagnosis of multiple sclerosis. Soon thereafter he dropped out of aviation and had retired to Brazil by 1916.

* * *

A delay of even a few years for the invention and patenting of the airplane could have had a significant impact on history, particularly on World War I, which began in July 1914. As it was, when WW I first began, the newness of aircraft meant the invention only played a small part in warfare. Not only was there a lack of trained pilots, but many lacked a vision of how the plane might be utilized, especially in warfare. However, by the end of the war fighter pilots had come on the scene and France, Great Britain, and Germany had each created air force branches of their military. To interrupt the development of the plane by even just two or three years could have greatly reduced the role of the airplane in the war and meant that some of the famous fighter pilots, such as the Red Baron (Manfred von Richthofen), might never have made their mark on history. In fact, without the plane, an argument could be made that the war to end all wars may have ended sooner.

Other possible impacts the death of Orville Wright may have had on history include some unusual and unexpected points of interest. For example, although it's impossible to estimate the civilian and military losses during WWI, certainly some lives would not have been lost—including von Richthofen and Lt. Quentin Roosevelt, the youngest son of President Theodore Roosevelt. Lt. Roosevelt flew with the 95th Aero Squadron and died being shot down in July 1918. Additionally, the concept of skywriting for advertising (developed in 1913) would have been affected, and airmail service, which began in 1918, would have been delayed. Finally, Henry "Hap" Arnold, who had been trained as a pilot by the Wright Brothers Flying School, may never have learned to fly. As a result, he might not have risen to the rank of Five-Star General and been given command of the US Army Air Forces in World War II. The long-term impact of the effect this might have had on WWII history is not possible to predict.

* * *

Orville died at age 76 of a heart attack on January 30, 1948 at home in Dayton, Ohio. In all his work he did not doubt the possibility of man's ability to fly. Together with his brother Wilbur, he revolutionized the field of aviation, transforming the world with the invention of the first practical fixed-wing aircraft. Their pioneering efforts culminated in the historic first powered flight in 1903, a milestone that forever changed transportation and military strategies globally, and blessed humankind abundantly. His achievements in aeronautics earned Wright the first Daniel Guggenheim Medal awarded in 1930. Orville's legacy endures as a testament to the transformative power of human ingenuity and perseverance. The miraculous preservation of his life likely altered the course of history.

Chapter 12: John F. Kennedy

Joseph Patrick Kennedy Jr. was the first-born son of Joseph and Rose Fitzgerald Kennedy. Born July 25, 1915, at Nantasket Beach in Hull, Massachusetts, Joseph Jr.'s birth had been heralded by his parents and grandparents as the beloved son who would break through barriers of bigotry against Irish Catholics to become a family triumph. His maternal grandfather, former mayor of Boston, told a reporter this new grandson would "be a captain of industry until it's time for him to be President for two or three terms. Further than that has not been decided. He may act as mayor of Boston and governor of Massachusetts for a while on his way to the presidential chair."[1]

With all the love and expectations placed on Joseph Jr.'s shoulders at such a young age, he seemed to accept his foreordained future with ready expectation. His parents, despite having eight additional children, lauded notable favor on Joseph Jr. as he worked hard to excel in school and in various sports. To prepare him for a career in politics, Joseph Jr. first attended a prestigious preparatory boarding school, then later to Harvard and graduate studies at the London School of Economics. When World War II broke out in Europe, Joe began officer training in the US Navy and became a naval aviator in 1942. "One of his squadron mates said that Joe 'had everybody's unlimited admiration and respect for his courage, zeal and willingness to undertake the most dangerous mission.'"[2]

Joseph Kennedy Jr. did everything right in preparing himself to be the success his parents and grandparents expected.

Until he died.

On the evening of August 12, 1944, while serving in Britain, Joe volunteered to fly in a secret bombing campaign, code named Operation Aphrodite. Partway through the mission, explosives on the plane prematurely detonated, killing everyone on board the flight. Military investigations never determined exactly what caused the early detonation. Joe's death devastated his parents; his father told a friend, "You know how much I had tied my whole life up to his and what great things I saw in the future for him."[3]

Joseph and Rose's second oldest son, John Fitzgerald Kennedy, 27-years-old, knew immediately on hearing about his brother's death that the family burden had now been firmly placed on his shoulders.

* * *

Unlike his beloved older brother, John F. Kennedy was the irreverent son. Despite an IQ of 112, his schoolwork reflected his laziness, with B and C grades. As a voracious reader with a deep interest in history and international relations, young Jack deeply disliked some required boring courses, such as Latin and French. Although popular with the other students, he disregarded authority figures and frequently instigated mischief—like the time he started the Muckers Club after the school principal used the term in a speech to reprimand boys who defied rules and did not live up to their responsibilities. Additionally, in contrast to his healthy older brother, Jack often felt sickly, making it difficult for him to compete on sports teams, as expected of Kennedy family members.

John F. Kennedy's first brush with death occurred in the late winter of 1920, at age two, when his family lived in Brookline, Massachusetts. While Rose Kennedy was in labor with her fourth child, Jack showed symptoms of scarlet fever: a bright red rash covering his body, a swollen throat, and a high fever. Jack's diagnosis caused "frantic terror"[4] in the home and his siblings and mother were kept away from his bedside. When Jack's fever reached 104, his father desperately searched for better medical care than the family physician could offer; Joe Sr. felt it would be safer for the whole family if Jack were in the hospital. Boston City Hospital had a special ward for patients with infectious diseases, but the 125 beds there were typically reserved for city residents.

Fortunately, Rose's father, former Boston Mayor John Fitzgerald, used his influence to get the hospital to provide a bed for his namesake in the isolation ward. Despite being admitted, Jack's battle with scarlet fever remained precarious for several more weeks as his temperature hovered around 102 degrees. Only Jack's father could visit; Rose remained home, still recovering from Kathleen's birth and needing to look after her other children. Joe Kennedy Sr. would leave work early each day to head to the hospital and sit by his son's bedside. As Jack's illness dragged on, his parents turned to their Catholic faith, praying for his healing. Joe even promised God he would give half his wealth to a Catholic charity if Jack would be able to recover.[5]

After nearly a month of illness, in mid-March 1920, little Jack finally began to show signs of recovery. Although his fever went down and the rash faded, Jack spent another month in the hospital. And then he spent an additional two weeks recovering in a care facility in Poland Springs, Maine with a private nurse. He finally returned home again in May, three months after falling ill, and just a few weeks away from his third birthday.

Scarlet fever is a bacterial infection that can occur after strep throat. In the early years of the twentieth century, particularly before 1921, scarlet fever had been one of the leading causes of death among children. "There were not yet medications like penicillin to fight the disease. For children, scarlet fever often meant death."[6] As an extremely contagious disease, scarlet fever required five weeks of quarantine and the local health department typically placed warning signs on homes where the infection had been diagnosed. In spite of their wealth, that Jack Kennedy survived scarlet fever at age two is miraculous considering the lack of treatment options available at that time.

The bout with scarlet fever proved to be only the beginning of John F. Kennedy's health problems. Rose Kennedy kept a notecard of each of her children's medical issues, and Jack's card showed he had many problems, including frequent upset stomachs and a variety of childhood diseases. "By the time he was five years old, he had endured not only scarlet fever, but also whooping cough, measles, and chicken pox. The string of sicknesses began a pattern of poor health that would plague him throughout his life."[7] By age 17, Jack had spent an entire year of his life laid up in hospital, clinic, and infirmary rooms. Sadly, in the Kennedy household illness was frowned upon; Kennedys were *not* sickly. Family members who felt ill were expected not to complain, and if they had to spend time in bed, it should be kept as brief as possible. As Jack grew up and continued to experience stomach problems, backaches, and fatigue, in true Kennedy fashion he learned to be stoic and to use humor to joke about his aches and pains.

At age 30, Jack would be diagnosed with Addison's disease. But he lived with the symptoms of the condition for at least 15 years before its identification. Addison's disease, also called adrenal insufficiency, occurs when the body doesn't produce enough of two hormones, cortisol and aldosterone. According to the Mayo Clinic, "Addison's disease occurs in all age groups and both sexes, and can be life-threatening."[8] Signs and symptoms of the condition include fatigue, weight loss, darkening of skin pigmentation, low blood pressure (resulting in fainting), depression, and even adrenal failure. Jack began experiencing all of these symptoms in his youth, even before going to boarding school. But the stress of being away from home led to more frequent occurrences of the symptoms and numerous hospital visits throughout his teen years.

For example, in the fall of 1930, 13-year-old Jack Kennedy left to attend the Catholic Canterbury boarding school in New Milford, Connecticut. Shortly into the fall semester he had a fainting incident after experiencing dizziness. The next semester Jack began having problems with fever, exhaustion, sore knees, blurry vision, and hives. Classmates teased him for his inability to participate in sports and for being frequently ill. To help him recover, Jack's parents sent him to Florida for Easter vacation, but after returning to school he collapsed with abdominal pain. After being rushed to a hospital in Danbury, he underwent an emergency appendectomy. A surgeon and nurse were flown in to attend to him as he slowly recovered. He never returned to Canterbury. With some tutoring, Jack passed his school exams at home.

At the end of the summer in 1931, Joe and Rose Kennedy decided Jack should be transferred to Choate boarding school in Wallingford, Connecticut, where his older brother Joe had begun flourishing. Once again, Jack struggled with his health; he had several confinements in the infirmary that fall and a two-night stay in a New Haven hospital. Constantly ill, he struggled to keep up with his schoolwork and had to do summer school to catch up.

As a 17-year-old junior at Choate in January 1934, Jack's white blood cell count plummeted and he collapsed. School administrators rushed him to the hospital in New Haven again, where doctors worried he might have leukemia or hepatitis. Desperate to get answers, Jack's parents sent him to the Mayo Clinic in Rochester, Minnesota. There he underwent a myriad of medical tests, making him uncomfortable and homesick. He lost eight pounds during his month at the Mayo Clinic, but still his condition baffled medical professionals. In the end, Jack remained ill despite a variety of dietary changes and medications meant to help. During Jack's stay in the hospital, special prayers for him were offered by clergy and the student body at Choate. He came very close to dying, noted close friend and classmate Lem Billings.

Modern-day doctors now recognize that on these occasions of severe illness, Jack Kennedy experienced what is today identified as adrenal crisis, or an Addisonian crisis. Each time he collapsed it had been a potentially life-threatening medical emergency. In fact, the mortality rate of those with Addison's disease is more than twice the average for the general population.[9] Those with undiagnosed Addison's disease often die because of cardiovascular disease, infectious diseases, and malignant tumors caused by the symptoms. But somehow Jack Kennedy survived. That he lived through his teens and 20s without being diagnosed is extraordinary considering the state of his health and the lack of care medical professionals were able to offer.

* * *

At age 20, Jack's father's position as the Chairman of the US Maritime Commission represented an opportunity to immerse himself in a favorite subject: international politics. During the summer of 1937, his father sent Jack and friend Lem Billings on a European tour, visiting France, Spain, Italy, Germany, and other countries. On the trip he sought out newspaper correspondents in various cities to ask questions about a variety of international concerns of the time. This critical thinking exercise related to European power and politics helped to separate Jack's opinions from those of both his father and older brother. He learned how to think for himself.

Then, in late 1937 FDR appointed Joseph Kennedy Sr. to the United States' most prestigious diplomatic post: Ambassador to Great Britain. In March the following year, Kennedy's large, rambunctious family (minus Joe and Jack) arrived in London and were instantly accepted into the highest ranks of British society. That spring, the family even spent an April weekend at Windsor Castle as guests of King George VI and his wife, Queen Elizabeth. Jack arrived in England in July 1938 to spend the summer working at the US Embassy in London. In August, a European crisis developed when Hitler threatened to annex Czechoslovakia's Sudetenland territory. Before the matter could be resolved, Jack returned to Massachusetts for the fall semester of his junior year at Harvard. But he soon obtained permission to take a leave during the spring semester to spend additional time in Europe researching a thesis on contemporary political affairs.

Jack began his senior year at Harvard in the fall of 1939 and arranged to write the promised senior thesis on the origins of Britain's (Chamberlain's) appeasement policy. With the help of his father, Jack traveled across Europe, staying in embassies, and interviewing diplomatic personnel in more than half a dozen countries. With the assistance of stenographers and typists, the thesis of 148 pages, titled *Appeasement at Munich*, took about three months to write in early 1940. Faculty members gave it mixed reviews, but Joe Sr. saw the thesis as an opportunity to increase Jack's credibility and visibility. After contacting a friend, Joe arranged for the thesis to be published in both the US and Great Britain. Retitled *Why England Slept*, the book sold about 80,000 copies and made $40,000 in royalties. Having personally witnessed the Luftwaffe's bombings of Britain, Jack had a desire to help British residents; he donated his British royalties to bombed out Plymouth to help the city rebuild.[10]

After graduating Harvard, Jack waffled on what to do next. With the war in Europe, and a high likelihood of the United States joining in, he wanted to be in the military. Jack knew his poor health would likely prevent him from enlisting, but it did not keep him from trying. "When, in 1941, Jack failed the physical exams for admission to first the army's and then the navy's officer candidate schools, he turned to his father to pull strings on his behalf."[11] Joe Sr. contacted Captain Alan Kirk, his former naval attaché, and current head of the Office of Naval Intelligence. One month later, in October 1941, Jack received a clean bill of health that enabled him to enlist as an ensign in the Naval Reserve; it was a complete fabrication that would not have been possible without family connections. Still, his acceptance into the Navy only lead to a safe but boring position as a paper pusher in Washington DC.

Over the next nine months, Jack continued to hide his stomach problems, although he did see a Naval physician about backaches. By July the following year, he received a transfer to a midshipman's school in Chicago in preparation for sea duty. He hoped to command a PT boat in the Pacific theater. Eventually, after Joe Sr. once again intervened on his behalf, Jack became one of fifty (out of over one thousand applicants) accepted for training. But the instruction posed an extreme challenge to Jack's health. "Riding in a PT, one expert said, was like staying upright on a bucking bronco. At full speed it cut through the water at more than forty knots and gave its crew a tremendous pounding."[12] Jack felt every blow.

By January 1943, 24-year-old Jack Kennedy had orders sending him with Motor Torpedo Boat Squadron 14 to help patrol the Panama Canal. But against his father's wishes, Jack pulled strings and got himself reassigned to the Pacific. Lieutenant Kennedy would be a replacement officer to Motor Torpedo Boat Squadron 2, based on Tulagi Island, immediately north of Guadalcanal in the Solomon Islands. On his arrival in March 1943, he immediately witnessed a deadly struggle. "As his transport ship approached Guadalcanal, a Japanese air raid killed the captain of his ship and brought the crew face to face with a downed Japanese pilot, who rather than be rescued by his enemy began firing a revolver at the bridge of the U.S. ship."[13] It wouldn't be long before Jack would face even greater danger.

At this point in the war, in the Solomon Islands campaign of the Pacific theater, the Japanese forces were supplied by a convoy of four destroyers that would sail from Rabaul, New Britain, New Guinea into the Blackett Strait under cover of darkness to deliver supplies to Vila. Three of the destroyers would be efficiently unloaded within 30 minutes. The fourth destroyer would patrol with the assistance of Japanese float planes. The Japanese were so effective at this operation that US forces nicknamed it the Tokyo Express. For months, American military leaders worked futilely to prevent the Tokyo Express from supplying Japanese forces. On the afternoon of August 1, 1943, an air raid on the Lombari PT boat base, where Lieutenant Kennedy was stationed, convinced base Commander Thomas G. Warfield that the attack had been an offensive move indicating the Tokyo Express would run that night.

He was right.

Warfield commanded that every available PT boat should be on patrol in the Blackett Strait that evening to try and disrupt the Tokyo Express. Fifteen boats were prepared, including PT 109, captained by Jack Kennedy. Thirteen men, including Jack, helped to man the boat. The fleet of PTs were divided into four squadrons, with only the lead boat in each squadron having radar capabilities. All boats were commanded to maintain strict radio silence during the operation, even though there would be great distances between them. By sundown—on a moonless night—the PTs departed Lombari while Commander Warfield stayed at the base.

Around 11 p.m., Jack's squadron encountered the four destroyers of the Tokyo Express and the Battle of Blackett Strait ensued. Two other PTs in his squadron, including the lead boat with radar, engaged by shooting their torpedoes; but the attack missed the intended target and the PTs retreated. With the code of radio silence and the cover of darkness, and unaware of the departure of the rest of the squadron, PT 109 remained behind as they continued to patrol. At some point a searchlight shone on PT 109 and it came under fire. Unbeknownst to Jack and his crew, the searchlight came from one of the Japanese destroyers near the shore. To avoid additional gunfire, PT 109 took evasive maneuvers and moved away from the area. After a time, PT 109 joined with PTs 162 and 169 to form a new squadron. The three boats made a picket line as they patrolled the Tokyo Express's escape route. A few planes fired on them, so they cut down to one engine to reduce their wake and be able to listen for enemy planes and vessels. Staying together proved challenging as they maintained a distance of a mile apart while patrolling.

At about 2 a.m. on August 2, one of the Japanese destroyers, the *Amagiri*, operating without running lights in the starless black evening, suddenly came upon PT 109. With only one of three engines running, PT 109 had limited speed and maneuverability. At the relatively high speed of at least 23 knots, the *Amagiri* approached quickly as it intentionally sought impact. There were fewer than ten seconds for Kennedy and his crewmates to react. The *Amagiri* rammed into PT 109, causing a massive explosion of fuel that caught the ocean on fire. "The PT's wooden hull hardly even delayed the destroyer."[14] Two of the crewmen were killed on impact and two others were badly injured and burned.

Only the forward hull of the boat remained afloat as the surviving crew members clung to life after the collision. In the aftermath, Kennedy and his men helped one another gather to the hull, feeling certain one of the other PT boats would soon come to their rescue. But both PT 162 and 169 left the area without searching the scene of the accident for survivors. Having seen the explosion from a mile away, they assumed no one could have possibly survived. Although the captain of PT 169 claimed otherwise, other crew members admitted "no valid effort"[15] had been made to look for survivors. In fact, when a few wanted to go back to search the next morning, Commander Warfield prevented the action because he wanted to avoid additional loss.

The 11 surviving abandoned men of PT 109 waited in vain for many hours to be rescued. It took more than three hours just to gather the survivors back to the floating forward hull. Ensign George H. R. "Barney" Ross, who had volunteered at the last minute to be a crew member on PT 109, described the situation as follows:

> "As the dawn came up we found ourselves on the boat with the boat under water all the way up to the bow . . . We were

expecting any minute to have the Jap launch come out and take us into custody."[16]

The Japanese-occupied town of Gizo stood approximately a mile and a half away, visible from the capsized hull, so the risk of being identified by plane or captured by an enemy boat was real. Jack ordered his men to stay as low as possible on the overturned boat to help prevent their detection. But the shark infested waters barred them from staying in the ocean.

By late morning, the boat hull had clearly drifted with the current and would not stay afloat much longer. After discussing the matter and taking a vote, they decided to swim to the smallest island visible in the opposite direction of Gizo. However, not all crew members knew how to swim, and Motor Machinist's Mate 1st Class Patrick H. "Pappy" McMahon had been severely burned and could not swim. The group devised a plan where an eight-foot-long piece of coconut timber, which had been on board the boat, became a floatation device non-swimmers could hold onto while others could push and pull it along. Unfortunately, McMahon's hands and arms were too burned to be able to grasp the wood like the others. Since Jack had previously been on the Harvard swim team, he took charge of helping Pappy. "It was to be an epic effort: Jack, with the straps of McMahon's life jacket like a bit between his teeth, swimming ahead of the others, tugging the badly burned McMahon behind him, and Thom alternately pushing and pulling the wooden log with four survivors clinging to each side."[17] They eventually covered three to four miles against the current, reaching Bird Island late that afternoon. When he finally pulled McMahon onto the beach five hours later, Jack collapsed, exhausted, onto the sand.

Bird Island, only one hundred yards in diameter, offered just enough brush to provide cover for the shipwrecked crew members. The island also had a few coconut palm trees that could provide some sustenance. Beyond this, the small isle lacked amenities and its placement did not allow the men to signal allies for rescue. But this didn't deter Jack from trying. Multiple times he swam out as far as he dared, hoping to flag down a passing ship or plane.[18] After his first attempt he likely experienced issues with his Addison's disease, exacerbated by fatigue: "Bouts of unconsciousness marked Jack's return swim to his crew, who had given him up for lost until he returned at noon" on August 3.[19] When he eventually crawled up onto the beach, his crewmates found him ill and vomiting.

After a few days on Bird Island the entire group, using the same coconut timber process, moved to the larger Olasana Island, which had more coconut trees, and a location closer to where allies would likely pass. On August 5, Jack and Ross swam to Cross Island in search of food and water. While there "they found a [broken] one-man canoe, a fifty-five-gallon drum of fresh water, and some crackers and candy. Jack carried some of the water and food in the canoe back to Olasana, where the men, who had been surviving on coconuts, had been discovered and were being attended to by two native islanders."[20] The next day, the natives took a message from Jack to the main PT base. Not having paper to write on, Jack used a pocketknife to carve a message onto a smooth coconut shell: NAURO ISL…COMMANDER…NATIVE KNOWS POS'IT…HE CAN PILOT…11 ALIVE…NEED SMALL BOAT…KENNEDY. Handing the coconut shell to the natives, he told them to take it to Rendova. They seemed to understand and, with coconut shell in hand, they paddled off in a canoe.

Although the native islanders had seemed trustworthy, Jack felt he should not assume a rescue would soon occur—especially after having mistakenly presumed the Navy would send a search and rescue party immediately following the shipwreck. Instead, Jack decided to take Ross with him in the leaky canoe and paddle out into the ocean in another attempt to flag down a ship. The men were able to fashion oars from a box that had been found on Cross Island, and they brought a broken coconut shell to use to bail water. But luck was not on their side; as they got further out into the ocean, the weather turned, and the canoe flooded over. After hours of fighting against currents, a wave finally tumbled them violently toward a reef. "[F]or the third time since the collision [Jack] thought he was dying."[21] Miraculously, he landed in an eddy and felt the reef below his feet enough to stand up. Ross, however, had been slammed against the reef and received lacerations from the coral on his right arm, shoulder, and feet.

Using the canoe paddles against the reef for Ross to step on, the two slowly made their way back to the beach where they collapsed and slept.

As it turned out, the Natives were to be trusted. They initially paddled twelve miles to a small island, where they informed a senior scout from New Zealand military forces of the discovery of the crew from PT 109. They then continued to paddle all night long in a better canoe to cover an additional 38 miles, through the same rough seas and weather, to deliver Kennedy's message to Rendova. When Commander Warfield finally received the news of PT 109's survivors on August 7, he sent two PT boats to rescue them. After six days, rescuers took the group of castaways back to Rendova where they could receive much needed medical attention and were able to contact worried family members. Within hours, word of Kennedy's survival and his heroic actions became national news. A *New York Times* headline announced, "Kennedy's Son is Hero in Pacific as Destroyer Splits His Boat." Jack's actions were eventually recognized, and he received the Navy and Marine Corps Medal, the highest non-combat decoration given for heroism.

* * *

Almost a year after John F. Kennedy was rescued in the Solomon Islands, his older brother Joe died in Suffolk, England. The irony of Joe's death is sobering. Joe had been the son intended for politics and the presidency; he had prepared his whole life for it. Jack, on the other hand, had resented the constant praise and attention his older brother received from their parents. As the ill son, unable to keep up in academics or sports, Jack felt he could never live up to Joe's accomplishments or successes. Disheartened, Jack chose in his youth not to compete with Joe's perfection. Instead, Jack lived recklessly, challenged authority figures, and pursued his own deep interest in international relations. In the end, fate favored the pluck and courage of the younger Kennedy brother.

Despite many differences, the two brothers had their similarities—not surprising considering the 22-month difference in age. Joe Kennedy had been described "as a young man[,] the most devastatingly attractive of them all with a 'magic smile,' a great flair for the ladies."[22] The same description could easily have fit Jack, too. The brothers both loved sports, particularly football (Joe played for Harvard). They were both outgoing and popular among their peer groups. And, as taught by their father, Joe and Jack were both fiercely loyal to family. With all these similarities, it begs the question: Why did Jack become the one who survived and went on to change history? What unique impact did John F. Kennedy make that his older brother could not, or would not, have been likely to make?

One of Jack Kennedy's unique strengths over Joe lay in his talent for writing. Both brothers believed being a writer could help to elevate a politician's prominence and visibility. But Jack held the edge over Joe in this regard. Despite his father's efforts, Joe's Harvard thesis was never published. Although Jack's Harvard thesis had sold well as a published book, he later admitted the writing had been weak. After WWII ended, however, he spent two years working as a journalist for the *Chicago-Herald American*. Initially, he covered the United Nations conference held in San Francisco, followed by some time in England to cover Churchill's campaign (and ultimate loss), and then to the European continent to travel with US Navy Secretary James Forrestal. During his travels as a journalist Jack met many of the world's most influential leaders, including Presidents Harry Truman and Dwight D. Eisenhower. In time, considering Jack's success as a news man, Joe Sr. thought Jack would take up writing as a career: "We were sure he'd be a teacher or a writer."[23]

After two years as a journalist, however, Jack decided he didn't want to be a reporter. He had come to the conclusion that he wanted to make a difference in the world, to be an agent of change. "A reporter is reporting what happened. He is not making it happen.... It isn't participating," he had decided.[24] Politics, on the other hand, represented a hands-on opportunity to have a real impact on the world. And knowing his father's political ambitions for him, Jack decided to make a career change into what he called "public service." In 1947 at the age of 29, he entered the race for a congressional seat representing Massachusetts in the House of Representatives. With his father working backroom channels and his mother and sisters holding social gatherings for constituents to meet the candidate, the election became very much a family affair. Even while running against several other candidates, Jack handily won the election with 40% of the vote.

Becoming a politician did not mean Jack would completely give up writing. In early 1954, now Senator Kennedy read *The People's Choice*, a 1933 book by American journalist, historian, and editor of *The Louisville Courier*, Herbert Aga. Aga's book took a critical look at the American presidency and touched on the subject of moral courage. The idea of moral courage deeply interested Jack and he pondered how much courage a politician needed to have and "at which point and on which issue he [a politician] will risk his career."[25] Thinking the concept might make a good magazine article, Jack showed his speech writer, Theodore Sorenson, Aga's book. He asked Sorenson to research and find senators who had demonstrated moral courage, risking their career to take a stand. Sorenson's research led to information on eight different senators—enough for a book instead of an article. "With assistance from research assistants [from] the US Library of Congress, Sorensen wrote a first draft of the book while JFK was bedridden with Addison's disease during 1954 and 1955, while recovering from surgery."[26] Although Sorenson drafted the initial chapters, Jack edited and oversaw the process of writing the book. Published in 1956, *Profiles in Courage* listed John F. Kennedy as the author. Despite rumors of Sorenson being the ghostwriter, *Profiles* became a best-seller. In April 1957, Columbia University announced that the book had won the Pulitzer Prize for best biography. Winning the Pulitzer gave John F. Kennedy prominence that would help propel him to the Presidency, and an air of wisdom and maturity he needed to be taken seriously as a politician.

Kennedy's writing abilities also helped to amplify his talent for public speaking. As a politician, he became well-known for several significant speeches that greatly influenced his legacy. The first of these speeches occurred in the spring of 1960 during his campaign running for President of the United States. The mood of the country felt tense with the rise of communism and McCarthyism. The Cold War deepened that year when a summit meeting between President Eisenhower and Soviet Premier Nikita Khrushchev collapsed after the Soviet's shot down an American spy plane over the USSR and captured the pilot. Many thought war with the USSR might be imminent. Kennedy chose as his running mate Lyndon B. Johnson, and promised voters he would not let communism overrun the world or the US. Both Kennedy and his opponent, Richard M. Nixon, "sought the support of the steadily growing suburban population and, for the first time, television became the dominant source of information for voters."[27] At 43, Jack's youth, charisma, and ability to speak to the camera had a significant impact in the televised debates. His aptitude for connecting with younger voters led to more time spent campaigning on college campuses.

Approximately a month before election day, Senator Kennedy campaigned on the University of Michigan campus in Ann Arbor while on a nine-whistlestop tour of the state. A crowd of about 10,000 gathered to greet JFK at 2 a.m. outside the student union. In his impromptu speech to the students, Kennedy proposed an idea he felt would encourage improved intercultural communication and help to reduce Cold War tensions in the world. He asked, "How many of you, who are going to be doctors, are willing to spend your days in Ghana? Technicians or engineers, how many of you are willing to work in the Foreign Service and spend your lives traveling around the world?"[28] The youth and optimism of those gathered yielded an extremely positive response; within a week over one thousand students willing to pledge time working in third world countries signed a petition in support of the idea. A few weeks later, on November 2, 1960, Kennedy again spoke about the idea of professionals willing to donate their time and efforts to help serve around the world. That same week, John F. Kennedy won the election in what is considered the closest presidential contest on record.[29] In the coming weeks, as over 25,000 individuals wrote letters expressing interest in his idea of the Peace Corps, President-elect Kennedy began taking steps to help make his campaign promise a reality. In March 1961, the Peace Corps was established by executive order with R. Sargent Shriver as its director. Within six months,

Congress approved the Peace Corps as an agency within the State Department and granted it funding.

Kennedy's public speaking abilities also had a tremendous impact on American involvement in space exploration. His vision for NASA involved landing a man on the moon, a goal that inspired technological advancements and fostered national unity during the Cold War era. Kennedy urged NASA engineers to go to the moon not only to advance scientific discovery but also to demonstrate American ingenuity and superiority. The goal directly challenged the Soviet Union, which had already achieved several milestones in space exploration. He saw the space race as a way to secure US leadership on the global stage. In a 1962 speech at Rice University, Kennedy famously declared, "We choose to go to the moon in this decade and do the other things, not because they are easy, but because they are hard."[30] This statement symbolized the nation's resolve to push boundaries and marked the beginning of NASA's lunar mission. Kennedy's charisma was contagious. Within nine months, astronauts Scott Carpenter, Walter Schirra Jr., and L. Gordon Cooper had each orbited Earth with successively longer missions. Ultimately, the United States became the first nation to reach the moon with its Apollo 11 mission in 1969, more than five years after JFK's death.

* * *

Both Joe and Jack Kennedy experienced discrimination while attending boarding schools in their youth. The students at the various schools they attended were prejudiced against both Irish and Catholics, for which the Kennedy family were well-known. It also didn't help that Joe and Jack's grandfather, John "Honeyfitz" Fitzgerald, had been a notorious, stereotypically loud Irish politician. As a result, classmates often called Joe and Jack "Irish" and "Catholic" in derogatory tones, accusing them of being dirty and dishonest. The Kennedy brothers reacted to the intolerance differently. Joe responded to the teasing and rude comments by challenging the bullies to a fight and taking out his aggression on the football field. Jack, being shorter, thin, and of ill health, would take bets on his brother's ability to win the fights; he acquired an impressive collection of marbles as a result of his spoils. More importantly, Jack long remembered both the marbles and the way it felt to be treated with prejudice.

Even as young adults, the two brothers responded differently to discrimination. Case in point: the antisemitism that accompanied Hitler's rise to power. Joseph Kennedy Sr. had been well-known for his isolationist position prior to WWII, as well as his belief that "the Jews had brought the Nazi persecutions upon themselves."[31] As the ambassador to Great Britain, Joe Sr. bought into ancient antisemitic beliefs about Jewish conspiracies to control the media[32] and dominate European governments. Joe Jr., working as his father's secretary, imitated the political stance on both isolationism and antisemitism. Prior to the war, in 1934, Joe Jr. had visited Berlin and been deeply impressed by the Luftwaffe. The German military, especially their airpower, seemed impervious. Later, "[w]hile in law school, he would form and lead an isolationist antiwar club at Harvard, and he eagerly corroborated his father's assessment of Jewish agitation against Hitler."[33] Like his father, Joe Jr. gave way to antisemitic scapegoating. Writing to his father, Joe Jr. commended Hitler's insight in realizing:

> The "... need of a common enemy, someone of whom to make the goat. Someone, by whose riddance the Germans would feel they had cast out the cause of their predicament. It was excellent psychology, and it was too bad that it had to be done to the Jews. The dislike of the Jews, however, was well-founded. They were at the heads of all big business, in law etc. It is all to their credit for them to get so far, but their methods had been quite unscrupulous ... As far as the brutality is concerned, it must have been necessary to use some."[34]

Jack, on the other hand, had a markedly different opinion about the Nazi treatment of Jews. His role as the second son gave him an observational vantage point for studying and reflecting, rather than merely accepting his father's point of view. This, combined with his health challenges, granted Jack greater freedom to explore, question, experiment, contemplate, and act genuinely.

Like his older brother, Jack had also visited Germany as a college student in 1937. But he paid more attention to the everyday man and "was viscerally offended by the arrogance of the Nazis and skeptical of the Third Reich."[35] And in his diary he noted the impact propaganda had played in Hitler's rise to power. At the end of the trip, instead of writing to his father about German might, he lamented the lack of awareness Americans had of the situation in Europe.

Although Jack had spent his earliest years trying to be his father's son, he would end up very much his own man.[36]

By the time JFK ran for president in 1960, the civil rights movement had been active for several years. During the campaign, Martin Luther King Jr. was arrested while leading a protest in Atlanta. Senator Kennedy called Coretta Scott King to express support and had his brother Robert contact the judge to ensure King's timely release. These actions led to an endorsement from King, helping to secure the Black vote, and likely Kennedy's win. From this start, the Kennedy administration made groundbreaking civil rights decisions; at the first cabinet meeting, each secretary received instructions to seek out ways to specifically increase opportunities for Blacks in their department. President Kennedy took numerous other measures: he appointed the first Black housing director to the Housing and Home Finance Agency. He established the Committee on Equal Employment Opportunity to expand the number of Black government workers at the federal level. The all-White Coast Guard received instructions to improve recruitment of Blacks. Two anti-segregationists were appointed by President Kennedy to the Civil Rights Commission. Then, two years into his administration, in June 1963, Kennedy famously federalized the Alabama National Guard to ensure two Black students could enroll in the University of Alabama. That same year, Kennedy worked hard to build bi-partisan support for a civil rights bill working its way through Congress. Tragically, President Kennedy's assassination took place in November before the legislation could be passed. Successor Lyndon B. Johnson took up the cause. Johnson "used his substantial political acumen, the assistance of Robert Kennedy's Justice Department, and the outpouring of emotion after President Kennedy's assassination to generate passage of the Civil Rights Act."[37]

* * *

As a child, Jack and Joe Kennedy once played a game of chicken. Joe dared Jack to race on bicycles in opposite directions around the block; when they approached each other, the first one to swerve away would be the loser. Not wanting to let his older brother get the satisfaction of winning yet again, Jack pedaled his bike as fast as he could, determined to be brave. As the two boys drew near each other, neither veered away. At full speed they crashed into each other. Being two years older and bigger, Joe came away unscathed. Jack, however, went flying off the bike and hit the pavement with force. It took 28 stitches to sew up all the cuts he received from the asphalt.

Jack Kennedy never forgot this experience. Thirty-five years later, as President, he would again play a game of chicken. The game began when Fidel Castro and Nikita Khrushchev formed a deal in July 1962 to place "Soviet nuclear missiles in Cuba to deter any future invasion attempt."[38] Within a few months, construction required for the installation of the missiles began. During a routine surveillance flight over Cuba in early September, aerial photos taken by US aircraft showed evidence of an arms build-up at the missile launch site at San Cristobal. In response to the intelligence gathered, President Kennedy publicly warned the USSR about placing nuclear missiles in Cuba. But Kennedy's warning went unheeded. On October 14 new aerial photos taken over San Cristobal clearly showed sites for both medium- and intermediate-range nuclear missiles were still being built. The Cuban Missile Crisis had begun.

President Kennedy met with his closest advisors for several days to try and determine the best course of action. Some recommended air strikes to take out the missile launch sites at San Cristobal, while others felt additional verbal warnings would be a safer option. Kennedy considered each possible action and counteraction with the goal to avoid nuclear war. He felt the use of nuclear weapons, by either side, would be catastrophic. In the end, Kennedy opted to take a moderate course of action between the two extremes offered by his advisors. "On October 22, he ordered a naval 'quarantine' of Cuba. The use of 'quarantine' legally distinguished this action from a blockade, which assumed a state of war existed."[39] He also sent a letter to Khrushchev stating unequivocally that the United States would not allow nuclear weapons to be delivered to Cuba; the letter also demanded that the missile launch sites be dismantled. That same evening, President Kennedy went on television to explain circumstances to the American public in a solemn, stern speech.

Two days later Khrushchev responded publicly to Kennedy by saying the 'quarantine' qualified as an act of aggression against the USSR. Despite these comments, some of the Soviet ships that had been sailing to Cuba turned around and went home; others found not to be carrying any missiles were allowed to proceed. However, new arial photos of San Cristobal found the launch sites were nearly ready. President Kennedy began to think only an attack on the launch sites would eliminate the threat; but he feared this too would end in yet another war. It appeared the two nations were at an impasse. To avoid nuclear war, one of them would need to flinch.

On October 26 a Soviet agent approached an ABC News correspondent with some indirect, back-channel information from Khrushchev meant for the White House. The communication proposed that the USSR would remove the missiles from Cuba if the US refrained from invading the island. That same evening, Kennedy received another long personal message from Khrushchev, which had been sent in the middle of the night USSR time. The contents of this personal message appeared to corroborate the back-channel message that had been sent through the Soviet agent and expressed readiness to remove the missiles. But the next day, a new message from Khrushchev said any compromise must include removal of US Jupiter missiles from Turkey. Tensions rose even further when the Soviets shot down an American reconnaissance jet over Cuba.

As military leaders prepared to make an attack on Cuba, Kennedy continued to search for a diplomatic resolution. He chose to respond to Khrushchev's initial late-night message, and to ignore the Soviet's more recent communication of October 27.

The decision was risky. But Kennedy felt anything that could potentially prevent a nuclear disaster worth trying. While the President talked directly and publicly with Khrushchev, his brother, Attorney General Robert Kennedy, met behind the scenes with the Soviet Ambassador to the United States. Robert's mission was to communicate privately that the US had already been planning on removing the missiles in Turkey, but that this action would not be a public acknowledgement in the resolution of the Cuban crisis. The combination of the direct and indirect communication with the USSR yielded positive results; the next day Khrushchev announced a plan to dismantle and remove Soviet missiles in Cuba. Kennedy had won.

But what if Kennedy had not won the face-off with Khrushchev? Or if JFK had died at a young age, leaving someone with less backbone to manage Cold War relations? If the Cuban Missile Crisis had turned into a full-blown conflict, what would have happened? Although predicting alternative paths of history typically leads to conjecture, most historians are certain of only one thing: A Cuban Missile War would have included nuclear bombs. The situation could have easily escalated into an all-out nuclear Armageddon, with the United States launching about 3,000 nuclear weapons and the Soviets sending about 250 of their own. The initial exchange would have likely been 50,000 to 100,000 times more powerful than the Hiroshima bomb. Some estimate a loss of over 200 million lives in North America alone. Cuba, Moscow, and Washington DC would have been flattened. And the damage from radioactive fallout as it encircled the globe—simply unimaginable. Former US Secretary of Defense William Perry, who analyzed intelligence data during the Cuban Missile Crisis, has said, "We can only wonder why Kennedy did not follow the combined recommendation of his Joint Chiefs of Staff. Had he followed it, we would have surely had a nuclear war. ...We were amazingly close to a civilization-ending nuclear war in Cuba."[40] Kennedy's intuition truly saved lives and changed world history.

* * *

When Joe Kennedy, Jr. signed up for the Naval Aviation Cadet Program in 1941 he wrote his father to explain why he had postponed his final year of law school to train to become a pilot. His reasons were primarily to protect the family reputation, since "people will wonder what the devil I am doing back at school with everyone else working for national defense."[41] The likelihood of sickly Jack ever being able to serve looked dim, so one of the Kennedy sons would need to go, reasoned Joe. Beyond that, Joe offered in the letter what proved to be a prophetic statement as a form of comfort to his father: "It seems that Jack is perfectly capable to do everything, if by chance anything happened to me."[42]

Jack was more than capable. In fact, it is likely he served more capably than Joe ever could have done. Although it is impossible to predict what kind of man Joe might have been if he had lived long enough to run for president, some historians doubt he could ever have been elected. "It was evident that Joe would never have been president because he was too much to the left."[43] Jack, on the other hand, had endured a childhood and adolescence suffering from life-threatening illnesses. He pursued his dreams, even when his parents disapproved of his decisions. Despite his relatively short presidency, Jack's leadership changed the world. Just as Joe's heart-rending early death left the Kennedy family in grief, JFK's tragic assassination in November 1963 left the nation in sorrow. The lost potential and unfulfilled promises of two brothers, their lives finishing too early, has reverberated through time.

□

Works Cited & Notes

Chapter 1: Harriet Tubman

1. "From the Nashville Rep.: A Shower of Meteors." *The Democrat*, Nov. 21, 1833, 1.
2. O'Keefe, Donal. "'They thought it was judgment day': The night the stars fell on the US south." *Irish Times*, Nov. 11, 2019, accessed July 7, 2022, https://www.irishtimes.com/culture/they-thought-it-was-judgment-day-the-night-the-stars-fell-on-the-us-south-1.4075652.
3. On August 21, 1831, Nathanial "Nat" Turner led a revolt of enslaved people. A slave himself, his mutiny led to a massacre of about 200 Black people. After the incident, a new wave of laws prohibiting the education, movement, and gathering of enslaved people was passed by both state and federal governments.
4. Larson, Kate Clifford. *Bound for the Promised Land*. (New York: Random House Publishing, 2004), 41.
5. Larson, *Bound for the Promised Land*, 40.
6. His exact name is not known, but Tubman later identified him this way. As quoted in Lowry, Beverly. *Harriet Tubman: Imagining a Life*. (New York: Doubleday, 2007), 79.
7. Larson, *Bound for the Promised Land*, 42.
8. Larson, *Bound for the Promised Land*, 42.
9. Lowry, *Harriet Tubman*, 79.
10. Larson, *Bound for the Promised Land*, 43.
11. Larson, *Bound for the Promised Land*, 43.
12. Seaberg, Maureen. "Harriet Tubman An Acquired Savant, Says Rain Man's Doctor." *Psychology Today*, accessed July 24, 2022, https://www.psychologytoday.com/us/blog/sensorium/201702/harriet-tubman-acquired-savant-says-rain-mans-doctor.

13. "How did Harriet Tubman escape?: Planning to escape and a new name." *Harriet Tubman Historical Society*, accessed July 24, 2022, http://www.harriet-tubman.org/escape/.
14. Harriet Tubman as quoted in Bradford, Sarah Hopkins. *Scenes in the Life of Harriet Tubman.* (Auburn, New York, 1869), Project Gutenberg, 2018, https://www.gutenberg.org/files/57821/57821-h/57821-h.htm. Note: wording and spelling has been standardized.
15. Lowry, *Harriet Tubman*, 158. Note: although the Underground Railroad became more organized after the passage of the Compromise of 1850, it did exist in part for many years prior. However, the Bloodhound Bill added a deeper level of danger for runaways; it was no longer good enough to help slaves reach a northern state where slavery had been outlawed. Those who escaped now had to reach Canada to avoid being caught and sent back. As a result, Harriet Tubman's niece, Kessiah, and her family moved on to Canada instead of staying in Philadelphia after their escape in November 1851.
16. Larson, *Bound for the Promised Land*, 90.
17. Larson, *Bound for the Promised Land*, 91.
18. Larson, *Bound for the Promised Land*, 100.
19. Clarke, James Freeman. *Anti-slavery Days.* (New York: John Lovell Company, 1883), 81-82, Google Books, https://play.google.com/books/reader?id=kBzVAAAAMAAJ.
20. Larson, *Bound for the Promised Land*, 101.
21. Many of the Ross family members changed their surname to Stewart after escaping slavery.
22. Hobson, Janell. "Family Portraits of a Legend: Conversations with the Descendants of Harriet Tubman." *Ms. Magazine*, accessed July 29, 2022, https://msmagazine.com/2022/02/09/harriet-tubman-family-descendants-slavery/.
23. As quoted in Brown, DeNeen L. "'Unflinching': The day John Brown was hanged for his raid on Harpers Ferry." *The Washington Post*, December 2, 2017, https://www.washingtonpost.com/news/retropolis/wp/2017/12

/02/unflinching-the-day-john-brown-was-hanged-for-his-raid-on-harpers-ferry/.
24. Kettler, Sara. "Harriet Tubman's Service as a Union Spy." *Biography*, accessed Aug. 1, 2022, https://www.biography.com/news/harriet-tubman-biography-facts.
25. Larson, *Bound for the Promised Land*, 207.
26. Larson, *Bound for the Promised Land*, 211.
27. Kettler, *Biography*.
28. The promised appointment was short lived, likely because Tubman was not getting paid for her work. Within a short timeframe she was forced to return home to Auburn where she could work to support her family. Tubman spent years petitioning the government for remuneration for her time helping the military.
29. Larson, *Bound for the Promised Land*, chap. 13.
30. Han, Edith, and Katherine Rivard. "A Beacon of Resilience and Love: Harriet Tubman." *NationalParks.org*. Accessed August 23, 2024. https://www.nationalparks.org/connect/blog/beacon-resilience-and-love-harriet-tubman.
31. Duffy, Jim. "'Now I'm Almost Home!' The Death and Funeral of Harriet Tubman, 1913." *Secrets of the Eastern Shore*, February 4, 2021. https://www.secretsoftheeasternshore.com/death-of-harriet-tubman-1913/.

Chapter 2: Mohandas Gandhi
1. "Satya means truth, the equivalent of love, and both are attributes of the soul; agraha is firmness or force. 'Satyagraha' is therefore translated Soul Force." Fischer, Louis. *Gandhi: His Life and Message for the World*. (New York: Signet Classics Penguin Books, 2010), chap. 8, Kindle.
2. Gandhi, M. K. *Mahatma Gandhi Autobiography: The Story of My Experiments with Truth*. (Mumbai, India: Sanage Publishing, 2020), chap. 136, Kindle.

3. Gandhi, *Gandhi Autobiography: The Story of My Experiments with Truth*, chap. 3.
4. Gandhi, *Gandhi Autobiography: The Story of My Experiments with Truth*, chap. 4.
5. Fischer, *Gandhi: His Life and Message for the World*, chap. 7.
6. Gandhi, *Gandhi Autobiography: The Story of My Experiments with Truth*, chap. 5.
7. Rolland, Romaine. 2020. *Mahatma Gandhi; The Man who Became One with the Universal Being.* Catherine D. Groth, translator. Project Gutenberg [ebook #61575], chap. 1.
8. Gandhi, *Gandhi Autobiography: The Story of My Experiments with Truth*, chap. 59.
9. "Mohandas Karamchand Gandhi." *South African History Online: Towards a people's history*, accessed May 22, 2022, https://www.sahistory.org.za/people/mohandas-karamchand-gandhi.
10. Fischer, *Gandhi: His Life and Message for the World*, chap. 6.
11. "Mohandas Karamchand Gandhi." *South African History Online.*
12. "38. Backlash from a Friend." *M.K.Gandhi.org*, Accessed May 27, 2022, https://www.mkgandhi.org/gandhiji/38backlash.htm.
13. Gandhi, *Gandhi Autobiography: The Story of My Experiments with Truth*, chap. 109.
14. Bhargava, Balram and Rajni Kant. "Health File of Mahatma Gandhi: His Experiments with Dietetics and Nature Cure." *The Indian Journal of Medical Research*, vol. 149, Suppl (2019), accessed May 24, 2022, https://www.ncbi.nlm.nih.gov/pmc/articles/PMC6515735.
15. Bhargava and Kant, *The Indian Journal of Medical Research*, vol. 149.
16. Gandhi, *Gandhi Autobiography: The Story of My Experiments with Truth*, chap. 109.
17. Klein, Ira. "Death in India, 1871-1921." *The Journal of Asian Studies*, Vol. 32, No. 4 (Aug., 1973), 639-659, accessed May 24, 2022, https://www-jstor-org.ezproxy.scottsdalecc.edu/stable/2052814.

18. As quoted in Iodice, Emilio (2017) "The Courage to Lead of Gandhi," *The Journal of Values-Based Leadership,* Vol. 10:2, article 12.
19. "Case Study 3 Background: The End of the British Empire in India." *The National Archives*, accessed May 26, 2022, shorturl.at/glEP8.
20. "Salt March." *History.com*, accessed May 27, 2022, https://www.history.com/topics/india/salt-march.
21. Nehru, Jawaharlal. "Nehru's iconic speech on January 30, 1948: The light has gone out." *National Herald India*, accessed May 27, 2022, https://www.nationalheraldindia.com/india/nehrus-iconic-speech-on-january-30-1948-the-light-has-gone-out.
22. Simeon, Dilip. "A New Kind of Force: Examining Charisma in the Light of Gandhi's Moral Authority." Excerpt included in "Gandhi's Charisma." *Berghahn Blog*, accessed May 28, 2022, tinyurl.com/278tmkh4.
23. Simeon, *Berghahn Blog*.
24. Simeon, *Berghahn Blog*.
25. Iodice, *The Journal of Values-Based Leadership*, article 12.
26. Orlando, Dominique. "The March that Made Gandhi the Mahatma." *The New Statesman*, UK Edition, accessed May 31, 2022, https://www.newstatesman.com/politics/2013/09/march-made-gandhi-mahatma.
27. "India Trip," *King Encyclopedia*, Stanford, CA: The Martin Luther King Jr. Research and Education Institute, accessed June 1, 2022, https://kinginstitute.stanford.edu/encyclopedia/india-trip.
28. The addition of -ji to the end of Mahatma makes the title a form of endearment.
29. Manju Seth, Amb. "Nelson Mandela's Umbilical Bond with Mahatma Gandhi." *Diplomatist.com*, accessed June 1, 2022, https://diplomatist.com/2020/07/23/nelson-mandelas-umbilical-bond-with-mahatma-gandhi.
30. It is interesting to note that although Gandhi was nominated five times for the Nobel Peace Prize, he never actually won the award; however, both Martin Luther King Jr. and Nelson

Mandela have received the honor based on their use of Gandhi's principles of nonviolent resistance.
31. Thomas, Dominic. "Mahatma Gandhi: The Track to Enlightenment: Mahatma Gandhi- UCA News." *ucanews.com*, accessed August 9, 2024. https://www.ucanews.com/news/the-track-to-enlightenment-mahatma-gandhi-and-mother-teresa/89527.
32. "What Would Dalai Lama Do Had Mahatma Gandhi Been Alive? A Lesson on 'How to Deal with China'." *News18.com*, accessed June 1, 2022, https://www.news18.com/news/india/what-would-dalai-lama-do-had-mahatma-gandhi-been-alive-a-lesson-on-how-to-deal-with-china-4714319.html.

Chapter 3: George Washington

1. Warren, Jack D. "George Washington's Journey to Barbados." *George Washington's Mount Vernon*, Mount Vernon Ladies' Association, 2002, www.mountvernon.org/george-washington/washingtons-youth/journey-to-barbados/.
2. Warren, "George Washington's Journey to Barbados."
3. Hasselgren, Per-Olof. "The Smallpox Epidemics in America in the 1700s and the Role of the Surgeons: Lessons to Be Learned during the Global Outbreak of Covid-19." *World Journal of Surgery*, Springer International Publishing, Jul. 2020, www.ncbi.nlm.nih.gov/pmc/articles/PMC7335227/#.
4. In the epidemic of 1764 in Boston "almost 18% of unprotected sufferers" died. Hasselgren, "The Smallpox Epidemics in America in the 1700s."
5. Hasselgren, "The Smallpox Epidemics in America in the 1700s."
6. Chernow, Ron. *Washington: A Life*. (United States of America: Penguin Publishing Group, 2011) chap. 2, Kindle.
7. Chernow, Washington: A *Life*, chap. 3.
8. The letter, placed in a sealed envelope, simply told Governor Dinwiddie that the discussion over the ownership of lands in the Ohio River Valley would have to be directed to the Marquis Duquesne in Quebec City, New France, and that St. Pierre did not feel obliged to obey Dinwiddie's demands.

9. Washington, George. *The Diaries of George Washington*. Vol. 1: 1748–65. Donald Jackson, ed. The Papers of George Washington (Charlottesville, Virginia: The University Press of Virginia, 1976), 93. http://www.loc.gov/resource/mgw.wd01
10. Barton, David. *The Bulletproof George Washington*. (Alledo, Texas: WallBuilder Press, 1990), 14.
11. Washington, *The Diaries of George Washington*, 156 (image 214).
12. Chernow, *Washington: A Life*, chap. 3.
13. Barton, *The Bulletproof George Washington*, 15.
14. Barton, *The Bulletproof George Washington*, 28.
15. Chernow, *Washington: A Life*, chap. 5.
16. Barton, *The Bulletproof George Washington*, 48.
17. Chernow, *Washington: A Life*, chap. 5.
18. Vickery, Dr. Paul. *Washington: A Legacy of Leadership* (Nashville, Tenn: Thomas Nelson, 2010) chap. 3, Kindle.
19. Vickery, *Washington: A Legacy of Leadership*, chap. 4.
20. Vickery, *Washington: A Legacy of Leadership*, chap. 4.
21. Meltzer, Brad and Mensch, Josh. *The First Conspiracy: The Secret Plot to Kill George Washington*. (New York: Flatiron Books, 2018), 24.
22. In one (likely apocryphal) story, Washington nearly ate poisoned peas, but was saved when a servant threw the plate out the window, where some chickens ate the deadly vegetables and later died.
23. The Life Guard was a regiment of the Continental Army that guarded General Washington, official military papers, and official funds.
24. Dr. William Eustis to Dr. David Townsend, June 28, 1776, *New England Historical and Genealogical Register* (1869), 23:206-09, https://books.google.com/books/about/The_New_England_Hi storical_and_Genealogi.html?id=F5yrNq-zNjgC.
25. McBurney, Christian M. *Abductions in the American Revolution: Attempts to Kidnap George Washington, Benedict Arnold and Other Military and Civilian Leaders*. (Jefferson, NC: McFarland & Company, Inc., 2016), 16. https://books.google.com/books?id=dxLaDAAAQBAJ&pg.

26. Barton, *The Bulletproof George Washington*, 69.
27. Brookhiser, Richard. *George Washington on Leadership*. (New York: Basic Books, 2009), 3, https://books.google.com/books?id=zI_alj7jkLYC&q.
28. McBurney, *Abductions in the American Revolution*, 16.
29. Vickery, *Washington: A Legacy of Leadership*, chap. 1.
30. Tasler, Nick. "Three Decisions That Defined George Washington's Leadership Legacy." *Harvard Business Review*, Harvard Business Publishing, 2 Nov. 2014, hbr.org/2014/02/three-decisions-that-defined-george-washingtons-leadership-legacy.
31. Stazesky, Robert C. "George Washington, Genius in Leadership," *Washington Papers*, University of Virginia, 2014, washingtonpapers.org/resources/articles/george-washington-genius-in-leadership/.
32. Chernow, *Washington: A Life*, chap. 17.
33. Tubbs, Brian. "What If George Washington Had Never Been Born?" *American Revolution and Founding Era*, Brian Tubbs, 19 Feb. 2011, americanfounding.blogspot.com/.
34. Chernow, *Washington: A Life*, chap. 43.
35. Tubbs, *American Revolution and Founding Era*.
36. Chernow, *Washington: A Life*, chap. 43.
37. Vickery, *Washington: A Legacy of Leadership*, chap. "Legacy."
38. Only workers previously enslaved by Washington were to be freed upon Martha's death; those whose enslavement Martha inherited from her first husband were to go to his estate and then be divided among his grandchildren when she died. Also, there were relationships, such as marriage, between the enslaved workers that made this extremely difficult even when Martha decided to set them free before her death. See *George Washington's Mount Vernon*, "A Decision to Free His Slaves." accessed Aug. 1, 2024, https://www.mountvernon.org/george-washington/slavery/washingtons-1799-will.

Chapter 4: Meriwether Lewis

1. As quoted in Jenkinson, Clay S. *The Character of Meriwether Lewis: Explorer in the Wilderness* (Washburn, North Dakota: The Dakota Institute Press, 2011), 249.
2. "Euro-American explorers were not the only ones to draw maps of the western country. As every visitor to Indian country soon learned, native people also made sophisticated and complex maps. Such maps often covered thousands of miles of terrain. At first glance Indian maps often appear quite different from those made by Euro-Americans. And there were important differences that reflected distinctive notions about time, space, and relationships between the natural and the supernatural worlds. William Clark was not the only expedition cartographer to struggle with those differences" ("Rivers, Edens, Empires: Lewis & Clark and the Revealing of America Lewis & Clark." *Library of Congress*, June 24, 2003. https://www.loc.gov/exhibits/lewisandclark/lewis-landc.html.).
3. Jackson, Donald, editor. *Letters of the Lewis and Clark Expedition, with Related Documents: 1783-1854*, 2nd ed. (Urbana: University of Illinois Press, 1978), 2:587.
4. Ambrose, Stephen E. *Undaunted Courage: Meriwether Lewis, Thomas Jefferson, and the Opening of the American West* (New York: Touchstone, 1996), 481.
5. Ambrose, *Undaunted Courage*, 24.
6. "Day-by-Day: September 16, 1805." *LewisandClark.org*, accessed March 31, 2024. https://lewis-clark.org/day-by-day/16-sep-1805/.
7. Lewis, Meriwether. "June 7, 1805," *Journals of the Lewis & Clark Expedition*, accessed April 1, 2024. https://lewisandclarkjournals.unl.edu/item/lc.jrn.1805-06-07.
8. Lewis, Meriwether. "June 30, 1806," *Journals of the Lewis & Clark Expedition*, accessed April 1, 2024. https://lewisandclarkjournals.unl.edu/item/lc.jrn.1806-06-30#lc.jrn.1806-06-30.03
9. In 1785 Jefferson authored Notes on the State of Virginia, in which he included detailed information on stream flow, lakes and coastlines, topography, soils, climate, minerals, plants,

and animals. Some consider this book the most important American book written before 1800. The US Geological Survey (USGS) still uses Jefferson's "Rivers" reports in Notes as a prototype for its own publications; the same is true for mineral commodity surveys produced by the USGS.
10. Brandt, Anthony, ed. *The Essential Lewis & Clark* (Washington DC: National Geographic Partners, LLC, 2002), "Jefferson's Instructions to Meriwether Lewis", Kindle.
11. Brandt, *The Essential Lewis & Clark*, "July 27 to August 26, 1804."
12. Brandt, *The Essential Lewis & Clark*, "July 27 to August 26, 1804."
13. Brandt, *The Essential Lewis & Clark*, "July 27 to August 26, 1804".
14. Captain Clark named them the Great Falls in his journal when he saw the water falls a few days after Lewis. The Great Falls no longer exist today as seen by Lewis and Clark due to hydroelectric dams built to generate power. Although limited in scope because of the dams, tourism to Great Falls, Montana to see the falls is common.
15. Lewis, Meriwether. "June 14, 1805," *Journals of the Lewis & Clark Expedition*, accessed April 1, 2024. https://lewisandclarkjournals.unl.edu/item/lc.jrn.1805-06-14.
16. Lewis, *Journals of the Lewis & Clark Expedition*, "June 14, 1805."
17. Lewis, *Journals of the Lewis & Clark Expedition*, "June 14, 1805."
18. Lewis, *Journals of the Lewis & Clark Expedition*, "June 14, 1805."
19. Lewis, *Journals of the Lewis & Clark Expedition*, "July 26, 1806."
20. Lewis, *Journals of the Lewis & Clark Expedition*, "July 27, 1806."
21. Lewis, Journals of the Lewis & Clark Expedition, "July 27, 1806."
22. Lewis, *Journals of the Lewis & Clark Expedition,* "July 27, 1806." Note: One of the alleged eight Piegans in this encounter may have been Wolf Calf. "[Wolf Calf] told

anthropologist George Bird Grinnell [in 1895] that he was with the war party that met the first two white men ever seen in the lower Blackfeet country. Their meeting was friendly at first, he said, but their chief told the rest to try to steal some of their things, which resulted in the death of a young man named Side Hill Calf" (Fifer, B. and Mussulman, J.A. "Wheeler on the Marias: Meeting a Blackfeet survivor," *LewisandClark.org*, accessed April 1, 2024. https://lewis-clark.org/legacies/wheelers-lc-trail/wheeler-on-marias/).

23. Brandt, *The Essential Lewis & Clark*, "Expedition Members."
24. Lewis, *Journals of the Lewis & Clark Expedition*, "June 14, 1805."
25. Lewis, *Journals of the Lewis & Clark Expedition*, "June 15, 1805."
26. Peck, David J. *Or Perish in the Attempt: The Hardship and Medicine of the Lewis and Clark Expedition.* (Lincoln and London: University of Nebraska Press, 2011), 277.
27. Jenkinson, *The Character of Meriwether Lewis*, 217.
28. "Corps of Discovery - What Did Meriwether Lewis Do after the Exploration?" *Lewis & Clark Online Exhibit*, State Historical Society of North Dakota. accessed August 26, 2024. https://www.history.nd.gov/exhibits/lewisclark/lewisafter.html.
29. "Lewis and Clark Corps of Discovery." *U.S. Army Center of Military History*, January 31, 2021. https://history.army.mil/lc/Explore/Army_Talk/at3.htm.
30. "Lewis and Clark: Historical Background." *National Parks Service*, February 22, 2004. https://www.nps.gov/parkhistory/online_books/lewisandclark/intro1.htm.
31. Grove, Tim. "The View from Lemhi Pass." *Historyplaces.wordpress.com*, December 23, 2013. https://historyplaces.wordpress.com/2013/08/17/the-view-from-lemhi-pass/.
32. Brandt, *The Essential Lewis & Clark*, "Jefferson's Instructions to Meriwether Lewis."
33. Ambrose, *Undaunted Courage*, 482.

34. Brandt, *The Essential Lewis & Clark*, "From June 13 to July 2, 1805."
35. Datt, Anirudh. "Lewis and Clark Expedition: Traversing the Uncharted Territories of North America." *Thomas-Earnshaw.com*, March 1, 2024. https://thomas-earnshaw.com/blogs/the-earnshaw-odyssey/lewis-and-clark-expedition-traversing-the-uncharted-territories-of-north-america.
36. Geiling, Natasha. "Lewis and Clark Only Became Popular 50 Years Ago." *Smithsonian.com*, June 5, 2014. https://www.smithsonianmag.com/history/what-did-lewis-and-clark-expect-find-180951467/.
37. Jenkinson, *The Character of Meriwether Lewis*, 249.

Chapter 5: Clara Barton
1. Charles Rivers Editors, *Clara Barton: The Life and Legacy of the Civil War Nurse Who Founded the American Red Cross* (Ann Arbor, Michigan: Charles River Editors, 2020), "Her Parentage and Infancy," Kindle.
2. Young, Charles Sumner, *Clara Barton: A Centenary Tribute to the World's Greatest Humanitarian* (Boston: The Gorham Press, 1922), 11. Project Gutenberg [eBook # 64967], 2021, https://www.gutenberg.org/cache/epub/64967/pg64967-images.html#Page_21.
3. Barton, Clara, *The Story of My Childhood* (New York: The Baker & Taylor Co., 1907), 35-36. Project Gutenberg [eBook #64704], 2021, https://www.gutenberg.org/cache/epub/64704/pg64704-images.html.
4. Charles Rivers Editors, *Clara Barton: The Life and Legacy*, "Clara's Early Years."
5. Barton, *The Story of My Childhood*, 60.
6. Barton, *The Story of My Childhood*, 81.
7. Parkman, Mary Rosetta, *Heroines of Service* (New York: The Century Company, 1921), 72. Project Gutenberg [eBook # 42451], 2013, https://www.gutenberg.org/cache/epub/42451/pg42451-images.html#III.

8. Parkman, *Heroines of Service*, 72.
9. Pfanz, Donald C., *Clara Barton's Civil War: Between Bullet and Hospital* (Yardley, Pennsylvania: Westholme Publishing, 2022), 11.
10. Oates, *A Woman of Valor*, 50.
11. Barton, *The Life of Clara Barton*, chap. XIV, Kindle.
12. Barton, *The Story of My Childhood*, 81.
13. Barton, *The Life of Clara Barton*, chap. XIV, Kindle.
14. As quoted in Pfanz, *Clara Barton's Civil War*, 50.
15. As quoted in Pfanz, *Clara Barton's Civil War*, 54.
16. Brockett, Lawrence Pierpont, and Mary C. Vaughan. "Clara Harlowe Barton." *Civilwar.com*, 2019. https://www.civilwar.com/history/significant-people-of-the-war/union-women/146800-clara-harlowe-barton.html.
17. Pfanz, *Clara Barton's Civil War*, 58.
18. Pfanz, *Clara Barton's Civil War*, 65.
19. Pfanz, *Clara Barton's Civil War*, 67.
20. Pfanz, *Clara Barton's Civil War*, 73.
21. Oates, Stephen B., *A Woman of Valor: Clara Barton and the Civil War* (New York: The Free Press, 1995), 47, Kindle.
22. Oates, *A Woman of Valor*, 275.
23. Prisoner exchanges had been deferred for over a year because the Confederacy refused to release Black prisoners.
24. "Clara Barton's Missing Soldiers Office: 1865-1868." *Clara Barton Museum*, August 11, 2021. https://clarabartonmuseum.org/mso/.
25. "Clara Barton's Missing Soldiers Office: 1865-1868." *Clara Barton Museum*.
26. "Clara Barton's Missing Soldiers Office: 1865-1868." *Clara Barton Museum*.
27. Oates, *A Woman of Valor*, 315.
28. Ultimately the work of the Missing Soldiers Office had to be shut down both due to lack of funding and to Clara's poor mental health.
29. Oates, *A Woman of Valor*, 368.
30. Young, *Clara Barton*, 156-157.
31. Charles Rivers Editors, *Clara Barton*, 42.
32. Young, *Clara Barton*, 157.

Chapter 6: Benjamin Franklin
1. Isaacson, Walter. *Benjamin Franklin: An American Life*. (New York: Simon & Schuster, 2003), chap. 2, Kindle.
2. Benjamin Franklin had signed a nine-year contract to serve as an apprentice to his brother, James. When James was arrested, he could not oversee the printing of his newspaper. Apprentices were not legally qualified to carry on the work. With an agreement that Benjamin would continue publishing the Courant, James signed Benjamin's apprenticeship papers, signifying its completion; however, a secret second set of apprenticeship papers had also been drawn up. While he carried the original signed papers, Benjamin was in violation of the second agreement.
3. Zall, Paul M. *Franklin on Franklin*. (Lexington, Kentucky: University Press of Kentucky, 2020), 80.
4. Zall, *Franklin on Franklin*, 80.
5. Finger, Stanley, and Ian S. Hagemann. "Benjamin Franklin's Risk Factors for Gout and Stones: From Genes and Diet to Possible Lead Poisoning." *Proceedings of the American Philosophical Society*, 152, no. 2 (2008): 190. http://www.jstor.org/stable/25478486.
6. While Benjamin Franklin had been in London in 1724-1726, Deborah Read had married a man named John Rogers. Soon after the marriage, Deborah learned John was deeply in debt and that he already had a wife back in England. Deborah left John and refused to acknowledge him as her husband. Later that year John was reportedly killed in the West Indies. When Deborah and Benjamin decided to wed in 1830, Pennsylvania laws did not allow for divorce on the grounds of desertion. And since John Rogers' death could not be documented, Deborah's marital status was left in limbo. Instead of a civil marriage, the couple decided to enter into a common law marriage.
7. Isaacson, *Benjamin Franklin: An American Life*, chap. 5.
8. Zall, *Franklin on Franklin*, 170.
9. Franklin, Benjamin. "Letter from Benjamin Franklin to [John Franklin] (copy), 25 December 1750." *Massachusetts*

Historical Society, Accessed June 16, 2022, https://www.masshist.org/database/viewer.php?item_id=1839&pid=15. Original spelling and capitalization retained.
10. Jorgensen, Timothy J. "When Benjamin Franklin Shocked Himself While Attempting to Electrocute a Turkey." *Smithsonian Magazine*, Accessed June 16, 2022, https://www.smithsonianmag.com/history/when-benjamin-franklin-shocked-himself-while-attempting-to-electrocute-a-turkey-180979094/.
11. Jorgensen, *Smithsonian Magazine*.
12. Isaacson, *Benjamin Franklin: An American Life*, chap. 5.
13. Isaacson, *Benjamin Franklin: An American Life*, chap. 5.
14. "Lecture 2: History Benjamin Franklin." Accessed June 20, 2022, http://www.atmo.arizona.edu/students/courselinks/spring13/atmo589/lecture_notes/jan15/lect2_history_benjamin_franklin.html.
15. Krider, Philip. "Benjamin Franklin and lightning rods." *Physics Today*, 59:1, 42, accessed June 20, 2022, https://physicstoday.scitation.org/doi/10.1063/1.2180176.
16. On his journey to England, Franklin wrote his wife about nearly being shipwrecked one night off the rocky Cornwall coast. He hypothesized the near crash was caused by an indraft heading up the English Channel. "We had a watchman placed in the bow, to whom they often called, 'Look well out before there!' and he as often answered, 'Aye, aye!' but perhaps had his eyes shut and was half asleep at the time, they sometimes answering, as is said, mechanically; for he did not see a light just before us, which had been hid by the studding sails from the man at the helm and from the rest of the watch, but by an accidental yaw of the ship was discovered, and occasioned a great alarm, we being very near it, the light appearing to me as big as a cartwheel. It was midnight, and our captain fast asleep; but Captain Kennedy, jumping upon deck and seeing the danger, ordered the ship to wear round, all sails standing, an operation dangerous to the masts, but it carried us clear, and we escaped shipwreck, for we were running right upon the rocks on which the lighthouse was erected." Franklin,

Benjamin. "The Electric Ben Franklin." *ushistory.org*, accessed June 30, 2022, https://www.ushistory.org/franklin/autobiography/page79.htm.
17. Isaacson, *Benjamin Franklin: An American Life*, chap. 10.
18. Brands, H.W. *The First American*. (New York: Doubleday, 2000), 502.
19. Brands, *The First American*, 503.
20. Isaacson, *Benjamin Franklin: An American Life*, chap. 11.
21. Brands, *The First American*, 507.
22. Isaacson, *Benjamin Franklin: An American Life*, chap. 11.
23. Isaacson, *Benjamin Franklin: An American Life*, chap. 13.
24. Heathcote, Charles William, Ph.D. 1956. "Franklin's Contributions to the American Revolution as a Diplomat in France." *Historic Valley Forge*, accessed June 28, 2022, https://www.ushistory.org/valleyforge/history/franklin.html.
25. Isaacson, Benjamin Franklin: An American Life, chap. 13.
26. Franklin, Benjamin. *Autobiography of Benjamin Franklin*. (New York: Henry Holt and Company, 1916); Project Gutenberg [eBook #20203], 2006, https://www.gutenberg.org/cache/epub/20203/pg20203-images.html.
27. Larson, David M. "Benjamin Franklin (1706-1790)." *Georgetown.edu*, Accessed June 30, 2022, https://faculty.georgetown.edu/bassr/heath/syllabuild/iguide/franklin.html.
28. Griffith, John. "Review of Franklin for the Many and the Few, by J. A. Leo Lemay, P. M. Zall, and J. A. Leo Lemay." *Early American Literature*, 21, no. 2 (1986): 168. http://www.jstor.org/stable/25056622.
29. Isaacson, *Benjamin Franklin: An American Life*, chap. 16.

Chapter 7: Winston Churchill
1. Herbert G. Nicholas, "Winston Churchill: prime minister of United Kingdom," *Britannica*, last modified Jan. 20, 2022, https://www.britannica.com/biography/Winston-Churchill/During-World-War-I.
2. Roberts, Andrew. *Churchill: Walking with Destiny*. (New York: Penguin Publishing Group, 2019). chap. 1, Kindle.

3. Roberts, *Churchill: Walking with Destiny*, chap. 3.
4. Churchill, Winston. *My Early Years*. (London: Thornton Butterworth, September 1931 [fifth impression]), chap. 1, Project Gutenberg Canada [eBook #1315], 2016, https://gutenberg.ca/ebooks/churchillws-myearlylife/churchillws-myearlylife-00-h-dir/churchillws-myearlylife-00-h.html. Note: Churchill was mistaken about it being double pneumonia, but his life was definitely endangered.
5. Vale, Allister and Scadding, John. *Winston Churchill's Illnesses, 1886–1965*. (Yorkshire: Pen & Sword Books, 2020), chap. 1, Kindle.
6. "Young Winston survives his preparatory schooling at Hove." *SussexWorld*, accessed Apr. 9, 2022, https://www.sussexexpress.co.uk/news/opinion/young-winston-survives-his-preparatory-schooling-at-hove-1280616
7. Vale, *Winston Churchill's Illnesses*, chap. 1.
8. "Young Winston survives his preparatory schooling at Hove." *SussexWorld*.
9. Vale, *Winston Churchill's Illnesses*, chap. 1.
10. Churchill, Winston. *Savrola: A Tale of the Revolution in Laurania*. (New York: Longman's, Green, and Co., 1899), chap. 12, Project Gutenberg [eBook #50906], 2016, https://www.gutenberg.org/cache/epub/50906/pg50906-images.html.
11. Churchill, *My Early Years*, chap. 6.
12. The 4th Hussars was a cavalry unit. An officer in the British army below the rank of captain.
13. Churchill, *My Early Years*, chap. 6.
14. Churchill, *My Early Years*, chap. 6.
15. Roberts, *Churchill: Walking with Destiny*, chap. 3.
16. Roberts, *Churchill: Walking with Destiny*, chap. 3.
17. Churchill, Winston. *My Early Years*. (London: Thornton Butterworth, September 1931 [fifth impression]), chap. 19, Project Gutenberg Canada [eBook #1315], 2016, https://gutenberg.ca/ebooks/churchillws-myearlylife/churchillws-myearlylife-00-h-dir/churchillws-myearlylife-00-h.html.

18. Hussey, John. "The Boer War Armoured Train Incident and Churchill's Escape, 1899." *The Churchill Project: Hillsdale College*. Accessed Apr. 21, 2022, https://winstonchurchill.hillsdale.edu/boer-escape/.
19. Roberts, *Churchill: Walking with Destiny*, chap. 3.
20. Roberts, *Churchill: Walking with Destiny*, chap. 3.
21. Churchill, John Spencer. *A Churchill Canvas*. (Boston: Little, Brown, 1962), 106.
22. Roberts, *Churchill: Walking with Destiny*, chap. 3.
23. Roberts, *Churchill: Walking with Destiny*, chap. 3.
24. Nicholas, Herbert G.. "Winston Churchill". *Encyclopedia Britannica*, 20 Jan. 2022, https://www.britannica.com/biography/Winston-Churchill. Accessed 29 April 2022.
25. Larson, Erik. *The Splendid and the Vile*. (New York: Penguin Random House, 2020), chap. 2, Kindle.
26. Holmes, Richard. *In The Footsteps of Churchill: A Study of Character*. (New York: Basic Books, 2005), 295.
27. Roberts, *Churchill: Walking with Destiny*, Introduction.
28. Larson, *The Splendid and the Vile*, chap. 4.
29. Larson, *The Splendid and the Vile*, chap. 4.
30. Roberts, *Churchill: Walking with Destiny*, Conclusion.
31. "WW2: Did Winston's Words Win the War?" *BBC Teach*, BBC, Accessed Apr. 29, 2022, www.bbc.co.uk/teach/did-winstons-words-win-the-war/zjdn7nb.
32. Churchill, Winston. 1940. "We Shall Fight on the Beaches." *International Churchill Society*, winstonchurchill.org/resources/speeches/1940-the-finest-hour/we-shall-fight-on-the-beaches/.
33. Ratcliffe, Susan, ed. "Winston Churchill 1874–1965." *Oxford Reference*. (Oxford: Oxford University Press, 2016), www.oxfordreference.com/view/10.1093/acref/9780191826719.001.0001/q-oro-ed4-00002969S.
34. Roberts, *Churchill: Walking with Destiny*, chap. 10.
35. Roberts, *Churchill: Walking with Destiny*, Conclusion.
36. Lewis, Adrian R. 2005. "Mulberry." *Encyclopædia Britannica*, Accessed Apr. 21, 2022,

www.britannica.com/topic/Mulberry-artificial-harbours-World-War-II.
37. Flint, Colin. 2019. "D-Day Succeeded Thanks to an Ingenious Design Called the Mulberry Harbours." The Conversation, Accessed Apr. 21, 2022, theconversation.com/d-day-succeeded-thanks-to-an-ingenious-design-called-the-mulberry-harbours-116933.
38. Roberts, *Churchill: Walking with Destiny*, chap. 22.
39. Brazier, David. "The Atlantic Charter: Revitalizing the Spirit of the Founding of the United Nations over Seventy Years Past." *United Nations*, United Nations, www.un.org/en/chronicle/article/atlantic-charter-revitalizing-spirit-founding-united-nations-over-seventy-years-past.
40. Roberts, *Churchill: Walking with Destiny*, chap. 30.
41. "Nearly Quarter of Brits Think Churchill a Myth: Poll." *ABC News Australia*, ABC News, 4 Feb. 2008, www.abc.net.au/news/2008-02-04/nearly-quarter-of-brits-think-churchill-a-myth-poll/1031856.

Chapter 8: Brigham Young
1. Ephesians 2:20.
2. *History of the Church* 2:196
3. Watson, Elden Jay, editor. *Manuscript History of Brigham Young, 1801-1844*. (Salt Lake City: Smith Secretarial Service, 1968), February 14, 1839.
4. Austin, G W. "The Epidemic of 1839." *Public health papers and reports*, vol. 4 (1878): 231-6.
5. Birch, D. "July 22, 1839: A Day of God's Power." New Era, (March 1971), 16.
6. Bush, Lester E. "Brigham Young in Life and Death: A Medical Overview." *Journal of Mormon History*, vol. 5, 1978, pp. 79–103. JSTOR, www.jstor.org/stable/23286038. Accessed 26 Sept. 2020.
7. Watson, *Manuscript History*, July 22, 1839.
8. Watson, *Manuscript History*, July 22, 1839.
9. Watson, *Manuscript History*, September 14, 1839.
10. Turner, J.G. *Brigham Young: Pioneer Prophet*. (Cambridge: Belknap Harvard, 2014), 65.

11. Watson, *Manuscript History*, March 9, 1840.
12. Watson, *Manuscript History*, November 26, 1842.
13. Bush, *Journal of Mormon History*, 79–103.
14. Watson, *Manuscript History*, November 26, 1842.
15. Watson, *Manuscript History*, November 26, 1842.
16. Smith, T. (2011, July 06). "Scarlet fever–past and present." *aetiologyblog.com*, Retrieved November 08, 2020, from http://aetiologyblog.com/2011/07/06/scarlet-fever-in-hong-kong/.
17. Jesse, D. "Brigham Young's family, part I, 1824-1845" *BYU Studies*, Vol. 18 No. 3 (Spring 1978), 311-327.
18. Lee, J. Doyle., Kelly, C. *Journals of John D. Lee: 1846-47 and 1859*. (Salt Lake City: Priv. print. for R. B. Watt by Western printing company, 1938), 194.
19. Bush, Journal of Mormon History, 84.
20. Esplin, R. (1997, March). *Brigham Young: Fire in His Bones*. Retrieved November 08, 2020, from https://www.churchofjesuschrist.org/study/liahona/1997/03/brigham-young-fire-in-his-bones?lang=eng.
21. Arrington, Leonard J., *Brigham Young: American Moses* (New York: Vintage Books, 1985), chap. 9, Kindle.
22. Christian, Lewis Clark (1981) "Mormon Foreknowledge of the West," *BYU Studies Quarterly*, Vol. 21: Iss. 4, Article 4, 414.
23. Arrington, *Brigham Young: American Moses*, chap. 9.
24. Bush, *Journal of Mormon History*, 85.
25. Bush, *Journal of Mormon History*, 85.
26. "Brigham Young." *The Brigham Young Center*, 2024. https://brighamyoungcenter.org/s/byp/page/home.
27. Bush, *Journal of Mormon History*, 88.
28. Bush, *Journal of Mormon History*, 91.
29. Walker, Ronald W. "Six Days in August: Brigham Young and the Succession," in *A Firm Foundation: Church Organization and Administration*, ed. David J. Whittaker and Arnold K. Garr (Provo, UT: Religious Studies Center, Brigham Young University; Salt Lake City: Deseret Book, 2011), 161–96.
30. Walker, "Six Days in August," 164.

31. Werner, M.R., *Brigham Young* (London: Jonathan Cape, Ltd., 1925), 191.
32. Jorgensen, Lynne Watkins (1996) "The Mantle of the Prophet Joseph Passes to Brother Brigham: A Collective Spiritual Witness," *BYU Studies Quarterly,* Vol. 36: Iss. 4, Article 8, 130. Available at: https://scholarsarchive.byu.edu/byusq/vol36/iss4/8.
33. Jorgensen, *BYU Studies Quarterly*, 139.
34. Arrington, *Brigham Young: American Moses*, chap. 11.
35. The Church of Jesus Christ of Latter-day Saints, *Caring for Those in Need: 2023 Summary*, 14, https://philanthropies.churchofjesuschrist.org/siteassets/humanitarian/welfare_2023_annual_report_caring_for_those_in_need.pdf.
36. Arrington, *Brigham Young: American Moses*, chap. 10.
37. Larsen, Gustive O., "The Story of the Perpetual Emigration Fund," *The Mississippi Valley Historical Review*, Vol. 18, No. 2 (Sep., 1931), 186.
38. "Brigham Young." *newsroom.churchofjesuschrist.org*, 2015. https://newsroom.churchofjesuschrist.org/article/brigham-young.
39. Monsen Jr., R. Joseph, "Reviews: Brigham Young and the American Economy," *Dialogue*, Vol. 1, No. 3, Autumn 1966, 160.
40. Turner, Brigham Young: Pioneer Prophet, 368.
41. "Development of the Utah Economy." *History of Mormonism*, September 1, 2009. https://historyofmormonism.com/2009/09/01/utah-economy/.
42. Larsen, Gustive O., "The Story of the Perpetual Emigration Fund," *The Mississippi Valley Historical Review*, Vol. 18, No. 2 (Sep., 1931), 194.
43. Arrington, *Brigham Young: American Moses*, Epilogue.

Chapter 9: Queen Victoria

1. Yale University's Ernest I. Kohorn has noted Princess Charlotte likely died of a pulmonary embolism than hemorrhage. "A mandatory autopsy was performed and the lungs were 'sliced' but the pulmonary arteries were not examined by opening

them. Death from postpartum haemorrhage is unlikely because all contemporary accounts, including the detailed description of her labour by her obstetricians, specifically state that there was no excessive external bleeding. The autopsy showed that the amount of blood . . . [was] unlikely to have caused death in an otherwise healthy young woman." See Kohorn, Ernest I. "The Death of the Princess Charlotte of Wales in 1817 Was More Likely Due to Pulmonary Embolism than to Postpartum Haemorrhage." *BJOG: International Journal of Gynecology & Obstetrics*, 53, no. 1 (2018): 1356–1356. https://obgyn.onlinelibrary.wiley.com/doi/pdf/10.1111/1471-0528.15261#:~:text=Princess%20Charlotte's%20death%20has%20been,95%3A683%E2%80%938).
2. Interesting fact: The Canadian Île Saint-Jean was renamed Prince Edward Island in 1799 in his honor. The island is well-known as home of the Anne of Green Gables series by L.M. Montgomery.
3. Wilson, A.N. *Victoria: A Life*. (New York: Penguin Books, 2014), chap. 2. Kindle.
4. Strahey, Lytton. *Queen Victoria*. (New York: Harcourt, Brace and Company, 1921), chap. II, Project Gutenberg [eBook #1265], 2006, https://www.gutenberg.org/files/1265/1265-h/1265-h.htm#link2HCH0002.
5. Worsley, Lucy. *Queen Victoria: Twenty-Four Days that Changed Her Life* (New York: St. Martin's Press, 2018), 63.
6. Worsley, *Queen Victoria*, 63.
7. Worsley, *Queen Victoria*, 64.
8. Worsley, *Queen Victoria*, 64.
9. Williams, Kate. "The Young Queen Victoria's Struggle to Gain the Throne." *HistoryExtra*, November 9, 2023. https://www.historyextra.com/period/victorian/young-queen-victoria-struggle-gain-throne-family-tree/.
10. Roberts, Stephen. "How Princess Victoria's Holiday in Ramsgate Nearly Altered the Future of the Royal Family." *Great British Life*, November 10, 2022. https://www.greatbritishlife.co.uk/people/22571422.princess-victorias-holiday-ramsgate-nearly-altered-future-royal-family/.
11. Worsley, *Queen Victoria*, 66.

12. The letters of Madame de Sévigné contain insightful observations of the major figures of the court of Louis XIV,; the letters were (and are still today) of interest to students of seventeenth-century French society. Victoria both enjoyed Madame de Sévigné's wit and stories, but also used the letters as a way to understand how life in a royal court functioned.
13. The Lord Chamberlain is the most senior official of the Royal Household. The office oversees all court ceremonies, and the arrangements for all state ceremonies, such as visits of foreign dignitaries, royal marriages, christenings, and some funerals. During Queen Victoria's reign, the Lord Chamberlain was an office appointed by the Prime Minister.
14. Wilson, *Victoria*, chap. 2.
15. Hoffman, R.G. (2015). "The Age of Assassination: Monarchy and Nation in Nineteenth-Century Europe". In: Rüger, J., Wachsmann, N. (eds) *Rewriting German History*. Palgrave Macmillan, London. https://doi.org/10.1057/9781137347794_7
16. Murphy, Paul Thomas. *Shooting Victoria: Madness, Mayhem, and the Modernisation of the British Monarchy*. (London: Bloomsbury Publishing, 2012), chap. 3, Kindle.
17. Murphy, *Shooting Victoria*, chap. 3.
18. Walker, Nigel. *Crime and Insanity in England*. (Edinburgh: Edinburgh University Press, 1968), 186.
19. Murphy, Shooting Victoria, chap. 3.
20. Queen Victoria. *Queen Victoria's Journals*. "Journal Entry: Wednesday 10th June 1840." Retrieved 9 July 2023, www.queenvictoriasjournals.org.
21. Murphy, *Shooting Victoria*, chap. 3.
22. Murphy, *Shooting Victoria*, chap. 2.
23. Murphy, *Shooting Victoria*, chap. 2.
24. Murphy, *Shooting Victoria*, chap. 3.
25. Murphy, *Shooting Victoria*, chap. 4.
26. Queen Victoria. *Queen Victoria's Journals*, "Journal Entry: Wednesday 10th June 1840."
27. Murphy, *Shooting Victoria*, chap. 6.
28. Murphy, *Shooting Victoria*, chap. 6.

29. Oxford spent the next 27 years in two different insane asylums in Britain, although much of that time his doctors felt he was perfectly sane. In 1867, at age 45, he was offered release on condition of permanently moving to Australia, never to return. Oxford accepted the deal and lived his remaining years in Melbourne. He passed away in April 1900, nine months before the death of Queen Victoria.
30. Although many of the would-be assassins did not properly load their weapons, this does not mean injury could not have occurred. In the case of William Hamilton's attempt in 1849, for example, a man standing nearby in the crowd was burned and injured when the shot was made.
31. Baird, Julia. *Victoria: The Queen: An Intimate Biography of the Woman Who Ruled an Empire.* (New York: Random House, 2016), chap. 17, Kindle.
32. Murray, E. B. (Ed.). *The Prose Works of Percy Bysshe Shelley* (Vol. 1). (Oxford: Oxford University Press, 1993), Oxford Scholarly Editions Online (2015). doi:10.1093/actrade/9780198127482.book.1.
33. Chambers, James. *Charlotte and Leopold: The True Story of the Original People's Princess.* (London: Old Street Publishing Ltd. 2015), Epilogue. Kindle.
34. Wilson, Victoria: A Life, chap. 27.
35. "What Is Hemophilia." *Centers for Disease Control and Prevention*, October 24, 2023. https://www.cdc.gov/ncbddd/hemophilia/facts.html.
36. Wilson, *Victoria: A Life*, chap. 1.
37. "While the Russian revolution and collapse of the Imperial Family was inevitably due to constant wars and lack of resources, it was Tsarevich Alexe's hemophilia that was the catalyst for the end of the Romanov dynasty. His condition, and the family's subsequent isolation from the public weakened the already unstable control the Romanov family had over their country, leading to their downfall" [Hoffman, Tessia A., "Bad Blood: Hemophilia and It's Detriment to the Russian Imperial Family" (2022). *Young Historians Conference.* 8.

https://pdxscholar.library.pdx.edu/younghistorians/2022/papers/8].
38. Hubbard, Lauren. 2022. "What Was Queen Victoria Like as a Mother?" *Town & Country*, May 23, 2022. https://www.townandcountrymag.com/society/tradition/a25835359/queen-victoria-children/.
39. Strachey, *Queen Victoria*, chap. IX.
40. Baird, *Victoria: The Queen*, chap. 22.
41. "Queen Victoria's Letters: Influence on Foreign Politics." *The Argus* (Melbourne, Vic. : 1848 - 1957). Sat. 17 Apr. 1926, p. 9. https://trove.nla.gov.au/newspaper/article/3746022.
42. Strachey, *Queen Victoria*, chap. IX.
43. Chambers, *Charlotte and Leopold*, chap. 24.
44. Baird, *Victoria: The Queen*, chap. 2.
45. Wilson, *Victoria: A Life*, chap. 27.
46. Baird, *Victoria: The Queen*, chap. 30.

Chapter 10: Martin Luther King Jr.
1. Frady, Marshall. *Martin Luther King, Jr.: A Life.* (New York: Penguin Publishing Group, 2002), chap. 1, Kindle.
2. Carson, Clayborne, editor. *The Autobiography of Martin Luther King, Jr.* (New York: Grand Central Publishing, 1998), chap. 7, Kindle.
3. Carson, *The Autobiography of Martin Luther King, Jr.*, chap. 7.
4. Carson, *The Autobiography of Martin Luther King, Jr.*, chap. 7.
5. Carson, *The Autobiography of Martin Luther King, Jr.*, chap. 7.
6. Frady, *Martin Luther King, Jr.: A Life*, chap. 1.
7. Rothman, Lily. 2015. "History: What Martin Luther King Jr. Was Like as a Child." *Time*, accessed May 12, 2022, https://time.com/3660258/mlk-childhood/.
8. *The Martin Luther King, Jr. Papers Project at Stanford University.* Stanford, CA: Martin Luther King Jr. Papers Project, 2002, 1:11, Web. https://lccn.loc.gov/2002567440.
9. *The Martin Luther King, Jr. Papers Project at Stanford University*, 1:13-14.
10. Olson, Robert. 2013. "'Jumping' and Suicide Prevention." *Centre for Suicide Prevention*, accessed May 13, 2022,

https://www.suicideinfo.ca/resource/jumpingsuicideprevention/.
11. Frady, *Martin Luther King, Jr.: A Life*, chap. 1.
12. "Crozer Theological Seminary," *King Encyclopedia, Stanford, CA: The Martin Luther King, Jr. Research and Education Institute*, accessed May 7, 2022, https://kinginstitute.stanford.edu/encyclopedia/crozer-theological-seminary.
13. Frady, *Martin Luther King, Jr.: A Life*, Introduction.
14. Garrow, David J. *Bearing the Cross: Martin Luther King, Jr. and the Southern Christian Leadership Conference.* (New York: Harper Collins, 1986), 57-58.
15. Garrow, *Bearing the Cross*, 58.
16. Garrow, *Bearing the Cross*, 58.
17. "Martin Luther King Jr.'s Home Is Bombed." *History.com*, A&E Television Networks, accessed May 10, 2022, www.history.com/this-day-in-history/martin-luther-king-jr-home-bombed-montgomery.
18. Carson, *The Autobiography of Martin Luther King, Jr.,* chap. 12.
19. Frady, *Martin Luther King, Jr.: A Life*, chap. 1.
20. "March on Washington for Jobs and Freedom." *King Encyclopedia, Stanford, CA: The Martin Luther King, Jr. Research and Education Institute*, accessed May 14, 2022, https://kinginstitute.stanford.edu/encyclopedia/march-washington-jobs-and-freedom.
21. Frady, *Martin Luther King, Jr.: A Life*, "The Far Country."
22. Sokol, Jason. The Heavens Might Crack. (New York: Basic Books, 2018), 41.
23. "Wilkins, Roy Ottaway." *King Encyclopedia, Stanford, CA: The Martin Luther King, Jr. Research and Education Institute*, accessed May 13, 2022, https://kinginstitute.stanford.edu/encyclopedia/wilkins-roy-ottaway.
24. Buckley, Tom. 1970. "Whitney Young: Black Leader or 'Oreo Cookie'?" *New York Times*. September 20, 1970, 245.
25. Abernathy, Ralph. *And the Walls Came Tumbling Down*. (New York: HarperCollins, 1989), 89.

26. King Jr., Martin Luther. *I Have a Dream: Writings and Speeches that Changed the World.* James M. Washington, editor. San Francisco, CA: HarperSanFrancisco, ix.
27. Geiser, Kelsey. 2013. "Stanford scholar Clarence Jones provides glimpse at words behind Martin Luther King's dream." *Stanford Report,* accessed May 15, 2022, https://news.stanford.edu/news/2013/may/jones-mlk-speechwriter-050913.html.
28. "Baker, Ella Josephine." *King Encyclopedia, Stanford, CA: The Martin Luther King, Jr. Research and Education Institute,* accessed May 16, 2022, https://kinginstitute.stanford.edu/encyclopedia/baker-ella-josephine.
29. Wilkins, Roy as quoted by Erin Allen. 2014. "The Power of One: Roy Wilkins and the Civil Rights Movement." *Library of Congress Blog,* accessed May 13, 2022, https://blogs.loc.gov/loc/2014/05/the-power-of-one-roy-wilkins-and-the-civil-rights-movement/.
30. King, Martin Luther. "Chapter 24: The Nobel Peace Prize." *The Martin Luther King, Jr. Research and Education Institute.* Accessed August 15, 2024. https://kinginstitute.stanford.edu/publications/autobiography-martin-luther-king-jr/chapter-24-nobel-peace-prize.

Chapter 11: Orville Wright

1. "When We Take to Flying: What has been done so far in the way of Aeronautics," *New York Times,* Feb. 23, 1896, 28.
2. Ironically, the first vaccine for typhoid fever was also developed that fateful year of 1896. Developed by Sir Almroth Edward Wright (a British bacteriologist and immunologist; no relation to Orville and Wilbur Wright), the inoculation was given to members of the British armed forces beginning in 1896. (Smith, Yolanda. "Typhoid Fever History." *News-Medical.net,* AZO Network, 29 Apr. 2021, www.news-medical.net/health/Typhoid-Fever-History.aspx.)
3. "The City's Health: Causes for Disease Set Forth by a Medical Society Committee." *Evening Star* (Washington DC), Jan. 23, 1896, archived

(www.newspapers.com/image/146204789/?terms=typhoid+fever&match=1: accessed Feb. 8, 2022, citing print edition), 8.
4. "The City's Health," Evening Star.
5. McCullough, David. *The Wright Brothers*, (New York: Simon & Schuster, 2015), chap. 2, Kindle.
6. Dr. Spitler knew the family well and had cared for their mother, Susan Catherine Koerner Wright, as she slowly died of tuberculosis between 1883 and 1889.
7. Wright, Milton. *Milton Wright Diaries: 1857-1917*. CORE Scholar, Wright State University, 1999, https://corescholar.libraries.wright.edu/cgi/viewcontent.cgi?article=1041&context=milton_wright_diaries, p. 458-459.
8. McCullough, *The Wright Brothers*, chap. 2.
9. Wright, Wilbur. "Letter Dated May 30, 1899." *Smithsonian Institution Archives*, Smithsonian Institution, 18 Sept. 2012, siarchives.si.edu/history/featured-topics/stories/letter-dated-may-30-1899.
10. McCullough, *The Wright Brothers*, chap. 4.
11. Kelly, Fred C., editor, *Miracle at Kitty Hawk: The Letters of Wilbur and Orville Wright*, (New York, Farrar, Straus & Giroux, Inc., 1951). Republished by Dover Publications in 1996.
12. Kelly, Fred C. "A Psychic Mystery of Aviation", *Michigan Alumnus Quarterly Review*, Aug. 9, 1958, vol. 64, 352-353.
13. Squier, George Owen. *The Present Status of Military Aëronautics*. Appendix No. 1. [N. P., ?, 1908] Pdf. https://www.loc.gov/item/09008785/.
14. Squier, The Present Status of Military Aëronautics. Appendix No. 1.
15. "Tragedy at Fort Myer." *Wright Brothers Aeroplane Company: The Wright Story*. Accessed July 1, 2024. https://www.wright-brothers.org/History_Wing/Wright_Story/Showing_the_World/Tragedy_at_Fort_Myer/Tragedy_at_Fort_Myer.htm.
16. "Modern Flying Machine a Dayton Product: Daring Men Make Notable Success of Aerial Navigation Experiments." *The Dayton Daily News*, January 25, 1902, 4, archived

(https://www.newspapers.com/image/397817140/?terms=aero nautical&match=1).
17. McCullough, *The Wright Brothers*, chap. 4.
18. Brooks, Shilo. "Why Did the Wright Brothers Succeed When Others Failed?" *Scientific American Blog Network*, Scientific American, 14 Mar. 2020, blogs.scientificamerican.com/observations/why-did-the-wright-brothers-succeed-when-others-failed/#.
19. McCullough, *The Wright Brothers*, chap. 4.
20. Stimson, Dr. Richard. "Propeller Design Demonstrates the Genius of the Wright Brothers." *WrightStories.com*, Dr. Richard Stimson, 2010, wrightstories.com/propeller-design-demonstrates-the-genius-of-the-wright-brothers/.
21. Even more remarkable is that modern tests of a 1911 Wright propellor achieved 77% efficiency, "amazing, when you consider that today's wood propellers are only 85% efficient"; see Stimson, *Wrightstories.com*.
22. Hazelgrove, William. "Why Wilbur Wright Deserves the Bulk of the Credit for the First Flight." *Smithsonian.com*, Smithsonian Institution, 1 Dec. 2018, www.smithsonianmag.com/smithsonian-institution/why-wilbur-wright-deserves-bulk-credit-first-flight-180970714/.
23. Kelly, Fred C., ed. *Miracle At Kitty Hawk, The Letters of Wilbur & Orville Wright*. (New York: Farrar Straus and Young, 1951), 21.
24. Langley, at age 50, was working on an unmanned flying machine he called an aerodrome. Wilbur and Orville Wright had been inspired by Langley's early work. Langley died in 1906.
25. Ader, born in 1841, was one of the oldest proponents of aviation. He had invented a bat-like steam-powered flying machine in 1886. Although he was able to get the machine off the ground, it was an uncontrolled flight. In 1909 he published a popular book on flying machines, which had 10 editions before the start of WWI. Ader is credited with the idea of naval aircraft carriers. He died in 1925.
26. Whitehead claimed to have flown a powered machine in 1901 and 1902. Although a Connecticut newspaper wrote about the

supposed flights, no photographs exist of them. Whitehead stepped back from aviation and public life by 1915 and passed away in 1927.
27. "The Case for Alberto Santos Dumont." *Wright Brothers.org*, Wright Brothers Aeroplane Company, www.wright-brothers.org/History_Wing/History_of_the_Airplane/Who_Was_First/Santos_Dumont/Santos_Dumont.htm.

Chapter 12: John F. Kennedy
1. Dallek, Robert. *An Unfinished Life*. (New York: Little, Brown and Company), chap. 1, Kindle.
2. "Joseph Patrick Kennedy Jr.: A Dream Unfulfilled." *John Fitzgerald Kennedy National Historic Site*, accessed August 25, 2022, https://www.nps.gov/articles/000/joseph-patrick-kennedy-jr-a-dream-unfulfilled.htm.
3. Dallek, *An Unfinished Life*, chap. 3.
4. Cooper, Ilene. *Jack: The Early Years of John F. Kennedy*. (New York: Dutton Children's Books, 2003), 7.
5. Joseph Kennedy Sr. did make a donation to the Guild of St. Apollonia for $3500 after Jack's recovery. But the donation was also made after the family purchased a new home, which was placed in Rose's name, and was therefore not counted as part of Joe Kennedy's wealth.
6. Cooper, *Jack: The Early Years of John F. Kennedy*, 5.
7. Cooper, *Jack: The Early Years of John F. Kennedy*, 33.
8. "Addison's disease." (2024, February 3). *Mayo Clinic*. https://www.mayoclinic.org/diseases-conditions/addisons-disease/symptoms-causes/syc-20350293.
9. Bergthorsdottir, Ragnhildur; Leonsson-Zachrisson, Maria; Odén, Anders; Johannsson, Gudmundur (1 December 2006). "Premature Mortality in Patients with Addison's Disease: A Population-Based Study". *The Journal of Clinical Endocrinology & Metabolism*. 91 (12): 4849–4853.
10. Kennedy bought a green Buick convertible with the American income.
11. Dallek, Robert. *An Unfinished Life*, chap. 3.
12. Dallek, Robert. *An Unfinished Life*, chap. 3.
13. Dallek, Robert. *An Unfinished Life*, chap. 3.

14. Hersey, John, "Survival: Long before he became President, J.F.K. battled to save himself and his men while adrift in the South Pacific," *The New Yorker*, June 10, 1944, https://www.newyorker.com/magazine/1944/06/17/survival.
15. Hamilton, Nigel. *JFK: Reckless Youth*. (New York: Random House, 1992), 577.
16. Hamilton, *JFK: Reckless Youth*, 581.
17. Hamilton, *JFK: Reckless Youth*, 583.
18. On one of the occasions where Kennedy swam out to a reef hoping to be able to signal a friendly boat or plane, he came across a barracuda: "It took half an hour to swim to the reef around the next island. Just as he planted his feet on the reef, which lay about four feet under the surface, he saw the shape of a very big fish in the clear water. He flashed the light at it and splashed hard. The fish went away. Kennedy remembered what one of his men had said a few days before, 'These barracuda will come up under a swimming man and eat his testicles.' He had many occasions to think of that remark in the next few hours (see Hersey, *The New Yorker*, https://www.newyorker.com/magazine/1944/06/17/survival).
19. Dallek, *An Unfinished Life*, chap. 3.
20. Dallek, *An Unfinished Life*, chap. 3.
21. Hersey, *The New Yorker*, https://www.newyorker.com/magazine/1944/06/17/survival.
22. "Forgotten Kennedy," *Kirkus Reviews*, accessed September 24, 2022, https://www.kirkusreviews.com/book-reviews/a/hank-searls-3/the-lost-prince-young-joe-the-forgotten-kennedy/.
23. Dallek, *An Unfinished Life*, chap. 4.
24. Dallek, *An Unfinished Life*, chap. 4.
25. Dallek, *An Unfinished Life*, chap. 6.
26. Hussain, Jehangir, "John F Kennedy as a writer," *The Daily Observer*, accessed September 26, 2022, https://www.observerbd.com/news.php?id=372172.
27. "Campaign of 1960," *John F. Kennedy Presidential Library and Museum*, accessed September 29, 2022, https://www.jfklibrary.org/learn/about-jfk/jfk-in-history/campaign-of-1960.

28. "Peace Corps," *John F. Kennedy Presidential Library and Museum*, accessed September 29, 2022, https://www.jfklibrary.org/learn/about-jfk/jfk-in-history/peace-corps.
29. Kennedy won the popular vote by 118,550 out of a total of nearly 69 million votes cast; and he won 303 electoral votes to Nixon's 219. The second closest presidential election was between Bush-Gore in 2000.
30. Dallek, *An Unfinished Life*, chap. 11.
31. Axelrod, Alan. *Lost Destiny: Joe Kennedy Jr. and the Doomed WWII Mission to Save London.* (New York: St. Martin's Publishing Group, 2015), Prologue.
32. To be fair, most of the Hollywood moguls of the day—many of whom were close friends of Kennedy—were Jewish.
33. Axelrod. *Lost Destiny*, Prologue.
34. Renehan, Edward. "Joseph Kennedy and the Jews." *History News Network*. Accessed January 1, 2024. https://historynewsnetwork.org/article/697.
35. Beauchamp, Cari. 2004. "Two Sons, One Destiny." *Vanity Fair*, December 2004. https://archive.vanityfair.com/article/2004/12/two-sons-one-destiny.
36. On the verge of Germany's invasion of Poland, Jack enabled hundreds of additional Jews to escape Warsaw when he suggested they apply for temporary (vs. long-term) visas under the guise of visiting the World's Fair in New York. And he personally helped process the paperwork submitted by many in order to expedite the applications. The ruse was used "at several American Embassies and secured hundreds of three-month tourist visas that were processed without question or delay." His actions likely saved the lives of several hundred Jews (see Beauchamp, "Two Sons, One Destiny," 397).
37. "The Modern Civil Rights Movement and the Kennedy Administration," *John F. Kennedy Presidential Library and Museum*, accessed September 29, 2022, https://www.jfklibrary.org/learn/about-jfk/jfk-in-history/civil-rights-movement.

38. "Milestones: 1961–1968: The Cuban Missile Crisis, October 1962," *Office of the Historian*, accessed September 30, 2022, https://history.state.gov/milestones/1961-1968/cuban-missile-crisis.
39. Axelrod. *Lost Destiny*, Prologue.
40. Perry, William. "The Risk of 'blundering' into Nuclear War: Lessons from the Cuban Missile Crisis." *Arms Control Association*, December 2017. https://www.armscontrol.org/act/2017-12/features/risk-blundering-nuclear-war-lessons-cuban-missile-crisis.
41. Axelrod. *Lost Destiny*, chap. 1.
42. Axelrod. *Lost Destiny*, chap. 1.
43. O'Connor, Joseph E. "Laski, Frida K.: Oral History Interview, JFKOH-FKL-01." *John F. Kennedy Oral History Collection*. John F. Kennedy Presidential Library and Museum, October 28, 2023.

RK IRVINE

Dear Reader,

Thank you for reading *Hinge Points in History*. I hope the stories of these world leaders were as fascinating to you as they were to me as I researched. If you can spare a few minutes, I would be extremely grateful for a review from you on Goodreads, Amazon, or even on your personal social media accounts. Reviews make a huge difference in every aspect of publishing, so I'm incredibly grateful for those who take time to share their thoughts on these platforms.

Thanks again for your support.

Kind regards, RK Irvine

Discussion Questions

1. Which world leader did you find most interesting to read about? Why? Did any of their trials, accomplishments, or stories surprise you? Share.
2. Did your opinions of the leaders included in *Hinge Points in History* change after learning more about them? If so, in what way? Explain.
3. Many people dismiss political leaders because their philosophical beliefs about life or government are fundamentally different from their own. How can learning about leaders from varied political backgrounds benefit us?
4. In the introduction, the author states that she purposefully avoided dwelling on the character flaws of the leaders discussed in the book. In your opinion, was this decision good or bad? Explain.
5. Most of the world leaders included in *Hinge Points in History* attributed their survival of near-death experiences to a higher power. Do you feel God intervenes in our lives to change the course of things? Why or why not?
6. Have you ever had a near-death experience? Share what happened and how the experience may have influenced your life going forward.

About the Author

RK Irvine is a graduate of Brigham Young University where she earned both Bachelor's and Master's degrees in Communication. She worked for over 15 years as a marketing research analyst. In addition to a love of writing, Irvine followed in her father's footsteps and became a college professor teaching communication. From 2017-2021 she served on the executive board of the American Night Writers Association. Reading, water coloring, and walking are some of her favorite ways to relax. Other books by Irvine include *Old English for Young Readers*, *Improving Family Communication*, and the *Let's Learn Together* series.

Follow RK Irvine on Facebook: @Rebecca Irvine or on Instagram: @author.rebeccairvine

Acknowledgments

About ten years ago I had an idea for an historical nonfiction book another author should write. Although I shared that idea with her at a writer's conference, the idea never fully left my head. When my author friend didn't act on my suggestion, I decided to try my hand at writing a chapter of it myself. Eventually I had 80% of a manuscript—but then got stuck when some key information eluded my research. But I felt more confident in my ability to write historical nonfiction. And as I ruminated about how to finish the other manuscript, the concept of looking at near death experiences of world leaders came to mind. When the idea met with the approval of one of my critique groups (Deb got goose bumps!), I decided to move forward with writing *Hinge Points in History*.

As I wrap up this book baby, I want to thank those who have provided me with feedback along the way. Without this love and support I would never have moved forward. Thank you to my ANWA critique group members for all the advice and support; you're the best! Thank you to Papa for your editing assistance. Thank you to my beta readers for providing insightful thoughts and ideas. And an extra big thank you to my husband Steve for being the best sounding board/thesaurus ever.

www.ingramcontent.com/pod-product-compliance
Lightning Source LLC
Chambersburg PA
CBHW060503090426
42735CB00011B/2093